"I thoroughly enjoyed reading Charles Heller's new book, *Prague: My Long Journey Home*, an insightful and inspiring glimpse into the life of a man who was forced to deny his ethnic roots after coming to his new country but sought to uncover his old identity years later. Mr. Heller's personal story, rather exceptional within the Czech-American community, touches upon several painful topics of our past and forces us to think about our identity in relations to our homeland. His authentic, powerful experiences present a better understanding of our history. I thank Charles Heller for having the courage to share his poignant and profound story with the world, in order to have a record of a history that should never be forgotten."

HIS EXCELLENCY PETR GANDALOVIČ
AMBASSADOR OF THE CZECH REPUBLIC

"It is not enough to record history; we must invigorate it. If generations after us listen and learn from history and make the world better for having done so, it will be because we told good stories. Charles Heller, by vividly recounting the story of his life, provides a window to the Czech-American immigrant experience, and makes an important contribution to the body of literature that will capture the hearts and minds of the future."

GAIL NAUGHTON, PRESIDENT/CEO
NATIONAL CZECH & SLOVAK MUSEUM & LIBRARY

"I enjoyed reading Charles Heller's *Prague: My Long Journey Home*. Having lived through the same times in occupied Czechoslovakia and later under Communists, coming to America 20 years after Dr. Heller, I understand and appreciate his experiences. His life is an example of tragedy, talent, enthusiasm, accomplishment, and of never giving up…"

KAREL RAŠKA, M.D., Ph.D., PRESIDENT
CZECH AND SLOVAK SOCIETY OF
ARTS AND SCIENCES (SVU)

"*Prague: My Long Journey Home* is a valuable read for its ability to capture the atmosphere of the destruction of a way of life."

iDNES/ZPRÁVY

"In the last days of World War II, nine-year-old Ota Heller picked up a revolver and fired it at a Nazi. He did not wait to see if the man was still alive."

RADIO PRAGUE

"The author manages to offer the reader humorous moments. He finds positives in a river of negatives and, between the lines, reminds us that neither war nor the loss of loved ones can destroy man's inner strength."

JAKUB EHRENBERGER, TOPZINE

"Charles Heller is completing his rich writing career as the author of his three-volume memoirs... Very interesting confirmation of the successful career of a twelve-year-old immigrant... a pleasurable read."

PETER HRUBY, KOSMAS JOURNAL

"Dramatic war story... Nine-year-old Ota (shot a Nazi)... told no one about the incident. It was a closed chapter. Simply, it was revenge for loved ones who departed and never returned."

JUDITA MATYÁŠOVÁ, LIDOVÉ NOVINY

"A thrilling account of a Central European Jewish (and Christian) family's trials during World War II... The Heller family saga reads like a living history of the horrors of the twentieth century in Europe. The story ends happily in America and the Czech Republic... the realization of the cosmopolitan dream."

FRANCIS RASKA, CHARLES UNIVERSITY

"The story of his childhood is very touching. One reads with admiration about his discovery of the United States, the assimilation of his family, and eventual building of a successful career."

LISTY JOURNAL

"Prague: My Long Journey Home is an entertaining, compelling, and valuable complement to books about Czech immigration to the U.S. It happened to a college classmate and professional colleague, not to someone's grandparents. It puts a human face on the many stories of suffering, torture, and determination to seek freedom and succeed that had been 'just on paper'."

BART CHILDS, Ph.D., PROFESSOR EMERITUS
TEXAS A&M UNIVERSITY

PRAGUE:

MY LONG JOURNEY HOME

A Memoir of Survival, Denial, and Redemption

To Mike —
Thank you for
your friendship.
Charlie

CHARLES OTA HELLER

abbott press®

A DIVISION OF WRITER'S DIGEST

PRAGUE: MY LONG JOURNEY HOME
A Memoir of Survival, Denial, and Redemption

Abbott Press books may be ordered through booksellers or by contacting:

Abbott Press
1663 Liberty Drive
Bloomington, IN 47403
www.abbottpress.com
Phone: 1-866-697-5310

ISBN: 978-1-4582-0120-1 (e)
ISBN: 978-1-4582-0121-8 (sc)
ISBN: 978-1-4582-0122-5 (hc)

Library of Congress Control Number: 2011961499

Printed in the United States of America

Abbott Press rev. date: 12/9/2011

A NOTE ABOUT CZECH WORDS

The Czech language, with few exceptions, is phonetic. There is no such thing as a "spelling" course in Czech schools because once one knows how to pronounce the letters in the alphabet, one knows how to spell every word. The exceptions are the letters "i" and "y," both of which are vowels, pronounced "ee." Most letters of the Czech alphabet are pronounced in much the same way as those in English. There are some complications. For one, there is "ch," which is considered a single letter and is pronounced the same as in the Scottish "loch." Then there are accent marks:

"*Čárky*" (pronounced "tchah-rky") are used to lengthen the sounds of vowels. "*Háčky*" (pronounced "hah-chky") are used to soften the sound of consonants. For example, "s" is pronounced the same as in English, but "š" becomes "sh." By far the most difficult Czech letter for English speakers is "ř," to which the closest approximation is a rolled "r," followed by "zh." Thus, the famous Czech composer, Antonín Dvořák, is pronounced "Antonh-een Dvor-zh-ahk."

Throughout the early part of the book, when my former (now, my middle) first name was Ota, some dialog contains the diminutive forms of my name, specifically: *Otíček* and *Otík*. When I address my parents as a child, I use the diminutive forms of mother (*maminka*) and father (*tatínek*). My mother's first name is Ilona; her friends call her *Iluška*. In most instances, the names are used to address a person; therefore, the vocative case is used. Generally, for males, the vocative version of the name ends with –*u*, and for females with –*o*. Women's last names generally end in "ová." For example, my father was Rudolph Heller, while my mother was Ilona Hellerová.

A final note: in Czech, the accent is <u>always</u> on the first syllable, something difficult for English speakers to remember, and they give Czech words a Russian tone by ignoring this rule.

In memory of my parents,
Rudolph and Ilona Heller,
the real heroes of this book and of my life.

CONTENTS

If I knew things would no longer be,
I would have tried to remember better.
Barry Levinson.

PREFACE

Soon after the overthrow of Czechoslovakia's communist regime in November 1989, I reunited with my closest boyhood friend, Vladimír "Vláďa" Svoboda. I had left him behind when my parents and I escaped from the country in 1948 and both of us were twelve years old. Now we were in our mid-fifties, and we had travelled along divergent paths – dictated by our respective environments.

"We should write a book together," Vláďa announced one day over a beer in a Prague pub. "Two boys grew up together. One escaped to find success and happiness in a free country. The other stayed behind and, because he refused to join the Communist Party, was unable to reach his potential and his goals in life. The contrast between living under democracy and totalitarianism would make for fascinating reading to people on both sides of the ocean."

Although I had been a part-time writer throughout my life, I was not enthusiastic about the proposed project. The logistics, geographic separation, and the fact that I would be writing in English while Vláďa wrote in Czech were reasons enough to question the practicality of the idea. The fact that I was working nearly one-hundred-hour weeks in the "day job" which put bread on our table, and thus had little time to write – while Vláďa was about to enter retirement in the mountains – rendered it impossible from my standpoint. But, I could not simply turn my friend down. I promised him that we would seek a professional opinion about the viability of such a book.

Alan Levy, senior editor of *The Prague Post*, had written a lengthy article about me and, subsequently, we had become friends. Alan had been a *New York Times* correspondent in Czechoslovakia, had written two wonderful books about life in the country under communism, and had won international acclaim for his most recent book, *The Wiesenthal File*. If anyone could advise us about the potential of Vlád'a's proposed book, it would be Alan.

On my next visit to Prague, he joined Vlád'a and me, along with our wives, for lunch at a French restaurant in *Obecní dům* (Municipal House). Alan's Czech was excellent "for an American," and he listened intently as Vlád'a explained the essence of the book. When the latter finished, Alan wiped the remnants of a chocolate éclair from his lips, scratched his head, and looked first at me and then at Vlád'a.

"I'm sure it will be a wonderful book," he said in Czech. "Your families will love it."

The late Alan Levy was a great writer partly because he could say so much using so few words. His two-sentence indictment killed the project.

Following the Velvet Revolution, Americans seemed to take a special interest in the small, far-off, country of Czechoslovakia. I responded to frequent inquiries of friends, acquaintances, and various organizations with stories and speeches about my youth – anecdotes about life during the Second World War, our liberation from Nazi oppression, the communist take-over, our escape, and life in refugee camps. I was told: "you must write your memoir" several hundred times. But, whenever I entertained the idea of putting pen to paper, I recalled Alan Levy's words. After all, who but family and friends could possibly want to read my story?

I was in a hotel room one night when a television skit called "Jaywalking" started me on the road to changing my mind. On "The Tonight Show," host Jay Leno was doing one of his man-on-the-street interviews during which he asked passers-by questions labeled by their low level of difficulty: "third-grade questions," "eighth-grade questions," and so on. On this particular night, he was standing on the campus of the University of Michigan and asking students "sixth-grade questions" pertaining to the Second World War. I sat with my mouth wide open in astonishment as I listened to one university student after another admit that he or she had no clue about the approximate years during which the war had taken place or who had been President of the U.S. during that time. When one student told Leno that Americans and Germans had fought side-by-side against the Russians in World War II, I nearly fell off my chair.

"Oh, my God!" I gasped.

Even worse, I was reading in newspapers and magazines about people – many of them know-nothing anti-Semites, but also a few who were articulate and educated – deny the existence of the Holocaust. With such denial rising just as the Holocaust generation is disappearing, I knew that I had to speak out, to bear witness, to help in setting the record straight. Later, when I looked into the faces of our three grandchildren – Sam, Sarah, and Caroline – I knew that I must record the story of the Heller/Neumann family and how it was affected by the upheavals of twentieth-century's greatest tragedy. After all, in a few more years, there will be no one left who can provide personal testimony.

The deal was sealed one day in the office suite of a wealthy Palestinian investor whom I will call Abdel. It was a nondescript conference room in a standard-issue office, located in one of hundreds similar steel and glass multistory buildings in the concrete jungle of the Washington suburbs. But, the expensive wooden furniture and the original oil paintings on the walls revealed the fact that Abdel had money. Lots of it. That was why we were there. My partners, Phil Samper and Rick Bolander, and I were raising money for our venture capital fund.

We were setting the tone for our well-rehearsed presentation which, we hoped, would convince this wealthy Arab businessman to invest in our fund. First came the usual icebreaking small talk that generally helped to establish a friendly, informal atmosphere before getting down to serious business. We touched upon a variety of current affairs, but with everyone carefully steering away from any controversial or sensitive topic. At least, that is how it went until someone brought up that morning's front-page story in *The Washington Post*.

"I <u>bet</u> she didn't know!" Abdel said suddenly, with sarcasm figuratively dripping from his curled, hateful lips.

In violation of the game of small talk, he was reacting to an article in which the writer had expressed doubt that Secretary of State Madeleine Albright had only recently discovered that she was more Jewish than Christian, despite having lived her entire life as a Roman Catholic, before becoming an Episcopalian.

"She <u>didn't</u> know!" I shouted, immediately realizing that I, too, had broken the rules of the game by screaming at a potential investor. It was obvious that my reaction had shocked everyone in the room. This was not an ideal way to make a sale.

After an embarrassed and uncomfortable silence, my partners proceeded with the fundraising meeting while I kept my mouth shut and thoughts to myself. An hour later, with the presentation finished, and with Abdel having promised to get back to us soon, I remained silent as we made our way down the elevator to the garage and to Rick's rented car.

As we drove away, Rick said to me: "I think Abdel touched a sensitive spot with you in there."

I nodded and explained that Ms. Albright had been baptized and raised a Roman Catholic. She had been a small child in pre-war Czechoslovakia when her family fled from the Nazis to London. I told Rick that she had grown up knowing nothing about her Jewish roots and only found out about her family's fate in the Holocaust after a reporter dug into her past.

"Thousands of us had similar experiences," I said, ending the conversation and leaving my colleagues to wonder what secret I may be harboring. It was clear that I had to start writing, not only for my family, but to add my voice to those who have borne witness. Whatever "secrets" I may have had, I had to reveal them.

Hundreds of books have been written about the Second World War, but only a small percentage of them have presented the story through the eyes of some of the millions of children who lived in Europe during the late 1930s and early 1940s and whose lives were shaped forever by the dangers, horrors and unsettling events they experienced. I was one of those children.

I began by writing vignettes about the early days of Nazi occupation, my father's escape and joining the Czechoslovak Division of the British army, our expulsion from our home by the Germans, my great-grandfather's departure for a concentration camp, my mother's suffering as she was first tortured by the Nazis and then taken to a slave labor camp, my life in hiding like an animal on a farm, and our eventual liberation. I wrote stories about our short period of freedom before a communist take-over of Czechoslovakia, our family's escape and subsequent life in refugee camps, and – finally – arrival in America and the beginning of a new life. I used family members' journals and old photos, along with information gathered through months of research, to connect the vignettes, to fill in missing pieces, and to provide historical context.

As the story began to take on the form of a memoir, I came to the realization that a single thread stretched through the pages. During the war, all losses, deprivation, and horrors to which we were subjected were explained to me with a simple statement: "the Germans are punishing us because your father is fighting against them." This made the suffering a point of pride for me. Little did I know that the explanation was a pious fraud. It was true that my father was fighting against the Nazis, but the real reason for our suffering was kept a secret from me. It would not be until I would reconnect with my native country many years later that I would put together the pieces of a puzzle and realize the truth. As this became a major theme of the memoir, I added chapters about returning to Prague, bonding with my native land, and dealing with the demons of this new realization.

Any memoir writer today must be mindful of hoaxes which have been foisted on readers in recent years. The occasional "memoir" which plays fast and loose with facts, and one even more rare that proves to be an outright lie, sullies the genre. At the outset, I want to tell the reader that this is my story, as I recall it. My favorite journalist/historian, William L. Shirer, asked: "Does memory, blurred and disjointed by the passage of time and fed by the imagination, lead you to recount more fiction than fact?" Obviously, it is impossible for me to remember the exact words of a conversation I had with my great-grandfather more than 70 years ago. While some of the dialog in my memoir may not be precise in terms of the words used, the meaning and impact on me are grounded in truth, as I remember it.

When anthropologists study an isolated native tribe in a previously-undiscovered part of a jungle, the researchers' presence changes the environment and the people they are observing. Thus, I must admit up-front that my own observations and recollections in this memoir are not uncontaminated by my biases, prejudices, the act of watching and reporting – and, of course, the passage of time. But, I repeat: this is my story, as I remember it.

Home is a name, a word, it is a strong one; stronger than magician ever spoke, or spirit ever answered to, in the strongest conjuration.

Charles Dickens

CHAPTER 1

Kde domov můj? (Where Is My Home?)

I pulled out a Walther revolver and shot a blond-haired, blue-eyed, Nazi in the waning days of the Second World War. I rejoiced as his female companion screamed in hated German from the doorway. In that triumphant moment, I felt as though I had won the war singlehandedly and taken revenge for six years of cruelty inflicted by the Germans on my country and my family, and for forcing me to hide like an animal. I was nine years old. It is now forty-five years later and I replay this scene in my mind as I look out the airplane window at a familiar countryside.

I am coming back to Czechoslovakia. It is 1990, a half-year after the nearly bloodless coup called the "Velvet Revolution," which has brought freedom to a country that was once my home, but one that I had forced into the recesses of my mind during my forty-one years in America. As the airplane banks into a left-hand turn, the port wing dips. I press my nose against the window. In the distance, past the green fields, I see the silhouettes of the church steeples of Prague. The pilot follows the track of a thin black snake of a road. I am startled. It's the Mělník highway! Suddenly, I feel a desperate and unexpected need and, with my index finger, trace a line on the window, following back toward the airplane's tail and along the road through two small towns. I am searching for a place I once loved. There it is – Kojetice! Only a couple of inches wide from this altitude, but I recognize it, and the memories come rushing at me. I am coming back to the home of my birth.

I see myself as three-year-old Ota Karel Heller. I am riding in the back seat of my father's Tatra convertible, with the top down. I laugh at the way Papa's curly, blond hair rises and falls in front of me like waves in a wheat field. I love the way the rushing air blows my own hair and forces me to squint. I lift my arms and let the wind fill my sleeves until they look like fat sausages. Papa and I are returning to Kojetice from one of our monthly shopping trips to Prague, only ten miles away from where we live. As always, he has bought me magazines which contain comic strips with my favorite characters – Shirley Temple, Mickey Mouse, and Donald Duck – all in Czech, of course. Additionally, Papa has selected a couple of American films with Czech subtitles, which he will project for the villagers in the Sokol Hall. I hope that at least one will be a western, starring my cowboy hero, Tom Mix, and his wonder horse, Tony.

The Mělník highway is an asphalt two-lane road which, immediately after leaving the outskirts of the city, enters a countryside of farms, forests, and prominent rock outcroppings. It is summer and I watch the fields of barley, hops, and corn roll by. I take deep breaths to inhale the sweet smell of freshly-cut wheat.

After passing through two small towns, we leave the motorway and turn right onto a dirt road leading to our 900-year-old village, population of a little more than 800. We are greeted by a sign, "Kojetice." The name on this sign would change three times in the future and become a reflection of the twentieth-century history of Czechoslovakia. Just one year later, the Germans would rename the village and change the sign to "Kojetitz." After the war, our so-called "liberators," the Red Army, would write it in Cyrillic letters, such that it would read "Koetue."

We drive past more fields before coming upon the first houses. On both sides of the road are cottages whose occupants work for the farms located on the other side of Kojetice or for our family's clothing company, the region's largest employer. The cottages are small, cozy, and pretty.

Some are made of brick and others of concrete. Grapevines climb up their white plaster walls. The tile roofs are red or brown, sometimes gray, and swallows build their nests beneath the overhangs. Czechs believe that fences <u>do</u> make for good neighbors, and each cottage is surrounded by a high wall. Most homes have beautiful flower gardens, with red and white roses and greenish-white, fragrant, mignonettes. In the back of each cottage is a fruit and vegetable garden, where radishes, peas, gooseberries, and currants grow. Often, an apple, pear or cherry tree provides shade on warm summer days. Some of the homes we pass belong to our family and are rented to company employees. The Neumanns (my mother's side of the family) and Hellers also own houses and other properties which they contribute to the community for recreational and cultural activities.

Driving toward the center of town, we pass the railroad station where trains going to and from Prague stop throughout the day and night. Just past the station, on the right side, stands a small hotel housing the town's only pub. Men gather here after work and on weekends to drink Pilsner beer, discuss politics and sports, and play *mariáš*, their favorite card game. Occasionally, Papa allows me to come in and watch.

The main street, lined with tall linden trees, passes several small side streets, turns right and begins a slow descent past a park on the right. The highlight of each year is *pout'* – a carnival which marks the end of harvest and brings hundreds of celebrants from surrounding villages to the park. As I gaze at the empty green space, I imagine the rides and the games and, most of all, the circus with its elephants, lions, and tigers – animals so much more exotic than the horses, cows, and oxen to which we are accustomed.

Past the park and on the same side, the butcher shop stands, with a pig, sliced longitudinally in half, hanging outside the door. The smell of sausages and salami strung outside the shop window is tantalizing, and I cannot wait to get home as my mouth waters for lunch. A road leading to the nearby industrial town of Neratovice bears off to the left as we continue our journey. Just past the turn-off rises a high wall that eventually melds into the outbuildings surrounding *Zámek* ("Castle"), which is how everyone refers to the mysterious mansion in the center of this large estate, a white chateau with a red roof and several towers, built in a baroque style by the nobleman who once owned all of the surrounding land. An enormous gate, through which horse-drawn wagons can pass, opens to a tunnel running through the outbuildings and leads to the large, lush, wooded grounds.

Just up the hill and on the opposite side of the street sits our next-door neighbors' farm. The Tůmas' house, barns, and stables are hidden by a high brick wall. The small pedestrian gate and the large one for animals and wagons both are made of heavy wood with rural scenes carved by a local artist.

Further uphill and across the street from our factory and home, the village centerpiece, the church of St. Vitus, stands on the same spot it has stood since 1271. This Roman Catholic house of worship has a special meaning to our mixed-religion family because both Mother and I were christened there, and I am one of the few privileged boys given the honor of pumping the huge pedal powering the pipe organ located on the balcony, although I am too small to do it without help. Occasionally, the priest even selects me to help pull the rope that rings the bell, calling the villagers to Sunday Mass. That is the ultimate thrill and distinction. Next to the church stands the post office, in a house owned by my great-uncle Ota Neumann, the mayor, who has loaned it to the village.

Below the church and across the street from our home is the elementary school, which I look forward to attending soon, and immediately behind it is one of my favorite places to hang out. Here, my godfather, Karel Šubrt, has his blacksmith shop. I spend hours sitting in the corner, watching him heat pieces of steel until they are glowing red, shape them into horseshoes, and then reheat them before putting them on a horse's foot. I follow him outside and am mesmerized by the sight, smell and loud sizzle when he lifts the horse's leg and applies the red-hot horseshoe to the hoof. Smoke rises from the foot and the hot odor of burning hoof is pungent and overpowering.

Up the hill above the church stands a monument to the village's fallen war heroes. It honors Kojetice citizens who died in the First World War.

As we approach home, I spot the tops of trees marking my favorite place of all, the woods on a hill above Kojetice, which we call *Skalky*. The name derives from the Czech word for "boulder," and for good reason. Among the hundreds of evergreen and birch trees are large outcroppings of shale, which make great hiding places when my friends and I play cowboys and Indians. The woods are dark and mysterious, and entering them is like stepping on a thick carpet, with many years' collection of dry pine needles and soft, green moss covering the ground. After a rain, bumps in the otherwise smooth groundcover reveal newly-grown mushrooms. My parents and I often join the villagers as we scatter through the forest in a hunt for the source of one of the Czech cuisine's most treasured delicacies.

Now we are at home. Our factory lies up the hill. The front building has a clothing store on the ground floor and our living quarters on the second. A large sign adorns the outside, with the original name of the business, that of my great-grandfather, Gustav Neumann, as well as the current English name of the firm, Labor, indicating that, in addition to women's dresses, it manufactures men's work clothes.

Over the top of the third-story window, under the center eave and sculpted in concrete, is our family emblem, the mountain Říp – a monadnock famous in the history of the Czech nation, and even more endearing to our family because my late great-grandmother, Luisa, had been born at its base. It is said that the forefather of the Czech nation – named Čech – surveyed the surrounding countryside from the top of Říp and declared: "This is the promised land, rich in game and fowl, overflowing with sweet honey." Thus, says the legend, our nation was born. The mountain's double connection to my family has become a point of pride to the Neumanns and the Hellers.

Behind the factory grows a two-acre garden, full of delicious fruits and vegetables. As much as my pals and I enjoy picking and eating cherries, currants, gooseberries, and peaches there, we find it much more exciting to sneak over the wall into the garden of the parish house next door and to steal similar fruits from our neighbor, Father Erhard, the priest, who chases us with a stick as we clamber back over the high wall.

My family lives in a huge, luxuriously furnished, apartment with contemporary blond, Danish furniture, crystal chandeliers, and original oils and watercolors of Prague and the Czech countryside. Upon entering, we put on our *pantofle* (slippers), following the Czech tradition of removing shoes as soon as one enters a home, and we walk along the shiny parquet floor. The sun's rays are reflected and refracted by the chandeliers' glass to create a strange psychedelic show that I find hypnotic. Prominent in the great room is a black grand piano on which my mother often plays pieces by Czech composers, Bedřich Smetana and Antonín Dvořák. My favorite is *Má Vlast*, Smetana's cycle of symphonic poems. Mother, who plays it with exquisite feeling, has explained to me that he wrote it in 1879 when he was deaf and that it is a musical description of our Czech lands. I am particularly fond of the *Vltava* (Moldau) piece which follows the river from its source in the Šumava mountains to Prague and eventually to its confluence with *Labe* (Elbe) in nearby Mělník, the capital of our district.

Papa takes my hand as we enter the dining room. Mother is sitting at the head of the table. Her brown eyes twinkle when she sees us. As always, I feel a warmth flow through my body when I hug her and she kisses me on the lips. My great-grandfather (*Dědeček*) is seated to her right. He smiles at me when I stroke his perfectly trimmed gray beard before I kiss his cheek. His sons, my grandfather (*Děda*) and my great-uncle (*Strejda*), are sitting on Mother's left. Both have black hair and black mustaches; I have trouble telling them apart, but I do not admit this to anyone. I give each a peck on the cheek and they smile and pat me on the head. All three Neumanns – Gustav, Artur, and Ota – are dressed in dark three-piece suits and ties; our family meals are formal occasions. Mother rushes over to embrace and kiss Papa, as I admire them and feel very proud to be the son of the most beautiful lady and the most admired man in our region.

"Welcome home, travelers," says Mother with a smile. My father and I sit down in the two empty chairs. We say "*dobrou chut'*" ("good appetite"), and I tackle my favorite Czech delicacy: *knedliky* (Czech bread dumplings) with eggs and ham, prepared by Tonička Řezáčová, our cook. I feel warm and comfortable in this large, brightly-lit room surrounded by members of my family who make it no secret that they love me and love and respect one another. At the same time, over the past few weeks, as we have sat down at meals, the looks behind the smiles on their faces have worried me. Something is wrong. The usual laughter and happy talk is shadowed by something I do not know – something I fear.

For a moment, my thoughts jump to the present. I am back on the airplane, which is less than half-full. People are not flying in 1990 because a rash of recent hijackings has created a global fear of air travel. The empty spaces around me exacerbate my own loss. I long to fill the vacant seats with my loved ones. Sadly, all but Mother are dead – and she is unable to travel. I take one last look at the black snake of a highway before we begin our descent into Prague's Ruzyně airport. My heart and mind juggle time as my past rises before my eyes. Once again, I am a nine-year-old child, holding a loaded revolver thrown away by one of thousands of escaping German soldiers at the end of the war. I have found it in a ditch. With it, I shoot an escaping Nazi standing not far from me as I crouch in the bushes. I am elated and think this act of revenge will erase forever the nightmare of the war. But now, back in the airplane, I know how wrong I had been. Children of war are sentenced to lives filled with memories and nightmares.

* * *

Although I was born in Prague, my boyhood home was in this ancient village of Kojetice, the history of which dates back to the year 1070. My early childhood was idyllic. Although my parents were strict disciplinarians who tried to keep me grounded, it was difficult for me to feel "normal." After all, none of my friends had nannies watching over them, cooks preparing their food or servants waiting on them. And as the only child at the crossing point of the Neumann and Heller families, I was the center of attention in our male-dominated household: *Dědeček, Děda, Strejda,* and my father, whom I called *Tatínek.* But, life in this safe and happy world would not last long. My first half-formed notions that things were different came in the fall of 1939, when I was three.

It was a Sunday at church. As Mother and I emerged from the darkness of St. Vitus, I blinked when the bright sunlight hit my eyes. Mass was over. I was happy to be free to spend the rest of the day playing with my toys on the roof above the sewing rooms of the family's factory. I was even happier when I saw my great-grandfather standing near the church gate, waiting for us.

Dědeček was my favorite relative, despite the fact that I was three and he was seventy-nine. When we were together, we were unaware of the difference in our ages. This venerable patriarch, with gray hair, gray beard, and wireless spectacles was revered by all, but to me he was just a buddy who would get down on the floor in his three-piece gray suit and play with me for hours, and who would tell me stories of faraway places he had seen. I loved him dearly, but I would not have him in my life for long.

On this Sunday, *Dědeček* told me that we would go for a walk in the woods. The day was sunny, warm, and breezy – a typical early fall day in Czechoslovakia. We rounded the church and climbed up the hill to Skalky. I felt the warmth not only of his body, but of his heart, as his large, calloused palm and fingers enveloped my tiny hand, guiding me along a path through the woods. When we came out of the darkness to a sunny meadow, *Dědeček* stopped.

"*Otíčku,* I want to tell you something," he said. His face changed. This would be a serious matter, and I stopped picking flowers and chasing bugs. "Terrible things are happening to our country. And terrible things may happen to our family. You're going to have to be very brave."

His words echoed whispered conversations in our home. I knew that something was wrong, but, protected child that I was, I was unaware on this sunny, fall day in 1939 that the Germans had been occupying our country since March.

"What do you mean, *Dědečku?*" I asked.

"I won't explain it to you now," he answered. "I just want you to promise that you'll listen to your parents and me, and that you'll always be brave."

"I will," I said solemnly. My young mind, obedient, respectful, and trusting, was troubled. But I was safe, wasn't I? I asked myself silently. I could not know that my family and I were about to enter the most brutal chapter in the already tumultuous history of our land. For me, so young, this new tyranny would bring immeasurable losses. For the Czech nation, tragic consequences awaited.

CHAPTER 2

Heart of Europe

The Czech Republic is an "island," protected by mountains and forests along its borders, and located near the geographic center of the continent. With great pride, its citizens refer to it as "the heart of Europe." The nation consists of Bohemia to the west and Moravia to the east, with the capital – *Praha* (Prague) – located near the geographic center of Bohemia. *Vltava* (Moldau), a river of romantic song and prose, flows from the south through Prague, until it meets *Labe* (Elbe), the river which carries its waters to the North Sea. Surrounded by Germany and Poland in the north, Slovakia in the east, and Austria in the south, the nation's location has been both a blessing and a curse throughout its history. Americans, who tend to be geographically challenged, often refer to the Czech Republic as being part of Eastern Europe. Doing so touches a very sensitive spot in the psyche of a Czech. When I hear someone make this reference, the conversation generally goes like this:

"Where is Vienna with respect to Prague?" I ask.

"I'm not sure."

"It's two hundred miles *east* of Prague. Do you consider Vienna part of Eastern Europe?"

"Of course not."

"Did I make my point?" I say. "The Czech Republic is in Central Europe, and Czechs consider themselves westerners."

The blessing is that the nation's location has accorded it exposure to cultural and intellectual developments of Western Europe. The curse is that being sandwiched between two of its historical enemies – Germany and Austria – has been the cause of living under foreign domination throughout its history. This curse is traceable back to the glory years of the Roman Empire, beginning in 14 A.D., although, according to *The Guinness Book of World Records*, the prehistoric settlement of Dolní Vestonice in southern Moravia is the oldest town in the world, dating back to 27,000 BC, during the Ice Age.

The Romans, who absorbed the Czech lands, named that part of their empire "Boihemum," after the Celtic tribe called "Boii" which lived in the region. The Slavic ancestors of today's Czech nation settled in Bohemia in the sixth century. Three hundred years later, the Slavs established a large country, Great Moravia, which encompassed today's Czech Republic, Slovakia, and parts of Poland and Hungary. The name Moravia (*Mähren* in German, meaning "marches") was coined by Germanic tribes that occupied the territories after the Celts. Due to its central location along the trade routes of Europe, Prague became an important business center.

It was during this period, the early 900s AD, that Jewish traders first settled in the area. Around the same time, two Christian missionaries, Cyril and Methodius, came to Great Moravia, where they devised a special phonetic alphabet – a predecessor to the Czech language – for the purpose of translating the Bible.

The Czechs were quite independent within the empire and had their own queen, Libuše, who married a peasant, Přemysl. The couple established a long-lasting dynasty of Přemyslid rulers, who were responsible for converting the majority of their subjects to Christianity. Not even a brief history of the Czech lands would be complete without the mention of *Svatý* (Saint) *Václav*, better known to English speakers as the Good King Wenceslas, who lived in the tenth century. One of the Přemyslid rulers, Václav built the original version of the nation's foremost landmark, the cathedral of St. Vitus, part of the Castle complex called *Hradčany*, on a hill overlooking Prague. More than nine hundred years later, in 1848, the second most famous site of the Czech Republic was named after the good king. *Václavské náměstí* (Wenceslas Square) is really a wide boulevard rather than a square; in 1913, the equestrian statue of St. Wenceslas, surrounded by four other Czech patrons, was erected near the head of the square, just below the majestic National Museum. It would become the rallying point for many patriotic events, including celebrations of independence in 1918 and 1989. In August 1968, western TV viewers would watch in horror as Soviet tanks would roll past the statue, while unarmed Czech patriots attempted to stop them with their bare hands.

In the tenth century, Great Moravia was conquered by the Holy Roman Empire, which was ruled from Germany. The Germans and Hungarians divided the spoils, with Slovakia becoming part of Hungary, while Bohemia and Moravia were absorbed into the Holy Roman Empire, controlled by the Catholic Church. Bohemia was afforded a great deal of independence and continued to grow and expand its borders. Its standing reached a peak in 1355 when one of its monarchs, *Karel IV* (Charles IV), was crowned Emperor and became ruler of the entire Empire, with Prague as its capital. During Charles' reign, the Czech nation thrived economically and culturally, and education became paramount. Today, many examples of great art and architecture from that era abound throughout Prague, and Charles University, established in 1348 as Central Europe's first institution of higher learning, continues as one of the world's great universities.

Jan Hus was eight years old when Charles IV died in 1378. Having achieved the rank of Rector of Charles University, he used his bully pulpit to criticize the Roman Catholic Church for gathering great wealth at the expense of ordinary citizens. Hus promoted reform of the church and the restoration of simple and pious Christian virtues. Although he was excommunicated for heresy, he continued to speak out and became a hero to thousands of Czechs longing for freedom from the German aristocrats of the Holy Roman Empire, who controlled much of Bohemia's wealth and power. When the Emperor, Sigismund, had Hus burned at the stake in

1415, he precipitated a hundred-year conflict known as the Hussite Wars. The Hussites fought against three powerful enemies: the Catholic Church, the rich and powerful Germans who had moved to the Czech lands, and the feudal lords who opposed religious and social change.

The powerful Catholic Church lumped together Hussites and Jews as heretics, thus bringing about an informal, yet strong, alliance between the two. Hundreds of Jews paid for their support of the Hussites by being expelled from several cities, including the capital of Moravia, Brno.

The Hussites were led by a brave, one-eyed, patriot named Jan Žižka, who in 1420 founded Tábor, a town in southern Bohemia which would become important in my life. Some 570 years later, I would play a role in helping to establish the Rotary Club of Tábor, a service group which would help to repair the damage sustained by the historic town during forty-one years of communist rule in the twentieth century. Reminders of the turbulent times of the Hussite wars can be found today in Tábor's street names, monuments, the ever-present symbol of the chalice, and in the Hussite Museum that is housed inside the Town Hall, where I and three of my fellow Rotarians from Annapolis, Maryland, would receive the key to the city. Žižka's soldiers were peasants and townspeople who were poorly equipped and trained, yet they scored great early victories over powerful armies from Germany, Austria, and Hungary. Ultimately, they ran out of fighting men and weapons, and were defeated and subjugated to the Holy Roman Empire.

But, Jan Hus and his followers had sparked a revolutionary movement away from the Catholic Church, one which made life easier for Jews living in the Czech lands. For many years, they had been allowed to practice only certain occupations, such as banking, and were required to wear yellow marks on their clothing whenever they appeared in public. The Hussites forced the elimination of such humiliation and strongly encouraged Jews to mingle with other citizens, in both their professional and social lives. The Czech Jewish community flourished during the reign of Rudolf II (1576-1612), who gave them the right to engage in nearly any occupation of their choice and promised them that they would never again be expelled from any part of their homeland.

The reforms of Jan Hus were carried on by Martin Luther, a German priest whose Protestant Reformation became popular among the Czechs, including the nation's nobility. When the Habsburg dynasty, which ruled much of Europe in the late 1500s and early 1600s, tried to force these Czech nobles into the Roman Catholic Church, a new conflict – the Thirty Years' War – erupted. In 1620, the battle of *Bíla Hora* (White Mountain), now on the outskirts of Prague, marked the end of the Hussite movement. The Czech Protestants were crushed by the forces of Ferdinand II, nationalism was obliterated, Catholicism was forced on the Czech people, and German was enforced as the language of the nation. Judaism was the only non-Catholic religion permitted by law. Bohemian nobility was wiped out and more than 30,000 families were forced into exile. At war's end, nearly one-third of the total Czech population had been killed. The Habsburg rule, which lasted for nearly 150 years, was oppressive, denied ordinary Czechs education, and reversed many years of cultural progress.

The small minority of Jews grew to 40,000 and continued to live peacefully among the Czechs for two hundred years, despite the Thirty Years' War and the subsequent destruction of the economy and decimation of the Czech population. This changed in 1726, when the Habsburgs established the "Familiant Laws," intended to decrease the size of the Jewish population by decreeing that only the first-born son of a Jewish family would be allowed to marry and to stay in Bohemia. Younger sons who wished to marry were forced into exile. In 1744, Empress Maria Teresa tightened the screws further by issuing an order to expel Jews from Bohemian cities, thus precipitating a migration to rural parts of the country and the formation of new villages. While I can trace the Jewish side of my own family only back to the beginning of the 19th century, I have found that all but a few lived in small towns and villages and practiced typical country trades. I suspect that my rural heritage is a direct result of Maria Teresa's decree. The origins of our two names, Heller and Neumann, are more difficult to discern. Under the Habsburgs, Jews were forced to take on Germanic names; it is likely that both names were made up under duress by my ancestors during that period.

Despite efforts to Germanize the Slavic nation, ordinary citizens continued to speak Czech and many intellectuals advanced the study of the Czech language. Carrying on the work of Jan Hus, who had simplified and formalized the language, men like Dobrovský, Jungmann, and Palacký took it further. František Palacký is honored as the first man to chronicle the history of the Czech people in their own language. This nineteenth-century period also marked a turning point for the Jewish population. Two writer friends – Václav Nebeský, a Christian, and Siegfried Kapper, a Jew – promoted the idea that Jews should be viewed as Czechs who happened to practice the religion of Judaism. The concept was revolutionary on a continent where Jews always had been regarded as a separate "nationality," regardless of where they resided or where they had been granted citizenship. Although a few prominent Czechs – such as the most widely read journalist of the period, Karel Havlíček Borovský – objected, the idea of Jews as Czechs was embraced by the majority of urban and educated Czechs, and the assimilation and acculturation finally began in earnest.

In 1841, Jews were permitted to own land for the first time and, within a few years, restrictions on movement, marriage, and economic activity were removed once again. Yet, all Czechs were destined to suffer one more indignity before being able to form a free nation with its own language. Otto von Bismarck, the Prussian chancellor, had said: "He who rules Bohemia, rules Europe." Not surprisingly, in 1876, someone decided to rule Bohemia once again. The Austro-Hungarian Empire was formed; Czechs and Moravians were subjugated by Austria, while the neighboring Slovaks came under the wing of the Hungarians.

Oppression and harsh economic conditions now drove many citizens into exile; thousands came to America. Nearly 100,000 of them came through Ellis Island, on their way to places which would become their urban and rural enclaves in New York City and Chicago, as well as Iowa, Nebraska, Minnesota, and Oklahoma. A large number of farmers, tradesmen, and laborers landed in Galveston, Texas, following The Reverend Josef Arnošt Bergman, who established a community in the small town of Cat Spring. By 1910, there were more than 15,000 Czech-born settlers in Texas, most of them Protestants from Moravia, who spoke a unique dialect. A few years later, they were followed by another large group, this one primarily Catholics from Bohemia, who spoke their mother tongue in its modern form. Today, Texas has one of the largest Czech-American minorities in the U.S., and communities with names like Praha and Tabor maintain many of the traditions of their native land.

While the nineteenth century generally saw Jews progress, it also marked another setback for their assimilation into the population as a whole. Since the majority had been forced to adopt German names many years before, and because German remained the language of Jewish intellectuals, many Czechs identified Jews with the hated Austrians. Once again, anti-Semitism reared its ugly head, and thousands of Czechs, encouraged by hateful teachings of the Catholic Church, took out their frustrations on the minority. New anti-Semitic laws were enacted, and the "Jews as Czechs" concept was embraced only by the most liberal thinkers among Czech intelligentsia.

* * *

During this subjugation at the hands of the Austrians, Czechs seemed to have lost their will to assert themselves, and something called *"Švejkism"* became a national trait that would characterize the nation throughout the twentieth century. Jaroslav Hašek, a Czech writer, invented the character of Josef Švejk and wrote of his escapades in one of the best-known pieces of Czech literature, *The Good Soldier Švejk and His Fortunes in the World War*. Like my paternal grandfather, Leopold Heller, Švejk is drafted into the Austro-Hungarian army at the beginning of the First World War.

Unlike the grandfather I never knew because he died in the war, Švejk goes through life with a child-like smile on his face, mocking his masters by acting like a fool. He subverts the Austrian army's precision and discipline through his obsequious behavior. Eventually, he is discharged from military service for "patent idiocy." Since the publication of his fictional adventures in 1924, Švejk has become a metaphor for the Czechs' passive resistance – some might call it spinelessness – first to the Austro-Hungarian Empire, then to the Nazi occupation, and eventually to 41 years of communist oppression.

In my family's struggles against the Nazis and the communists, we would be aided by many heroes and betrayed by a few traitors. But mostly, we would fall victim to the indifference of a nation of Švejks.

* * *

Tomáš Masaryk is the most important figure in modern Czech history. Born in 1850 to a poor, working-class family in Moravia, he worked as a blacksmith before becoming a student of philosophy at universities in Brno, Vienna, and Leipzig. In 1882, he became a controversial professor at the University of Prague. He angered Czech intelligensia by challenging the validity of long-standing literature which promoted chauvinistic nationalism.

Masaryk enraged the majority of the populace by defending publicly Leopold Hilsner, an innocent 23-year-old Jewish vagrant, who was accused of a ritual murder of a 19-year-old Christian girl, despite the fact that there was no evidence against him. Masaryk's intervention led to the commutation of a death sentence to that of life imprisonment. Interestingly – from my own personal standpoint – when Hilsner was released from prison in 1918, he was taken in by a family named Heller from the village of Polná. Consequently and coincidentally, he changed his name to Leopold Heller – the name of my paternal grandfather who had died two years before while fighting as a soldier in the army of the Empire. Adding to the coincidence, the grandson of Hilsner's adoptive family is named Charles Heller; he lives in Toronto and is the author of a 2008 play called "The Trial of Leopold Hilsner."

Masaryk appreciated the fact that Jews adhered to their traditions and their faith, despite the fact that they had been persecuted for both for thousands of years. However, he found it impossible to embrace total assimilation. While he believed firmly, and supported totally, equal rights and decent treatment of Czech Jews, he considered them "a distinct element within a nation." Later in life, he admitted to writer Karel Čapek:

"When did I overcome in myself this popular anti-Semitism? Sir, I feel that perhaps never; only intellectually."

Educated Jews themselves were split into two factions. There were the Zionists, whose commitment was to the renaissance of Judaism in Palestine, rather than to the Czech nation. On the opposite side were my forebears and their colleagues, who spoke Czech, sent their children to Czech schools, and were fervent supporters of an independent Czech nation.

The upper echelons of the nation's Jewish population – literati such as Franz Kafka and Max Brod, as well as captains of textile and other industries – disagreed with their future president and thought of themselves strictly as Czechs. Many even changed the spelling of their names to make them less Germanic and more Czech. For example, names such as "Schweikert" and "Leipzig" were changed to the phonetic Czech, "Švajkrt" and "Lajpcik," respectively.

During World War I, Masaryk won the admiration and gratitude of his countrymen when he fled the country and began agitating for Czech and Slovak independence, first in Switzerland and then in Italy, England, and the U.S. In Cleveland and Pittsburgh, he and a group of patriots in exile signed agreements to form an independent nation called *Československo* (Czechoslovakia). Masaryk formed a network of Czech revolutionaries who provided intelligence that proved critical to the Allies' victory. He married an American champion of women's rights, Charlotte Garrigue, and he took her maiden name as his own middle name. Finally, at the conclusion of the war, he and American President Woodrow Wilson jointly wrote the Czechoslovak constitution. On October 28, 1918, Masaryk declared the nation's independence, while standing on the steps of Independence Hall in Philadelphia. Now beloved by Czechs, Tomáš Garrigue Masaryk – like Charles IV before him – became known as the father of his country, this one the country of Czechoslovakia, and became its first president. The period of his leadership would come to be known as the First Republic.

Unlike other, homogeneous, European countries, the new nation included a number of minority groups: Germans, Hungarians, Poles, Ruthenians, Gypsies, and Jews. Its Declaration of Independence, modeled after that of the United States, guaranteed equal rights to all. But laws and the good intentions of their authors did not eliminate anti-Semitism. Jews may have chosen to be nonobservant, but many Czechs decided that they were still Jews. In the early, unsettled, days of the First Republic, riots against Jews, accompanied by beatings and looting, took place in Prague and some smaller cities. The rioters, frustrated by their post-war economic difficulties, accused Jewish shopkeepers of profiteering. But, things changed in a short time. Soon, Czechoslovakia became the richest nation in Europe by virtue of having inherited nearly three-quarters of the industrial capacity of the former Austro-Hungarian Empire. After some early difficulties in absorbing this new capability and having to create new markets for products, the country became one of the most modern and industrialized in the world. Jobs were plentiful, culture flourished, and all Czechoslovaks – including the minorities -- truly enjoyed their freedom.

Czechoslovakia's Jewish citizens, no longer subjected to bigotry and mistreatment, thrived in this paradise of Wilsonian democracy. Despite his hidden feelings, Masaryk's humanitarian leadership brought about unprecedented interaction between Christian and Jewish Czechs at all levels -- social, cultural, and professional. This resulted in intermarriage rates unlike those seen anywhere in the world. When my parents – one a Jew, the other a Catholic – married in 1934, nearly one-third of Czech

Jewish grooms were marrying Gentile brides. Although only 2.5 percent of the population was Jewish, nearly one-fifth of all university students were Jews. They made significant contributions to the nation's culture – music, art, theater, literature, and science – while others thrived as businessmen, lawyers, and physicians.

Although intermarriage was more common in Czechoslovakia than elsewhere in Europe, there were many unions between Christians and Jews in other nations. One of these is of particular interest to those of us who suffered at the hands of Hitler's henchmen. In Austria, a 42-year-old Catholic woman named Maria Anna Schicklgruber worked as a cook for a wealthy Jewish family, the Frankenbergers. The latters' 19-year-old son and the cook had an affair, out of which a son was born. This Jewish-Catholic son eventually changed his name to Hitler and fathered the greatest Jew-hater of them all, Adolf.

Post-war Czechoslovakia was Masaryk's idyllic nation, a European mirror of the United States of America, a country in which all people were said to be created equal and all citizens had the opportunity to be the best they could be. Like their fellow citizens, my parents worshipped the first president, and his photos seemed to hang everywhere in our home. Some were portraits, while others showed him kissing children in native dress. In my room, he was pictured sitting on a horse, dressed in riding britches and a military cap, with a red-white-and-blue ribbon stitched to the lapel of his dark coat. He appeared – and truly was – a heroic figure to whom elderly Czechs refer as *tatíček* ("daddy") even today. Tomáš Garrigue Masaryk died on September 14, 1937, when I was less than twenty months old.

The family is one of nature's masterpieces.
George Santayana

CHAPTER 3

Czech Families Neumann and Heller

My birth on January 25, 1936, marked the first intersection of two Czech families, Neumann and Heller. Or, at least, so I thought for most of my life. It turns out that our story is as entangled as that of the Czech people. My study of the history of the Czech nation leads me to the conclusion that, when the Habsburgs forced Jews to take on Germanic names, the then-senior member of the maternal side of my family decided to become a *neu mann* ("new person"). By the same token, my guess is that during the same period, the head of the other side of my family may have been a minor banker who decided to adopt the name of the smaller unit of Austrian currency, the *heller*. Perhaps if he had been a big-time financier, my last name would be Schilling. But, all of that is speculation.

My primary window into our history is a journal kept by my maternal great-grandfather, Gustav Neumann. *Dědeček* memorialized our geneology in a black notebook, writing on quadrille paper, in neat, formal, cursive Czech, with a fountain pen. In an attempt to shield me from the horrors suffered by members of our family, and in order to protect me from a stigma they imagined would be associated with the revelation of my true ethnicity, my parents kept many secrets from me. Consequently, I was left only with those stories they chose to tell me, the recollections of friends, photographs, various notes and articles, my own memories, and – after Mother's death in 2006 – her incomplete diary and *Dědeček's* journal. The latter provides amazing detail about members of both the Neumann and Heller families. At the same time, it creates a mystery of which I was unaware until I started on a journey of discovery of my family's roots.

The first intriguing question in attempting to construct a "wiring diagram" of our genealogy comes from the appearance of the name "Neumann" on both sides of the family. It was the name of my maternal great-great-grandfather, Phillip, born in 1832, whose surname was passed through the generations all the way to my mother. But, Neumann was also the maiden name of my *father's* mother, Otilie, who was born in 1887. Although I was intrigued by this find, I considered it a mere coincidence because "Neumann" was, and still is, a fairly common name in the Czech Republic. Among several Czech Neumanns who have gained fame are St. John Neumann, the first Czech-born Roman Catholic saint and, more recently, Kateřina Neumannová, gold medalist in cross-country skiing at the 2006 Winter Olympics (Czech women's surnames generally end with *ová*, to indicate the feminine gender).

But, further digging into *Dědeček's* journal produced a thunderbolt. On the Neumann side of the family, there appears a man named Rudolf Heller, a cousin of Otakar Neumann, and thus a second cousin of *Dědeček*. Rudolf Heller was also the name of my father. The two are not the same; the former passed away in 1926, when my father was 16 years old, ten years before I was born. But, amazingly, the two were not only namesakes, but they came from the same small town. Moreover, with the exception of my maternal grandmother, all of my relatives on both sides, dating back at least to 1800, came from an area circumscribed by a circle with a diameter of only twenty miles. Is all this a coincidence? Unlikely. As the only child of Rudolf Heller and Ilona Neumannová, both only children, I had believed that I was the single connecting point of the Neumann and Heller clans. Now, I am convinced that, like the royal families of Europe, these two families were connected already through a complex web of earlier marriages. But, that, too, is simply speculation on my part and, of course, the reference to royalty is made in jest.

Gustav Neumann, my maternal great-grandfather *Dědeček*, who became the patriarch of our family, was born on August 17, 1860, in the ten-house village of Lobeček, only two miles from the home in which the man who would become the most famous of Czech composers, Antonín Dvořák, had been born 19 years earlier. *Dědeček's* parents, Phillip Neumann and the former Marie Friedová, squeezed out a living by running a food store. In order to feed their seven children, Phillip moonlighted as a glazier and an accordion player. The family moved to the nearby town of Luboč when Gustav was two years old.

Gustav apprenticed with a number of merchants and married Luisa Deutschová, one year younger and from the nearby town of Roudnice nad Labem, practically in the shadow of the mountain Říp, a monadnock prominent in the legends of ancient Czech people. In 1883, the young Gustav was ready to open his own business. He was made aware of a small general store for sale in a village with a railroad station, a post office, and a nearby state highway, his requirements for building an entrepreneurial enterprise. The village was Kojetice, located less than ten miles north of Prague. House numbers in those days were assigned in the order that the homes were built, and Gustav bought #24, containing the store and a small household for himself and Luisa.

In addition to selling shoes, belts, brooms, and buggy-whips, eventually he began importing, repairing, and renting out Singer sewing machine. This led to an idea which would result in great entrepreneurial success. He hired a lady who had been his first customer, Anna Červinková, and he trained her to sew clothes. Overnight, he was in the clothing business, making and selling aprons, trousers, shorts, and underwear. He hired out sewing to other women and brought on a tailor. Just before the turn of the twentieth century, he purchased a larger house, #7, and opened a retail clothing store in the front, with the cutting and sewing performed in the rear.

Luisa and Gustav had three children. The youngest, Ida, passed away at the age of seventeen and was buried in nearby Kostelec. Sons Ota and Artur went to work for their dad. In 1927, *Dědeček* purchased the house next door, knocked it down, and built an addition to what was now a full-fledged clothing factory with forty-eight employees. Three years later, the firm called "Gustav Neumann" was the largest manufacturer of work clothes in Central Europe. It was a major player on the Czechoslovak industrial scene with 295 employees.

Then came a difficult time. Even as the company celebrated its fiftieth anniversary in 1933, it was hit by the effects of the worldwide Great Depression. People stopped buying. Unlike other employers who made drastic cuts in their workforces, my great-grandfather laid off no one. He kept all his workers on the payroll, the majority working out of their homes. He paid them to produce goods he could not sell in order to enable them to support their families. When the depression finally ended, he had a dedicated workforce and a large inventory. The firm morphed into one called "Labor" and became a major exporter to countries throughout Europe, as well as Morocco and Palestine. The Neumanns were revered for their generosity, as they donated land and houses for community activities, sponsored athletic teams, financed the arts, and treated their employees like family members.

My father, Rudolf – whom I called *Tatínek* when we spoke Czech and "Papa" later in America – was born on Saturday, December 17, 1910, at 41 Římská Street, in the Vinohrady section of Prague, to Leopold and Otilie Heller. Before young Rudolf got a chance to know him well, his father was drafted into the army of the Austro-Hungarian Empire and was killed in action in the First World War. Leopold Heller, my paternal grandfather, was buried in Budapest twenty years before I was born.

After Leopold's death in World War I, Otilie found it impossible to care for herself and her young son, and both were taken in by her brother, Emil Neumann (there is the name "Neumann," on the *Heller* side of the family!), and his wife, Zdeňka. They lived in the town of Kralupy, about 15 miles down the Vltava River from Prague, where Emil owned a store which sold construction materials and equipment. Young Rudolf attended school in Kralupy and helped out in the store. I remember my great uncle

Emil and his wife only vaguely because the last time I visited them, I was just four years old. Soon thereafter, unbeknownst to me until much later in life, their entire family was exterminated in Nazi gas chambers. Sadly, I know Papa's other uncles and aunts only from brief written notes. There were Rudolf and his wife Emma in Prague, and Jula and Kačka, who resided in Vienna before being herded away by the Germans and eventually murdered in a concentration camp, too.

My father had begun elementary schooling while still in Prague, on Purkyňovo Square. At the age of twelve, after having completed grammar school in Kralupy, he began several years of commuting to Prague – first, to attend gymnasium (high school for university-bound students) at Na Smetance in Vinohrady and then to Bergmann Business College, from which he graduated in 1930. The fact that he was able to obtain a college education was attributable to President Masaryk, who insisted that Czechoslovakia, unlike all other countries in Central Europe, must not have Jewish quotas imposed on higher education.

Rudolf stood five feet, eight inches tall, and had the powerful build of an athlete. He excelled in soccer, volleyball, and table tennis, and he and a friend would set the European singles kayak distance record by paddling their homemade boats from Neratovice (a town near Kojetice, on the river Labe) all the way to Hamburg – a total of nearly eight hundred miles. Papa was handsome, with blue eyes and blond hair, wavy like an on-rushing surf. His manner was stern and formal to those who met him for the first time, but friendly and warm toward his family and those who became his friends.

My mother, Ilona, was born out of wedlock on November 21, 1915, in Vienna, Austria. Her mother, Marie Kozuschniková, a Sudeten ethnic-German, Czech Catholic, was not married to the father, Artur Neumann. For this reason, Ilona's last name at birth was that of her mother when she was christened in a Roman Catholic church in Vienna VIII, Alservorstadt. She became Ilona Neumannová when she was adopted by Artur a month later.

"Officially, I was adopted by my father," Mother would tell me many years later. "But, actually, I was adopted by three men and one lady. I was brought up by the trio of my father, my uncle Ota, and my grandfather Gustav, as well as my grandmother Luisa. I had the best childhood any girl could ask for, and I was spoiled rotten."

Mother was known not only as the richest girl in the region, but also as the most beautiful. About five feet six inches tall and slender, she had brown eyes and her black hair was short and upswept in the style of the period. Her radiant smile revealed a gap between her upper front teeth and lit up every room she entered.

Back then, no one seemed to notice that the elder Neumanns were Jewish. Like the Heller side of the family, they did not think of themselves as Jews. They did not speak German or Yiddish, nor did they belong to any Jewish organizations. They were totally assimilated Czech patriots. Mother was raised a Catholic and even became the first-ever girl altar-"boy" in the 700-year-old Church of St. Vitus across the street from our home. After attending elementary school in Kojetice, she graduated from the English School in Prague. Always something of a tomboy, she played soccer and volleyball with the boys, and she hung around with them when they smoked secretly "behind the barn."

The year 1932 marked a turning point in my parents' lives. It was the year Rudolf Heller came to work for Labor. He continued to live in Kralupy and made the daily commute by train to the industrial town, Neratovice, and then covered the last two miles to Kojetice on foot. Besides becoming absorbed in the challenges of helping to build Gustav Neumann's firm into an international powerhouse, Rudolf became romantically involved with the boss' granddaughter, Ilona. Within a few short months of his arrival, they fell in love. My father found it difficult to court my mother without personal transportation, and he was tired of riding a train which took nearly two hours to travel 20 miles. So, he made the first major purchase of his life, a beautiful, red, Czech-made, Jawa motorcycle.

The couple traveled the countryside on weekends, spending much of their time sipping Ludmila wine at their favorite spot, the castle in Mělník, high on a hill surrounded by vineyards and overlooking the confluence of the country's two great rivers, Vltava and Labe. In 1934, Papa established his own company, a textile finishing business, as a sister company of Labor. In July of that year, he and Mother announced their engagement at a grand party in Kojetice, attended by relatives and friends from both sides. Following Czech tradition, the future maid of honor smashed a tea cup on the floor and each attendee received a small shard of the broken china as a keepsake. Papa grabbed the largest fragments and had them set in a golden frame in the shape of a heart. The memento of that happy day hung on a wall of our home when I was a small boy.

Five months later, one day before my father's twenty-fourth birthday, my parents were married at city hall on *Staroměstké náměstí* (Old Town Square) in Prague – on December 16, 1934. I treasure the photo of my 19-year-old mother in a white wedding gown and Papa in a winter coat with fur collar, coming down the steps, with little Tommy Eisner – who would one day become my "big brother" in America – standing behind them.

The wedding reception was held at the Hotel Esplanade, across the avenue from the Woodrow Wilson train station, in Prague. The father of one of Mother's closest Kojetice friends, Denise Opeltová, was the general manager of the Esplanade and he prepared an elegant setting in the ballroom for the event. Of the many wedding gifts the couple received, the most treasured was a brand new Czech-made Tatra convertible, presented to them by my future namesake, my great-uncle Ota. When the newlyweds returned from a delayed honeymoon at the Winter Olympics in Switzerland, Papa assumed the role of chief executive officer of Labor, with the elder Neumanns – Gustav, Artur, and Ota – acting as his board of directors. In addition to being the largest employers in the region, my parents also became leaders in the community. Both were active in the patriotic gymnastic society, Sokol, the most influential and most popular organization in the nation.

Founded in 1862, Sokol (Czech for "falcon") embodied the national ideal and its aim was "the physical, and in part also the moral, education and improvement of all the nation, its nurturing for the enhancement of its strength, bravery, refinement, and defense." The strength of Sokol, and its threat to enemies of the Czech nation, is best exemplified by the fact that it would be among the first organizations to be shut down by both the Nazis and the communists when they seized power. Mother became leader of the Sokol girls and women of Kojetice, while Papa led the boys and men.

On Saturday, January 25, 1936, Mother gave birth to their only child in Jerrie's Maternity Ward of Prague's Vinohrady hospital. I was named Ota Karel, my first name in honor of my great uncle, now also the mayor of Kojetice, and my middle name taken from the man who would become my godfather, our neighbor and village blacksmith, Karel Šubrt. Many years later, when I was a parent myself, I would ask Mother why I had been an only child. Mother explained that she and Papa had wanted to have two children. She became pregnant again a few months after I was born.

"But, then I was climbing one of those high ladders in the factory warehouse, helping to get cloth for the seamstresses," she explained. "I strained something, and the baby was lost." My parents tried once more, and Mother became pregnant for the third time.

"But, then the Nazis came..." Her voice trailed off, and she did not explain further. There was no need. It would be the only time we would discuss the subject. But, I wondered often, as I do today, if my brother- or sister-to-be was an uncounted victim of the Germans.

My great grandmother, Luisa, passed away less than five months after my birth at the age of 75, on June 23, 1936, and she was buried next to her daughter, Ida, in the nearby town of Kostelec nad Labem. My only memory of Grandma Neumannová is a single photo of her holding me in her arms in our garden. Unbeknownst to all at the time was the fact that she would be the last member of our once-large family to die a natural death for the 52 years that would follow.

CHAPTER 4

Occupation: The Nazi Circle

Just prior to my birth, in late 1935, Tomáš Garrigue Masaryk stepped down, and diplomat Dr. Edvard Beneš became the second president of the young nation. This was already a tumultuous time in Europe, with Hitler flexing his muscles and declaring that Austria belonged to the Germans. If Germany would annex Austria, Czechoslovakia would be surrounded by the Nazis. Simultaneously, much of the German ethnic population of Czechoslovakia – numbering two-and-a-half million and located primarily in the Sudeten territory, along the borders with Germany and Austria – was beginning to identify more closely with Hitler than with the nation to which they had pledged allegiance after the First World War. Led by an obscure schoolteacher named Konrad Henlein, these Sudetens, as well as their brethren on the other side of the border, began agitating for annexation of this territory by the German state, as part of Hitler's call for the unification of all his countrymen under one great empire.

President Beneš, a mild-mannered intellectual, was summoned by Hitler to Berchtesgaden, Germany, to discuss the Sudeten issue. Beneš declined the invitation.

"If I went, it would end in disaster because I would never accept his insults," he explained. "I would have to answer him, and as such a creature is impervious to reason, the only answer would be to take a hand grenade in my pocket and, when he started to shout, simply to throw it at him."

Beneš was referring to the Führer's lunatic rantings about Czechoslovakia, its ethnic German population, and its president. Just prior to ordering Beneš to meet with him, Hitler had screamed insults at the Czech people:

"The creation of this heterogeneous Czechoslovak Republic after the war was lunacy. It has none of the characteristics of a nation, whether from the standpoint of ethnology, strategy, economics or language. To set an intellectually inferior handful of Czechs to rule over minorities belonging to races like the Germans, Poles, Hungarians, with a thousand years of culture behind them, was a work of folly and ignorance. The Sudeten Germans have no respect for the Czechs and will never accept their rule. After the (First World) War, the allied powers declared that Germany was unworthy to govern blacks, yet at the same time they set second-rate people like the Czechs in authority over three-and-a-half million Germans of the highest character and culture..."

Foreseeing an invasion, Beneš ordered the immediate building of fortifications along the Czech-German borders. When Germany annexed Austria in the Anschluss in the spring of 1938 and this border became even longer, he ordered the building of many more reinforced concrete pillboxes in the south.

The Sudeten Germans continued to scream, and Hitler threatened more. The allies were still looking for a peaceful resolution and, this time, they asked the Italian dictator, Benito Mussolini, to act as a mediator. *Il Duce* called for a conference among Hitler, British Prime Minister Neville Chamberlain, French Prime Minister Edouard Daladier, and himself – with the Czechoslovaks excluded – to be held in Munich in September 1938. On the 30th of September, the treacherous document called the "Munich Agreement" was signed by the attendees. It called for the ceding of all borderland areas of Czechoslovakia to Germany. Chamberlain declared "peace in our time," and both he and Deladier were welcomed enthusiastically back in their homelands, having amputated a defenseless small country. To this day and forever forward, the word

30

"Munich" means only one thing to Czechs and Slovaks: the sell-out of their nation by their supposed friends. Sadly, the isolationist America of the 1930s not only looked on this travesty with disinterest, believing that the expanse of the Atlantic Ocean would insure her peace and prosperity, but her president approved of the sell-out. Franklin D. Roosevelt sent Chamberlain a telegram: "Good man," it read. "I am not a bit upset over the final result."

The Czechoslovak government at first refused to abide by the Munich Agreement, but then it gave in under the weight of demands from its British and French "allies." In response, the Czechoslovak public revolted with a general strike and demanded a change in government. They succeeded. Beneš's newly-constituted cabinet refused to recognize the Hitler-Chamberlain agreement and immediately declared a general mobilization, with all young men required to begin training to defend their nation.

My great-uncle Ota, the mayor of Kojetice, wanted my father to be the first man in the district to join the army, as a sign of our family's patriotism. So, Papa joined immediately and was assigned to a unit in Piešt'any, Slovakia. He drove all the way across the country to his new base, flying the flag of the patriotic organization, Sokol – a red banner with a white falcon – from the antenna of his Tatra convertible, as a gesture of resistance. I recall a day when I was three years old and Papa came home on leave from the mobilized army in the middle of the night. He sat down at the foot of my bed. When I awoke, he held and kissed me, and then gave me a red metal airplane with red-white-and-blue Czechoslovak markings on its wings. The airplane would become my most prized possession during the next few years. After Papa returned to his unit in Slovakia, I carried it everywhere, even to church on the day of my christening, much to the chagrin of Mother and the priest.

The pressure from the Germans, the British, and the French for Czechoslovakia to permit the secession of the Sudeten lands grew in intensity. Naïvely, the western powers thought this would prevent war.

Finally, Beneš and his new government had no choice but to accept the Munich pact. The mobilized army was dissolved. My soldier father, the Czechoslovak army, and the entire nation were angry by this betrayal and humiliation. Many Czechs and Slovaks developed a deep distrust for the West, one which – only a few years later – would help to drive the country toward a disastrous concord with the Soviet Union.

Beneš abdicated and flew to London, where, anticipating Hitler's total destruction of Czechoslovakia, he prepared to form a government in exile. Papa came home, hung up his army uniform in a closet, resumed his civilian life, and wondered what would happen next. He gave me his army cap, which I would continue to wear within the confines of the various homes I would occupy throughout the war. With it on my head and the red airplane held high, I would run around pretending I was bombing and killing Germans.

Emil Hácha, an intellectual and ineffective judge and poet, became president of the carved-up country. On March 14, 1939, he was summoned to Berlin by Hitler, ostensibly to discuss the fate of Slovakia. Instead, he was bullied into signing an agreement to permit Germany to integrate Czechoslovakia into its empire. He put his name on the paper at 3:55 a.m. of the fifteenth of March, unaware of the fact that the German army was massed on his country's border, prepared to cross.

※ ※ ※

At 6:00 a.m., Hitler's army invaded Czechoslovakia. Immediately, Germans took over all government functions, keeping Hácha as a figurehead president of the newly-named Bohemia and Moravia Protectorate. Slovakia was split away and became a separate fascist country, with Monsignor Josef Tiso, an anti-Semitic Roman Catholic priest, as its president.

Hitler's secret goal after the conquest of Czechoslovakia was to conquer country after country throughout Europe. After that, he would be strong enough to vanquish and subjugate the remainder of the world. On August 23, 1939, Germany and the unknowing leadership of the

Soviet Union also signed an agreement: a nonaggression pact. This folly led to the partition of Poland. While Britain and France had no problem in sacrificing Czechoslovakia, they drew the line of their tolerance of Hitler's ambitions at the Polish border. When Poland was invaded, they declared war.

Soon, the Germans began the process of depriving Jewish citizens of their homes and property. The world would find out later that the Nazis had long-term plans to eradicate all Jews, as well as some racial groups and nationalities, from the European continent, in the building of their perfect Aryan world.

They constructed a "totem pole" of nationalities, which grouped Europeans into eleven groups. At the top were the "Reichsdeutsche" – Germans living in Germany. At the bottom were the easternmost Slavic groups: Russians, Ukrainians, Belarusians, Serbs, Turks, and Slavic Muslims. We Czechs, as well as Poles, Estonians, Lithuanians, and Finns, were two rungs up from the bottom – "subhuman and racially inferior." Unbeknownst to all, millions of people belonging to the inferior groups were scheduled for eventual extinction or deportation to Siberia and other lands east of the Ural Mountains.

I use the first-person-plural pronoun "we" because everyone in my family considered himself or herself a Czech, whether Catholic or Jew. There were three types of Jews in Czechoslovakia. First, there were those whose language was German. They were intellectuals (such as the writer, Franz Kafka) who wrote and spoke German, and thus, despite their secularity, were considered a separate community from the Czech mainstream. Second, a small minority of religious Jews practiced Judaism and spoke German or Yiddish, or both. They, too, lived outside the mainstream. The third, and largest, group consisted of Czech Jews who were secular and totally assimilated into Czech society. They did not practice their religion and, in fact, observed such holidays as Easter and Christmas according to their nation's traditions. They spoke Czech exclusively, had "Christian" Czech first names, and were fervent patriots. Jewish members of the Neumann and Heller families belonged to the latter group. But, the Nazis thought otherwise. Most of our family eventually would be separated out as Jews, a racial group residing below the bottom of the Nazi totem pole.

As we were to learn, the race-conscious Nazis used anthropological examinations to determine if a person belonged to one of the races inferior to the Master race – Jews, gypsies, Slavs. But, because of the common practice of religious intermarriage in Central Europe, they had problems, at least early on, defining who was Jewish. As it became obvious to European Jews that the Germans would eventually occupy their countries and, when they did, that they would discriminate against them, the Jews took actions which they thought would protect them. They saw the prevailing Christian religion, Roman Catholicism, as their means of escape from harm. Jews who married Gentiles immediately converted to Catholicism and, encouraged by missionaries with promises of safety, even Jews who were not in mixed marriages became Catholics.

According to Jewish Law (*Halacha*), a person is considered a Jew if born to a Jewish mother or if he or she has formally converted to Judaism. Having been born to a Christian mother – who, herself, was the daughter of a Christian mother – and having been a Roman Catholic since birth, I was quite irrefutably a Christian. Furthermore, the fact that I had not been circumcised made me even less Jewish. Mother, too, was clearly a Christian. Both of us were baptized Catholics, and the only religious education we had ever received was that of the Roman Catholic faith. Neither of us knew anything about Judaism.

The Germans, determined to safeguard the purity of race, had other ideas. In 1935, they established the Nürnberg Laws, which decreed that anyone with three Jewish grandparents was a Jew, regardless of religious affiliation or self-identification.

Within a week of the occupation of Czechoslovakia, General Alois Eliáš, who would be named prime minister of the government of the Bohemia and Moravia Protecrorate, brought forth a proposal to the

Germans, asking for a more lenient definition of Czech Jewry. His plan defined a Jew as a person born to four Jewish grandparents who "belong to the Jewish community." In case of less than four such grandparents, or if a grandparent had not belonged to the Jewish community on or after November 1, 1918, a Jew who had no criminal record, was not a Communist, and whose family had resided in the country for fifty years or more, could apply for an exemption from being classified as a Jew. Under this proposal, our entire family would have been exempt as a result of not having belonged to the Jewish community, and Mother and I would have been doubly exempt because neither of us had four Jewish grandparents.

Unfortunately for all of us, after a great deal of discussion between the Protectorate government and the Germans, and within Nazi high-level circles, it was decreed that Czechs, like the Germans, would follow the Nürnberg Laws. By now, these had been expanded and consisted of typically precise German formulas for a people considered inferior to the Master Race, people said to be responsible for all that was wrong with the world. A Jewish person was defined as one who met any one of four conditions: having three or four Jewish grandparents; or having two Jewish grandparents who belonged to the Jewish community on September 15, 1935, or joined thereafter; or being married to a Jew on September 15, 1935, or having married one after that date; or being the offspring of a marriage or extramarital affair with a Jew on or after September 15, 1935.

My Christian mother who had married a Jew in 1934 and was the offspring of a Jewish-Christian coupling qualified as a Jew under two of the categories. I, that devout little Catholic boy, had both three Jewish grandparents and a Jewish father, and thus also met two of the Nazi definitions. Once the Czech government was forced to accept the Nürnberg Laws, both of us were in trouble – unless the authorities could be convinced that *Děda*, Mother's father and my grandfather, was a Christian – which he was not. In that case, Mother, though not I, would be in the clear. But more on this later.

In addition to those Jews who had taken recent action in order to avoid Nazi persecution, throughout Europe there were thousands of Jews who had converted to Catholicism in the late nineteenth and early twentieth centuries. This, along with intermarriage between Christians and Jews, primarily in Europe's cosmopolitan cities, created problems for the Germans' insane objective of creating a continent of a racially pure Aryan society. Thus, they went a step further and came up with definitions of, and rules for, people who were not classified as Jews but whose veins contained drops of Jewish blood. Using the term *Mischlinge* – "hybrids" or "mongrels" – they added two levels of impurity.

Mischlinge of the first degree were those with two Jewish grandparents. Mischlinge of the second degree had one Jewish grandparent. In October 1942, the Germans would decide that all first-degree Mischlinge would be sterilized, while those of the second degree would continue to be subjected to previously-established restrictions. The sterilization would never be carried out, but many Mischlinge of the first degree, especially those who, according to German criteria, looked or acted Jewish, would die in concentration camps. Ironically, as documented by American author Bryan Rigg, as many as 150,000 Mischlinge of both degrees would end up fighting in the German armed forces, and several would even reach the ranks of general, admiral, and field marshal.

Before the Nazis came up with the "Final Solution," the mass murder of all Jews, they devised laws which placed limitations for Jews on employment, use of public transportation and private automobiles, and shopping. Restrictions on Mischlinge were less severe, but they existed nevertheless. They extended to housing, use of telephones, and use of public toilets. Later, as the Germans began to tighten the screws, Jews and Mischlinge were not allowed to leave their homes without displaying a yellow Star of David on their outer clothing.

Stressing the superiority of the Aryan race, the Germans went far beyond classifying Jews, as they divided populations of occupied countries into different groups, according to racial purity. The rights of each group

– food rations, living quarters, use of public transportation, ability to send children to schools – depended on where each group stood on the purity scale. Curiously, although impure by Nazi standards, 13,000 Japanese were allowed to live comfortably in Germany during the war; because their country fought as part of the Axis, they were considered "honorary Aryans."

People in the Protectorate, the racially inferior Slavs, were not as lucky. Food rationing for all citizens began in the fall of 1939. Soon thereafter, goods of all kinds began to disappear from the shelves of stores, as Czech industry and agriculture was forced to support the German war machine. For Jews, things were much worse. They were allowed to shop only during designated hours, after that day's available goods had been picked over by non-Jewish shoppers.

A total of 118,000 citizens were classified as Jews. In those very early days of the occupation, approximately twenty percent of this targeted group managed to emigrate. Only 14,045 of those who stayed would survive the war; Slovakia's number of Jewish survivors would be only slightly smaller.

Czechs showed their resistance to the German occupation in typical, Švejk-like, ways. On April 20, 1939, they ignored Hitler's birthday and, instead, lay hundreds of flowers at the base of the Jan Hus monument in Old Town Square. On May 5, they placed wreaths and flowers next to the statue of Woodrow Wilson across the street from the train station which had borne his name.

A week later, the Prague Symphony Orchestra played Bedřich Smetana's patriotic suite, *Má vlast* ("My Country"), at the National Theater. It is difficult for citizens of free nations to comprehend how pieces of music – in the case of Czechs, *Má vlast* and the national anthem, *Kde domov můj?* – can bring out deep, almost uncontrollable, emotions. This is because Americans and a few others have never been occupied, oppressed, and forbidden to listen to, or sing, their patriotic songs. Smetana's suite is a cycle of symphonic poems, the last telling of a glorious Czech liberation. *Vltava* is the second symphony, and it portrays the nation's favorite river.

The river begins in the southern forest of Šumava and flows through the Bohemian countryside. It crashes over rapids before it reaches Prague, where it seems to pause to admire the great rocky fortress, *Vyšehrad*, and the ancient seat of the Czech nation, *Hradčany*. After passing through the historic capital, Vltava flows through fields and valleys once more, before merging with the river Labe. On that day in May 1939, the playing of *Má vlast* was followed by a fifteen-minute, emotional, thunderous, standing ovation and the conductor kissing Smetana's score. Immediately, the Germans banned the playing of *Má vlast* and *Kde domov můj?* for the next six years. In so doing, they deprived us of a part of our essential being: the story of our country through our own poetic language. Through obliterating the arts, one can obliterate a people.

When asked directions on the street by German soldiers or officials, the *Švejks* of Prague would reply: *"Nerozumím"* ("I don't understand") despite the fact that most spoke at least some German. City workers refused to erect new German street signs. Drivers of cars "forgot" that the Germans had announced only eleven days after the occupation that, effective immediately, driving was being changed from the left side of the road to the right. Such "forgetfulness" caused many accidents and tie-ups.

On October 28, 1939, the twenty-first anniversary of Czechoslovakia's independence, resistance groups organized a protest against the occupation. After gathering on Wenceslas Square, the marchers descended on a hotel housing the Gestapo, demanding the release of political prisoners. They managed to free one man but, as the demonstrations continued, the Nazis, aided by Czech police, decided to take action. They shot two of the patriots. One died instantly. The other, a medical student, survived, but died two weeks later. His death brought about violent protests by university students. This, in turn, gave the Germans the excuse to shut down all universities in the Protectorate. Moreover, it was the end of any public opposition to the occupiers.

***

Early on in the occupation, my parents, like most Czech citizens, were unaware of the complex German ethnicity formulas, and they thought that Mother and I, both Catholics, were safe from prejudice or persecution. For that reason, she and I were last on our household's schedule for escaping the country. My father was to flee first. He put together a complex scheme for getting to the west, where he would then orchestrate escapes for the rest of us. But, that plan was foiled when his schedule was accelerated. On February 21, 1940, he kissed Mother and me goodbye as usual, before leaving for work, without knowing that these would be our last kisses for more than five years. After a day of meetings in Prague, he headed for home. As he turned from the highway onto the road to Kojetice, he was flagged down by a friend who was waiting for him at the intersection.

"Don't go back home tonight," she warned him. "There is a warrant for your arrest, and the Gestapo is waiting for you in the village."

It turns out that my father had been convicted of an unspecified crime and sentenced to six months in prison and a fine of one million Czech crowns. But, he knew that the consequences would be much harsher than that. Without even a toothbrush to his name, he drove to the Smíchov section of Prague, where he knocked on the door of the apartment of an old schoolmate. His friend let him hide there for five days, a period during which he made contact with the "underground railroad" that was assisting hundreds of escapees. He sent word to Mother that he was leaving and that he would arrange for us to follow in the near future. He headed for Slovakia, where he crossed the border into Hungary, traveling partly by train and mostly on foot. Using a false passport, he managed to get to Yugoslavia. He had been told that the British Army, with assistance from the Yugoslav Partisan organization, was recruiting Czechoslovak escapees in Belgrade to form a new unit to fight in the Middle East. Papa went to the Czech embassy, where he received no help from the ambassador or his staff. Yugoslavs were helpful, but they feared their pro-Nazi regime and could not offer anything beyond an occasional meal. Papa spent more than two months trying to make the connection which would help him reach the Brits. He whiled away the days by studying English. Then, carelessness almost cost him deportation back to the Protectorate and, most likely, his life.

Sitting in a park and reading *The London Times* with the aid of a Czech-English dictionary, he was arrested by the police. He was thrown into prison, where he awaited trial on espionage charges. For three weeks, he slept on the floor of his cell with little food and no water for washing or shaving. Finally, a Serbian guard came to bring him to trial. He brought him to the court waiting room on the fourth floor of the building housing the prison. After several minutes of standing in the middle of the room, the guard whispered in Papa's ear:

"I'm a member of the Resistance. I'm going to turn my back for half a minute, and I don't want to see you when I turn back."

The only problem was that there were five doors leading out of the room. Papa stood there, trying to determine which one to try. He could eliminate the one through which they had entered, but the others could have led anywhere – to the court, to someone's office. He had only one chance. What to do?

"Suddenly, one of the doors opened, and a clerk emerged with a stack of files in his arms," Papa would tell us after the war. "I felt as though I was pulled to this guy by a magnet. I followed him through another door and stayed on his heels, down four floors, past sentries, past the prison entrance, and all the way to the street. Then, I ducked into the nearest cellar."

Unshaven, dirty, wearing wrinkled clothes and shoes without laces, he could not walk the streets in the daytime. When night came, Papa crept out, sneaked into the room he had been renting to wash, shave, change clothes and pick up his money, and then walked to the outskirts of Belgrade. From there, he made his way to the countryside, where he hid in haystacks for two days until he felt sufficiently safe to find a railroad station. After studying a map of the country, he caught a train for the seashore. He had enough money to rent rooms in various small hotels and, for nearly five months, pretended to be a tourist in search of surf, sand and sun. But, he was not enjoying his "vacation" at the beach, was worrying about Mother and me, and was anxious to continue his journey. In October, seven months after his escape from Czechoslovakia, he determined that the air had cleared sufficiently and he returned to Belgrade.

There, finally, he made contact with Yugoslav Partisans, who took him to a safe house, where he joined a small, informal Czech army unit, the first group permitted to pass through Greece and Turkey. In Istanbul, the British Mission dispatched the rag-tag group to Messina, a Mediterranean port, where the would-be soldiers awaited transport either to Syria or Palestine. Two weeks later, a Polish ship, *Warsaw*, took the unit, which by now had swollen to 150 Czechs and Slovaks, aboard for the journey across the sea. They landed in Jaffa, a port near Tel Aviv, where the British Army had its receiving camp. There, they were officially conscripted into the service. Finally, my father was safe and a soldier ready to fight the hated Germans.

In the end, we will remember not the words of our enemies,
but the silence of our friends.
Martin Luther King

CHAPTER 5

Persecution

Before his arrest in Belgrade, Papa had made arrangements for the escapes of my grandfather, Artur – *Děda*, and my great-uncle, Ota – *Strejda*, and then for Mother and me. I do not recall ever having said "goodbye" to *Děda* and *Strejda* . One day, they simply disappeared, and I was ordered by Mother not to ask questions and not to discuss their absence with anyone. Now, Mother, *Dědeček*, and I were alone and I was thoroughly confused by the upheavals that had taken place in our close-knit family.

It turns out that my grandfather and great-uncle were brought out of the Protectorate by the same "underground railroad" which had assisted Papa in his escape. Although we would never be able to determine their exact fate, we would be informed at the end of the war that something had gone wrong and that they had been captured by the Germans somewhere in Yugoslavia. The Nazis shot Ota dead, and they murdered Artur by poisoning him.

Father also had arranged for, and paid, a Yugoslav diplomat to go to Prague. He was to bring Mother and me to his country's embassy and then to leave the country, with Mother as his wife and me as their son. Falsified Yugoslav passports were prepared for us, a courier delivered the message with the plan, and we were packed and waiting. But, our chances for flight to freedom disappeared with a telephone call from a friend, warning Mother to unpack immediately because the Nazis had discovered the scheme. The Gestapo interrogated and tortured Mother for weeks in their infamous Peček Palace headquarters in Prague, but she pleaded ignorance. My strong and courageous mother never wavered, despite the beatings and threats administered by her captors. She maintained her story that she had no idea of the whereabouts of her husband. He had simply disappeared one day, and she had not heard from him since. As far as she was concerned, she told the Nazis, he had deserted his family. She must have been convincing because the Germans did not punish us. Unaware of the fact that Papa had planned our escape, I could not understand why he had not sent for us; I expressed my anger to Mother. It was only then that she told me that Papa was somewhere fighting against the Germans, and that I was to keep it a secret, lest our lives would be in danger. My anger turned to pride in my heroic father, fighting for our freedom.

Mother, my great-grandfather, and I were now the only family members remaining in the village of Kojetice. In July 1940, *Dědeček* was informed that Josef Hollman, from Warnsdorf, Germany (formerly Varnsdorf in the Sudeten part of Czechoslovakia), had "purchased" our factory in Kojetice as well as our apartment building in Prague. We were being evicted from our spacious and beautiful apartment at the factory so that the Nazi and his family could move in and run the business. We were ordered to leave all furniture and to take with us only those belongings which we could carry away.

The Germans' requirement for process and procedure, even in the act of stealing, made it necessary to document the Hollman "acquisition." This stretched our stay in our apartment until December. Our next-door neighbors, Vladimir Tůma and his wife, Marie Tůmová, owned one of the larger farms in Kojetice and graciously offered to let the three of us move in with them, with the stipulation that Mother would pay rent with money and labor.

When she was growing up in Kojetice, my mother, Ilona Neumannová, worked hard at being just another village kid. Despite the wealth and family standing which could have set her apart from the other children who came from families of modest means, she fit right in. In her early years, she attended the public elementary school, rather than being packed off for boarding school like other kids from wealthy families. She played soccer and volleyball with the boys, and she was usually the instigator in pulling pranks throughout town. Even in her late teens – when she departed for the English School in Prague and vacationed with her family on the Riviera – she had time to socialize with her village pals.

Now, some of those old friends came to our rescue. During the fall, Mother's former schoolmate, Vojtěch Řezáč, whose wife had been our family's cook, gathered a small group of his strong, young teammates from the town soccer team. They defied the Germans' orders and, over several nights, carried some of our most valuable furnishings, including a grand piano, out of our second-story apartment, across the factory loading area, down the street, across the farm courtyard, and up a ladder to a hiding place in the loft of one of Tůmas' barns. How they managed to accomplish this remains a mystery and stuff of legend in Kojetice even today.

We settled into life on the farm. Mother, the refined lady who had been surrounded by servants all her life, now worked in the fields digging potatoes, stacking hay, and collecting sugar beets. As September approached, I looked forward to starting school across the street from the factory which had been ours. One evening, I asked Mother if we would be going to Prague so that we could buy a leather backpack in which I would carry my school books like the other kids. Mother looked at me for what seemed a long time, without answering. Finally she put her arms around me and held on. I could feel her hot tears streaming down the back of my neck.

"*Otíčku*," she sobbed. "I'm very sorry, but you won't be going to school."

I had been told not to ask too many questions about all the strange things which were going on in our lives, but now, through my own tears, I wanted to know why all my friends would be going to school and I would not be going with them.

"The Germans won't allow you to attend school because your father is in the British army, fighting against them," Mother explained.

Of course, I was unaware of the fact that Mother was only guessing, having no idea where Papa was, if he was really fighting against the Germans, or if he was even alive. Nor did I know that this would become the "party-line" used to explain to me why we were being selected by the Nazis for special maltreatment, suffering, and humiliation. It was the beginning of hiding from me any hint of Jewishness in my ancestry, a deception which would continue even throughout my adult life. Still the devout Catholic, I had not a clue that the Germans considered me a Jew and that, effective August 1940, Jewish children were not permitted to attend Czech schools. Determined to protect me from the Nazis, Mother wanted me to know nothing about my ethnic origins – and she succeeded.

Yet, despite my pride in my heroic father and a feeling that my suffering was my patriotic duty, I could not help but wonder:

"Why are the other children in the village going to school, playing hide-and-seek, riding bicycles, visiting relatives? What makes me different from them?"

Mother was concerned about my education and asked one of the teachers, Mr. Rech, if he or his daughter would be willing to tutor me. He declined, admitting that he was afraid to anger the Germans and their Czech collaborators.

Dědeček helped with some light household chores and spent many hours each day with me, walking in the fields and the woods, and teaching me to read. As each other's only companions for months, we became inseparable – an 80-year-old worldly gentleman and a five-year-old boy. We must have made a strange sight for the villagers: a distinguished, white-haired, bearded and bespectacled, old man in a three-piece gray suit, holding the hand of a pudgy, blond-haired kid skipping on the dirt roads. As an only child of two only children, I was unlucky in that I never had real uncles or aunts, but I had the rare privilege of not only knowing my great-grandfather, but of having him as my best friend.

In the summer of 1941, I became ill. It began with a sore throat and fever. A few days later, I developed a rash over the upper part of my body. I was taken to Bulovka hospital in the Libeň section of Prague, where I was diagnosed with *spála* (scarlet fever), and placed in isolation. Mother was terribly upset by the fact that she could not visit me due to the quarantine. I was frightened because I had been removed from my remaining small family. My only human contact was with ghostly, scary figures in white frocks and masks, who entered my room only occasionally. I imagined that they were Germans who had kidnapped and banished me. When I began to improve and could walk around the room, Mother came each day, a half-hour train ride and another half-hour walk from the station to the hospital. Every day, she stood on the sidewalk for nearly an hour, just to be able to see me at the window. Then, she returned to the railway station and to Kojetice. I was terribly lonely and homesick, and I wanted to jump from the third-story window in order to be with her and away from the ghosts.

Each night, I prayed to *andělíčku, můj strážníčku* ("little angel, my little guardian") to reunite me with my beloved mother. Finally, after fifty days, I was released from the hospital. On the train ride back to Kojetice, Mother held me close and I felt safe again as I pressed against her strong body. I looked into her brown eyes and traced her eyebrows, nose, and mouth with my forefinger.

"*Maminko*, you are the most beautiful lady in the whole world," I whispered so that the other passengers would not hear. She smiled sadly and kissed me on the lips.

Dědeček was waiting for us at the station, and I was overjoyed to be reunited with my only remaining family as he and Mother held my hands while we walked through the village on our way home to Tůmas' farm. The only aftereffect of my illness was a heart murmur, which would stay with me until my early teens.

* * *

The following spring came the most devastating moment of my young life. The morning of April 21, 1942, I came into the farm kitchen for breakfast. To my great surprise, I found *Dědeček* standing there, dressed in his gray suit, and wearing a gray overcoat with a six-pointed, yellow star with the strange word "*Jude*" (German for "Jew") at its center, sewn to his lapel. Next to him, on the floor, stood a suitcase.

"Where are you going, *Dědečku?*" I asked.

"I have to go away for a little while," he lied. "But, don't worry. I'll see you again soon."

He, Mother, Mrs. Tůmová, and I climbed aboard a wagon pulled by two horses, and Mr. Tůma drove us to the railroad station on the other side of town. Mother and I stood on the platform with *Dědeček*, awaiting a train to Prague. To this day, *Dědeček's* last words to Mother echo in my head and touch my soul:

"You take care of *Otík* and yourself. I'm sure that something will be left here when it's over, and you'll be able to start all over again."

The train carried him to Prague, where he and hundreds of other prisoners were assembled in the Exposition Hall of the Trade Fair grounds near Stromovka. The next day, he and hundreds of Jews, each carrying one or two suitcases, were marched through the streets of Prague to another train station. There, they were squeezed into cattle cars of a train that made a slow three-hour trip to the concentration camp in Terezín. Known as Theresienstadt to Germans, Terezín is a historic fortress 60 kilometers north of Prague, named after Empress Maria Theresa. In late 1941, the Nazis moved out the town's citizens and converted it to a ghetto for Czech Jews. The fortress, with barracks built to accommodate 5,000 people, became a prison for 50,000 inmates. It was important in the Nazis' holocaust strategy, in that they used it as a "model ghetto," to be shown to the International Red Cross as an example of German kindness to Jews. For the purpose of this show-and-tell for the world, the inmates had their own symphony orchestra, a theater, and art studios for the children. As soon as the Red Cross observers would leave the camp, the musicians, actors, and artists would be shipped to death camps, only to be replaced by other talented prisoners for the next show-and-tell. In reality, Terezín was but a stop-over on the way to annihilation. Most inmates were sent on to the ovens of Auschwitz-Birkenau, while others were transported to Treblinka.

Coincidentally, *Dědeček* arrived in Terezín at about the same time, and perhaps even on the same transport, as the three Jewish grandparents of future U.S. Secretary of State, Madeleine Albright, whose Czech background and ethnicity stories are nearly identical to mine. Two of her grandparents died there from undetermined causes, and the other perished at Auschwitz.

Mother received word from a friend that *Dědeček's* health was good and that he was being helped by friends during his short stay in Terezín. But, on October 15, 1942, the Germans put him on a transport to Treblinka, a death camp located in Poland, north of Warsaw. The head of the camp was Franz Stangl, an Austrian police officer who became a Nazi extermination expert, having been credited with the gassing of 100,000 people at the Sobibor camp before assuming his duties as Treblinka commander. After the war, he would be tried by a German court, but would manage to escape to Syria and then to Brazil. He would be caught and extradited in 1967, dying in prison in Düsseldorf five years later. Before Treblinka was closed in 1943, following a revolt by inmates, it is estimated that 700,000 to 1,000,000 people were put to death in its gas chambers.

One of the few survivors of the Treblinka revolt was a Czech named Richard Glazar. He wrote that, immediately upon arrival by transport, all but strong, young men who could be used as laborers in the camp, were ordered to strip and that, as soon as their baggage and clothing were taken away, they were shot. It is quite certain that my elderly great-grandfather, my beloved *Dědeček*, was murdered on October 17, 1942, and that the lightest of the ashes of his burned body rose to the sky on that fateful night.

The numbers of concentration-camp deaths are so large and incomprehensible that they become impersonal. To me, this would become very personal and tragic once I would be able to comprehend it. My great-grandfather and best friend, Gustav Neumann, was murdered by Stangl and his Nazis at Treblinka only six months after we said goodbye to him at the Kojetice station, and less than two months after his eighty-second birthday. Of course, we knew nothing of his whereabouts or fate, and we would find this out only after the war.

Along with all the members of my father's family, my paternal grandmother, Otilie Hellerová, too, was murdered by the Germans. According to the International Tracing Service (ITS) at the United States Holocaust Memorial Museum, Grandma was sent to Terezín on February 22, 1942, and was transported from there to Izbica, a small Polish town in the valley of the river Wieprz, on March 17, 1942. She was 54 years old. According to the ITS:

> "Izbica was a 'transit ghetto' for holding Jews pending their 'resettlement,' in the euphemistic Nazi jargon. But there are no extant lists to inform us of when the temporary residents of Izbica were taken away to their deaths, in successive transports throughout 1942 and 1943. The actual process mass murder proceeded at Belžec for many of them."

During the entire war, we received only one piece of correspondence from a concentration camp. It came from Grandma Hellerová, and, though it is undated, I believe that she sent it from Izbica. Written in pencil on thin, lined, paper, it is addressed to my mother and reads in part:

> Dear Iluška [Czech diminutive for Ilona]
> …We will endure this, nothing lasts forever, but you are young so take care of yourself. You are in my thoughts and I pray that God will hear me…
> Love, Grandma

Although Izbica is not nearly as well known as Auschwitz, Treblinka, Mauthausen, Bergen-Belsen, and other Nazi death factories, my search for Grandma's fate has led me to horrifying possibilities. According to an eyewitness account given to the Holocaust Education & Archive Research Team (HEART), exactly one week after Grandma arrived, on March 24, 1942, the "sleepy town was awakened by shots. Another roundup! Frightened

Jews quickly dressed, ran and hid. On the hills encircling Izbica, silhouettes of armed soldiers began to appear. The whole area was surrounded. Bands of Ukrainian collaborators rushed into Jewish homes. They took every Jew they encountered – children, old men and women, even cripples." I hope Grandma was shot that day, so that she was not subjected to even greater suffering of those who stayed behind and either became targets for the camp commander, the psychopathic murderer Kurt Engels, who *"enjoyed shooting Jews in the early morning hours, before breakfast,"* or were sent to Belžec or Majdanek to be gassed.

* * *

Of course, Mother knew nothing of the fates of any of our relatives at that time, but, despite the fact that both of us were Roman Catholics, she feared the worst. Accordingly, she turned to our family's pre-war lawyer, Dr. Zapletal, in Prague. He concocted a plan to ask her ethnic German Catholic mother, Marie Kozuschniková – my other grandmother – to swear in court that my grandfather Artur, Mother's father, was not Jewish. This would be an outright lie because *Děda* was a Jew. But, if the Germans would buy it, we would have a chance of avoiding transport to a death camp.

In the early days of the occupation, there had been protection of children of mixed marriages, until they reached their fourteenth birthdays. Although this protection was spotty, some weeks, one was protected and other weeks, a child could be called to a transport, any protection was better than none. Giving me the best chance possible to avoid being taken to a concentration camp drove Mother to this desperate attempt to deceive the Germans and their Czech fascist collaborators.

At first, Grandmother refused to go along with the lie because she feared the Nazis. But, Mother's best friend, Aša Hahnová, visited her at her home in Ostrava and managed to convince Grandma to do this in order to save our lives. Grandma came to Prague, where, on August 18, 1942, she swore before a judge and jury that the father of her child,

Artur Neumann, was a Christian. If the jury of Germans and their Czech collaborators would accept this lie, Mother would be considered "100% pure Aryan" and probably safe, with the only mark against her being her marriage to a Jew. At the same time, I would be upgraded to a first-class Mischlinge, having only two Jewish grandparents, and I would have a better chance to survive.

After a three-hour trial, the jury recommended that Mother be sent for a racial examination. Two weeks later, she paid 1,500 Czech crowns to be examined at Charles University in Prague. The "racial experts" there measured her nose, size of forehead and ears, and other potential "Jewish characteristics." Knowing that the ruling may be a matter of life and death for both of us, Mother was terrified as she awaited the results. Despite Dr. Zapletal's continual prodding, the court never responded. But, when Mother received notice that she and I were to report to Prague for a transport to a concentration camp on December 12, 1942, it was evident that she had failed the test. She lied to me that we would be moving to another part of the country for a while and packed two suitcases for us. Mother instructed me not to ask questions, and I did not. Consequently, I was confused because I did not understand why we would be moving from Kojetice. Mother was mortified because she *did* understand.

Then, she decided to defy the Germans. When the appointed day came, our suitcases remained packed, but we stayed in Tůmas' farmhouse. Miraculously, the Nazis did not come after us. Mother never found out why. Later, she received two more notices for us to report to transports. Again, she defied them – and again, nothing happened.

With our case apparently unresolved, Grandmother Kozuschniková again came to the rescue. Despite the fact that she was weak following stomach ulcer surgery, she made four long train trips to Prague to appear before the racial court, where she continued to swear under oath that my Jewish grandfather was a Christian. Her weight was down to 110 pounds by the time Dr. Zapletal informed her that she had made a great impression on the court and that, this time, the Nazis believed her testimony. Finally, she was able to go home to Ostrava to rest and to care for her other family. In spite of her failing health and her safe standing as an ethnic German, she had spent two years risking her life by lying to the Nazis in order to save Mother and me. Sadly, I was unaware of any of this at the time.

* * *

All this came at the time of the greatest repression of Czechs of all ethnic origins. One part of the Germans' grand plan for Europe was the destruction of the Czech nation. Consequently, Reichsprotektor of the Bohemia and Moravia Protectorate, Konstantin von Neurath, and State Secretary Karl Hermann Frank submitted a proposal to Hitler to Germanize one-half of all Czechs and to expel the other half. The proposal became strategy, and the Acting Reichsprotektor, Reinhard Heydrich, set out to implement it with great enthusiasm. The 37-year-old Heydrich had been chief of the German security office and number three in the Nazi hierarchy. He was driven both by the orders of his superiors and his fervent hatred of Slavs and Jews. For good reason, he became known as the "Butcher of Prague."

Interestingly, post-war records would show that Heydrich was blackmailed by some of his Nazi competitors because he, himself, may have had drops of Jewish blood. If the rumor that he had one Jewish grandparent had been brought to light, he would have been classified as a second-degree *Mischlinge*.

In September 1941, Heydrich acted quickly to subjugate the Czechs. Any display, no matter how small, of Czech nationhood was strictly forbidden. He ordered the arrest of the prime minister of the Proctorate, General Alois Eliáš, because the latter, while appearing to cooperate with the Nazi occupiers, was working with the London government in exile and supporting resistance movements. Heydrich declared martial law. A month later, he made a secret speech in the beautiful Spanish Hall of Prague Castle, which made clear his intentions for the Czech people:

"This region must become German space, and the Czech has no business being here."

Heydrich's arrogance knew no bounds. At one point, he demanded to be shown the nation's crown jewels, the ancient crown of the revered St. Wenceslas. The power-mad German could not resist the temptation to place the crown on his head. No doubt, he was not aware of the Czech legend that anyone who wears it unrightfully will be severely punished. Furthermore, he did not know that President Beneš and his government in exile were concerned about the fact that Heydrich's crackdown had caused a cut-off of intelligence reports from the Czech underground to London and that resistance to the Nazis had been brought to a halt. In order to reestablish an intelligence network, Beneš ordered 160 British-trained Czechoslovak paratroopers to be dropped into the country. Most significantly, he and his military advisors hatched an ultrasecret plan for a small group of these soldiers to kill Heydrich in order to boost the Czechs' morale.

On November 28, 1941, a Halifax bomber dropped sixteen airborne troops into their native country. Of this group, three men – Sergeants Jozef Gabčík, Jan Kubiš, and Josef Valčík – had a single assignment: kill Heydrich. The three men spent the next six months preparing an elaborate plan of assassination and escape. On May 27, 1942, Heydrich was being driven in a big, green Mercedes to his country residence, one stolen from a Jewish family, in Panenské Břežany, following a schedule and route reported to the underground by a Czech carpenter employed at the estate.

Heydrich's route ran only two blocks from our family's apartment building in the Libeň section of Prague. The parachutists were waiting for him about a mile north of our building, alongside a sharp curve in the road in Kobylisy. As the car approached, Gabčík ran out into the road, pretending that he was trying to catch the #3 streetcar, which was leaving a station. Suddenly, he stopped, turned, aimed his Sten submachine gun straight at Heydrich, and fired. Incredibly, the gun jammed. The quick-thinking Kubiš stepped in and threw a hand-grenade at the car, destroying a portion of it, and causing it to crash into the curb. Heydrich's driver jumped out and took off after Gabčík, but the latter had a second gun and shot the driver in the leg. Then he hopped on another passing tram, heading for the center of Prague. Kubiš was slightly wounded by shrapnel from his grenade, but he was able to jump on a bicycle and ride down the hill toward Libeň. Valčík, too, managed to escape.

Heydrich survived the attack. He was taken to Bulovka, the same hospital in which I had spent thirty days with scarlet fever just a few months before. At first, it appeared that he would make it through several surgeries. But, then complications set in due to an infection contracted from horse hair in the car's upholstery which had entered Heydrich's body during the explosion. On June 4, Hitler's foremost henchman and butcher died. After a state funeral in Germany, martial law was declared in the Czech lands, and more than 3,000 people were murdered in reprisal. A huge manhunt for the assassins began. Although the Gestapo was able to find many of the objects used in the shooting and the escape – pistols, raincoat, grenade, bicycle – they had no clue as to the whereabouts of the perpetrators.

Vladimír "Vláďa" Svoboda, a six-year-old boy who would become my best friend after the war, lived with his parents in a Libeň apartment across the square from our family's apartment building. Six thugs of the dreaded SS, dressed in brown shirts with swastikas on the sleeves, crashed through the door of the Svobodas' home and searched every room for any sign of the assassins. In the process, they examined the family's radio to make certain that it had been gutted of ability to pick up foreign broadcasts. They conducted similar searches in every apartment in the building, while other SS groups duplicated the effort throughout Libeň. Satisfied that the Svobodas had not assisted the parachutists, and that their radio was legal, they left without a word.

"Of course, that evening we listened to the BBC broadcast, *Volá Londýn* (London calling)," Vláďa would recall many years later.

For the bounty of two million Reichsmarks, a parachutist from one of the other two units dropped on the same day, decided to betray the assassins. Hiding at his mother's home in Třeboň, a town in the southern part of the country, Karel Čurda came to Prague and told everything he knew to the Gestapo. Although he did not know where the assassins were hiding, he gave the Germans names of people who had helped them along the way. Torture of the young son of the Moravec family, members of the patriotic Sokol and hosts of the assassins, finally revealed that the three were holed up in the Church of St. Cyril and St. Methodius on Resslova Street in the New Town section of Prague. A fierce battle took place as the Germans, with help from the Prague fire department, attempted to force the Czechs out of the church. One of the patriots was killed by the Nazis and, when all seemed hopeless, the others took their own lives.

In retaliation for the assassination, the Germans committed one of the greatest atrocities of the war, outside the death camps. They concocted a story that the citizens of the small village of Lidice, located between Prague's Ruzyně airport and the city of Kladno, had provided assistance to the assassins. This was an outright lie. Lidice consisted of 503 people, 106 houses, a school, and a small baroque church, and no one in this farming community had a clue about the plot. Mother and I could hear the gunfire on June 10, 1942, when the Germans shot 192 men and seven women in Lidice. They burned the entire village to the ground, and they shipped 196 women to the Ravensbrück concentration camp. Most of Lidice's 96 children were murdered in gas chambers and a few, those who were lucky enough to have Aryan features – blond hair, blue eyes – were put into German families to be raised as good Nazis. Less well known is the fact that the Germans also wiped out the small village of Lezáky, with 32 murdered and 11 shipped away, only two weeks after the massacre of Lidice. In Great Britain, Winston Churchill was so incensed by the Lidice and Lezáky atrocities that he wanted to bomb German villages in retaliation; however, his wish was not heeded by other members of his government.

While the world was shocked by these Nazi reprisals, few paid attention to the fact that many more Jews than Gentiles were murdered as part of the Nazis' revenge for Heydrich's death. One thousand Jews from Prague were packed into a transport named *Attentat auf Heydrich* (Assassination of Heydrich) and another two thousand were selected from Terezín, all bound for death camps in Poland. Only one man is known to have survived.

In the most blatant demonstration of *Švejkism*, nearly three hundred thousand Czechs gathered in Wenceslas Square, raised their right arms and screamed *"sieg heil!,"* demanding punishment for those who had assisted the killers of Heydrich. As much as these cowards might have tried, it did not endear them to their Nazi occupiers.

Although there were no additional mass killings in the Protectorate, the Nazis continued their efforts to annihilate the Czech nation. Many symbols of Czech history and identity were destroyed. German soldiers threw the remains of the Czechoslovak Unknown Soldier into the Vltava river; they removed thousands of books from libraries; they forbade the display of our Czechoslovak flag.

* * *

For Jews, life in the cities became nearly impossible. Progressively, they were forbidden to purchase clothing (except from pawn shops), tobacco, alcohol, shaving cream, and specific food items including fruit of any kind, cheese, fish, chicken, jams and jellies, and even honey. They were not allowed to use public transportation or to hail a taxi. They could not go to bars, restaurants, parks, swimming pools, post offices or to use public rest rooms. In the winter, Prague Jews had to report for snow-shoveling duty every day, and they were slapped or beaten along the way by Germans and Czech fascists.

In December 1942, Jews who had not yet been taken away were forced to give the Germans fur coats, wool underwear, and sweaters, to be sent to soldiers fighting on the Eastern Front. By then, they were forbidden to go nearly anywhere in Prague, except with a special work pass. One of very few exceptions was Troja, where Jews were allowed to stroll along the bank of the Vltava, but, incredibly, only in the direction of the river's flow. The Nazis' ability to humiliate knew no bounds.

As a step toward the "final solution," Jews were marked for separation from the rest of society. On September 1, 1942, K. H. Frank, the Protector of Bohemia and Moravia, issued an order requiring Jews to wear a yellow, six-pointed, Star of David, with the inscription, *Jude* ("Jew" in German). There were a few expressions of solidarity by patriotic Czechs with Jews, such as all workers at a chocolate factory showing up for work wearing the stars. But, these dissipated quickly under threats from the Germans.

Once again, Mother was summoned to Peček Palace, the Gestapo headquarters in Prague. After waiting for several hours in a cold, large room with wooden benches resembling church pews, she was escorted by two German goons down a long hallway. Here, she could hear the screams and cries of prisoners being tortured in cells on both sides of the corridor. She had heard about the electric-shock and bone-crushing instruments, as well as the infamous guillotine, with a blade weighing some 130 pounds, on the other side of those doors. She was terrified, but she would not be tortured, at least during this visit.

Once brought into an interrogation room, Mother was told that, going forward, she would be required to wear the yellow star whenever she would be outside her home.

"I'm a Catholic. Why do I have to wear the star?" Mother asked the Gestapo officer in her best German.

"Because you're married to a Jew. Things have changed," he said. "Moreover, you're not allowed to use public transportation, use a telephone, go to the theater – just like the rest of the Jews."

"Do I have any rights at all?" she asked.

"For now, at least, you have the right to live."

Heydrich may have been dead, but the plan of President Beneš to revive the spirit of the Czech people had failed. Nazi repression was total. Shamefully, less than 2,000 German officials controlled a Czech population of nearly ten million, with the dirty work being performed by 350,000 Czech bureaucrats.

CHAPTER 6

Survival

The most striking structure in our village of Kojetice was a beautiful, tall, white chateau with a red roof and several small towers. As a small child before the war, I had imagined that a beautiful princess lived in one of the towers of this magical place which the villagers called *Zámek* ("Castle") and that someday I would rescue and carry her away. The majority of the estate around the Castle was surrounded by a ten-foot concrete wall. The portion which abutted the main road through town consisted of buildings which, prior to the war, had housed workers and stables for many riding and work horses. Inside the large compound, there were evergreen and fruit trees, a large pond, vegetable gardens, and an outdoor bowling alley. Early in the war, Mr. Vávra, the owner, had been permitted to continue to run the large and to live in the Castle, but now he had to share the large chateau with his workers and their families, numbering about fifty.

Across the road from the entrance to the estate, Mother and I continued to live on Tůmas' farm. I was lonely and bored from spending my days with goats and evenings with adults who spoke only about the war. Marie Tůmová was a warm and generous lady who tried to treat me like the child they never had. Her husband was not mean to me and he tried to teach me to perform useful chores around the farm. But he was distant and somewhat cold. I missed the nurturing of my parents and the elder Neumanns, all of whom had once focused so much of their love and

59

attention on the only child in the family. Now, all but Mother were gone and she worked in the fields six days a week and came home exhausted each evening.

Each night after she came home, I begged Mother to let me go out into the village, so that I could see the places where I had played before the war and to get a glimpse of people I had known. Mother was reluctant because on two occasions in the past, when I had been outside the farm walls, I had worn Papa's old army hat and carried my red metal airplane, proudly telling everyone within earshot:

"I'm Papa, shooting Germans from the sky."

Mother worried, too, because it was difficult to hide my existence from the Germans and their collaborators in a small village, where everyone watched and gossiped about the lives of neighbors.

Finally, one evening, Mother relented to my constant pestering. She told me that I could go out into the street only this one time, but that I must not make any statements about the Germans and that I must wear a Star of David on my jacket. Not having the slightest idea what this six-pointed yellow star with the word *Jude* meant, and remembering from pre-war days that sheriffs wore stars in American cowboy movies, I agreed enthusiastically. The following day, I waited until mid-afternoon when I knew that school would be letting out. I went out the gate and crossed the street to the sidewalk adjacent to the wall of the Vávra estate. I walked slowly up the hill toward the school. A group of boys, carrying their leather school bags on their backs, was coming down the hill on the other side of the street, just below our factory. Suddenly, they spotted me.

"There he is! Let's get him!" yelled one of the boys.

They picked up stones from the side of the dirt road and began to pelt me with them. Several hit me in the arms and chest. Many more missed and rebounded off the brick wall and cracked the plaster covering. I was scared and confused. I ran back toward the Tůma farm as fast as I could. A few more stones hit my legs as I crossed the road. Once safe inside the gate, I began to cry. Slowly, I walked to the house, where Mrs. Tůmová was preparing dinner. Tearfully, I explained to her what had happened. I told her that I did not understand. I had not done anything to these boys.

"They're just stupid," she said, referring to the boys. "They'll get theirs someday. But, don't tell your mother about this when she gets home from the fields. She has enough worries."

Having been taught not to ask questions and to follow orders, I kept my silence. I looked down on the yellow star sewn onto my jacket and wanted to ask:

"Does this have something to do with the kids hating me?"

But, as always, I had to adhere to the code of silence. Although I did not comprehend the meaning of the stoning at the time, it did make it clear to me that not all our neighbors were our friends. Most people in Kojetice were decent to us during the war, but now I knew that there were exceptions.

❊ ❊ ❊

The repressive atmosphere of the occupation created a fierce hatred of Germans among the Czech populace. However, centuries of foreign occupations had brought about the birth of *Švejkism*, the Czechs' preference for suffering in silence and resisting their conquerors peacefully, rather than fighting back. This national characteristic is a source of jokes during good times, but it is one of which Czechs are not proud. During World War II, the overwhelming majority of Czechs chose to live their lives as *Švejks*, carefully and quietly awaiting liberation. At the same time, a small minority took risks, helped the Allies from within, and assisted those who were most oppressed by the Nazis. Then, there were those collaborators who actively helped the Germans in exchange for food, fuel, housing, and other favors. Of course, I was too young to understand all this at the time.

The anti-Semitic Czech collaborators and nationalists who considered Jewish citizens something other than "real Czechs," may have had second thoughts after the war when news spread of the events of March 8, 1944.

This was the day of the greatest slaughter of Czech citizens in modern history. On that day, 3,792 Czech Jews demonstrated their patriotism and defiance by singing *Kde domov můj?* – the national anthem – as they were herded into the gas chambers of Auschwitz-Birkenau.

Many years after the end of the war, I would become a charter member of the U.S. Holocaust Museum in Washington, DC. On my first visit to this incredibly haunting place, I stared at a map of Europe which showed some grim statistics: the number of Jews murdered in each country. Poland – 3,000,000; Soviet Union – 1,000,000; Czechoslovakia – 277,000; Hungary – 200,000; The Netherlands – 106,000; and so it went. Then, my eyes stopped abruptly as they came upon the country of Denmark. The number was <u>77</u>! How was this possible? Denmark was occupied just like all the other countries and it, too, had a significant Jewish population. How could the number be so miniscule? I asked one of the docents if this had been a mistake and someone had omitted some zeroes.

"No, we didn't," he smiled. "Unlike all other occupied nations except Albania, Denmark resisted the deportation of its Jewish citizens. On the day that Jews were ordered to wear the Star of David on their outer clothing, the Danish royal couple had the stars sewn on their coats and thousands of Danes followed suit. When they discovered that Jews were to be rounded up, Danes warned the Jews and hid them throughout the countryside. It was a remarkable act of decency and bravery by an entire nation."

While I continue to be proud of my Czech heritage, I am sad that the great majority of Czechs chose to be *Švejks*, rather than Danes – 277,000 vs. 77.

＊ ＊ ＊

By 1943, the Germans had taken all of the Tůmas' horses and several of their oxen. Mr. Tůma was left with one ox to plow and otherwise work his fields, in addition to three goats, a few chickens, several rabbits, some pigs, and a flock of geese. I spent many days on Skalky, the rocky forest beyond the fields of Kojetice, reading books and daydreaming while supervising the goats as they gorged themselves on any grass they could find. Each day was the same as the last. The only breaks from tedious sameness came through new adventures I shared with my friends Robinson Crusoe and his sidekick, Friday, and my Indian hero, Vinnetou. When I put down the books by Daniel Defoe and Karl May, I closed my eyes and let my imagination take me to my greatest hero, Rudolf Heller – my father. One minute, I would be sitting behind him in the cockpit of a Spitfire and we would be blasting German tanks from the air. The next minute, I would be carrying a Czechoslovak flag, running through sand, a step behind Papa who was leading a charge through the African desert, chasing Nazis into the Mediterranean Sea.

Inside the farm compound, I was engaged in a real and continuous battle – with the geese. Each time I stepped into the courtyard, they came after me with a vengeance, hissing and trying to bite my legs. Even trips to the outhouse were adventures. But, I got my revenge against my enemy. On many days, Mrs. Tůmová prepared in her kitchen little delicacies called *šišky*: round, two-inch-long, mixtures of corn, wheat, and flour. She brought them to a barn, where Mr. Tůma had rounded up a few geese which had been selected for future dinner tables. There, Mr. Tůma held a goose, his wife placed a *šiška* into the bird's mouth, and I massaged his long neck, working the little "bomb" down toward the stomach. Little did my enemy know that he was being fattened up for a future feast. Revenge was sweet, and the taste of roast goose was even sweeter.

The greatest feasts on the farm followed the occasional slaughter of a pig. This was a highly illegal activity because all pigs were to be fed and then turned over to German soldiers for their meals. Thus, the killing of a hog was done in the middle of the night, and it was followed by frenzied activities consisting of stripping everything edible from the carcass before daylight. Although I avoided the killing, I was allowed to stay up all night to watch the making of sausages called *jitrnice*, the frying of my favorite *škvarky*, the hiding of meat in the smokehouse to become ham at a later time. In the end, nothing but bones was left. These were ground up the next day and thrown away.

Once we ran out of pigs and geese, our meals consisted primarily of potatoes, brown bread, jam, cucumbers, radishes, apples, cherries, and gooseberries. Fortunately, there was never a shortage of my favorite, *sádlo*. When translated into English, the word "lard" sounds horrible and unworthy of human consumption. But, containing small hunks of *škvarky*, spread on bread and salted, *sádlo* constituted a cholesterol-laden delicacy for the discriminating wartime Czech palate.

* * *

At the east end of Kojetice, just outside of town and on the opposite side of the road from the woods of Skalky, was the town soccer field – the field which my grandfather, Artur, had donated to the town. Next to it, on a hill behind the small grandstand, was a huge haystack. Occasionally during the war, I sneaked out from the farm and walked through Skalky to the field in order to watch a soccer game between our Kojetice team and a league opponent from a nearby town. Although many villagers were aware that I was being hidden at Tůmas', I hung back and stayed near the haystack in order to be as unobtrusive as possible.

On one such Sunday, I was watching a game from the hill when a couple of boys came over and suggested that we play hide-and-seek in the haystack, a popular pastime for the village kids. I joined in and began to burrow a hiding place for myself in the hay. Suddenly, my hand hit something solid. It was a body! And then the body moved! I was terrified, reversed course, and crawled back toward daylight as fast as I could. I yelled to the boy who was "it" about my discovery. He screamed and ran toward his parents in the grandstand. A large group of adults followed him back to the haystack, and they arrived just as the person who had been hiding in the hay began to crawl out.

He was covered with straw and dressed in a dirty and wrinkled uniform of a British pilot. A policeman in the crowd drew his pistol and led him off, as I ran back toward the woods and to the farm, crying and confused about what I had done. Later, at the dinner table, I listened while the Tůmas discussed the arrest of an RAF pilot who had bailed out of a disabled airplane over Neratovice and how he had been caught hiding in a haystack. I said nothing, but I would wonder for many years if, unwittingly, I had been responsible for the capture of one of my secret "friends in the sky." At night, when I prayed for the safety of my family and myself, I included the pilot in my conversations with God and Jesus.

With Tůmas' farm stock depleted, there was no work for Mother. Besides, the Tůmas were getting signals that soon the Germans would take over their entire farm. It was time for us to move on. On January 15, 1943, we were taken in by the Novák family, which lived in a two-story house in a section of Kojetice called Močidlata. The latter was actually a long, unpaved street that ran from the main road nearly to the railroad tracks, with houses on one side and Kojetice creek on the other. Mother and I moved to the second floor of the Novák house, where we had a bedroom with a single bed and a bathroom with a toilet. The only heat was provided by a pot-bellied stove near the foot of the bed. Because coal was rationed, we used the stove sparingly, and let the fire go out completely during the night. Prior to going to bed, we heated a brick on top of the stove and placed it under the goose-down comforter near Mother's feet. Mother and I then knelt side by side on the floor, with our elbows resting on the mattress, and prayed for the safety of Papa, *Dědeček, Děda, Strejda,* our other family members and friends, and ourselves. By morning, the brick was cold and we were freezing. My morning job was to start a small fire in the stove and, after washing, Mother placed two slices of bread on top of the stove to make our breakfast toast. After heating the bread, she spread garlic on both sides, and we ate the toast, accompanied by ersatz coffee for Mother and a strange concoction resembling diluted cocoa for me.

Mother went to work on the farm of Mr. Urban. My most vivid memory of this farmer is a story which was told about a British fighter pilot shooting one of his oxen. The RAF often bombed the German railroad depot and chemical plant outside the neighboring town of Neratovice, only a couple of miles from Kojetice. Usually, the bombers were accompanied by Spitfire fighter aircraft. Early in the war, whenever Neratovice was being bombed, people in Kojetice took cover. Later, it became such a common occurrence that many of us treated the bombings as entertainment, and we watched and listened in awe, as the bombs whistled while descending to earth, followed by huge explosions which shook the earth, with black smoke rising to the sky. On one such day, Mr. Urban continued to plow his field, with an ox pulling his plow and the farmer walking behind, steering. A Spitfire pilot who must have been bored because the Nazis were not shooting *flak* that day, flew very low over the fields from Neratovice toward Kojetice. When he reached Mr. Urban's field, he fired one shot. It hit the ox in the head and killed him on the spot. People would say after the war that the pilot returned to Kojetice, found Mr. Urban, paid him for the ox, and apologized. Nice story; I hope it is true.

While Mother worked in the fields, she tried to make my life in hiding as normal as possible. In March 1943, I began taking violin lessons from Mr. Böhm. I dreamed of becoming another Paganini, but the teacher considered me less than a virtuoso. He whacked me across the knuckles with his bow each time an awful screech resonated from the strings of my violin. But, I enjoyed playing and, after a few weeks, actually managed to generate real music with my instrument.

As the war entered its fourth year in 1943, Mother continued to worry that I – now seven years old – was not receiving a formal education. She approached a local teacher named Kotmel about tutoring me. He came three times before he told Mother that he was too busy to continue. No doubt, he realized the danger of teaching a child whose education was forbidden. Then, a long-time employee of our factory, a gentle, patient, educated gentleman named František Volt stepped in and became my secret teacher. The Volts lived next door to the Nováks, so, three times a week, I simply climbed over the wall after dark for my lessons. Mr. Volt taught me reading, writing, Czech grammar, mathematics, history, and geography, and he became my good friend. I enjoyed helping him work in his garden. Both he and my violin teacher were not only kind, but also brave, because they defied the Germans and their collaborators and placed themselves and their families in danger by helping a boy who was on the occupiers' enemies list. While there may have been a few Nazi collaborators, and many more *Švejks* who looked the other way, there were citizens of our village who helped us – directly, as well as indirectly by saying nothing about our existence.

I spent my days doing homework and reading books borrowed from the Volts and the Nováks. During the warm seasons, I whiled away the time on the flat roof of a small building in Nováks' backyard, where they stored gardening tools and machinery. The roof was my castle, and I imagined that the yards, orchards, and fields around me were my kingdom. Sometimes, I was Robinson Crusoe, and the roof was my deserted island. At other times, I became another of my heroes, Norwegian explorer Roald Amundsen, surveying the South Pole from my dog-drawn sled.

Although I was lonely, I was never bored while living in this fantasyland. Once, with the help of a lady named Mrs. Slunečková, Mother managed to get tickets to the National Theater in Prague. Although Nazi law forbade us to attend any theater, we saw *Z pohádky do pohádky* ("From Fairy Tale to Fairy Tale") in the afternoon; in the evening we attended the performance of the Czech national opera, *Prodaná nevěsta* ("The Bartered Bride"). I was thrilled. Although I was not particularly fond of opera, I loved Bedřich Smetana's gift to the Czech nation. Mother recorded my reaction in her journal:

> *"Ota told me 'You know, Mother, fairy tales are not for me anymore.' But, his eyes lit up when the orchestra played a 'Bartered Bride' polka which he had learned to play on his violin. I would love to take him to the National Theater more often but, unfortunately, that is impossible."*

Besides Aša Hahnová, whom I called Aunt Aša, Mother's other dearest friend throughout the war was Anna Panchartková, a wonderful lady of small stature and huge heart who never married and considered us her family. Aunt Anča, as I called her, started to work for my great-grandfather's firm, Labor, in the 1930s, and continued there under the German owner, Hollman. She and her two sisters, who lived in the town of Mladá Boleslav, owned a small cottage in the mountains. Twice during the war, she brought me there, and I played with toy boats in a nearby mountain stream and went with her on hikes, all the while wearing Papa's Czechoslovak army hat. For me, these were idyllic breaks from the routine of life in Kojetice, where I was a virtual prisoner, but I missed Mother and wished that she could join us.

At the beginning of 1944, Mother was transferred to the Vávra estate, where she worked only four hours a day. She had more time, but even less money, than before. She and Aunt Anča shared their food ration coupons and shopped together for the three of us. Anča was able to eat workday lunches at the company cafeteria. Mother cooked dinner, and Anča came over each evening for our family meal. Mother, who had never cooked a meal prior to the occupation, became a creative cook, having to concoct various combinations out of bread, potatoes, carrots, cabbage, and peas. Meat was now nonexistent, and I spent many hours imagining myself with a hunk of hard salami and a piece of cheese. Perhaps because I was deprived of them for so long, I would become a salami and cheese fanatic in future years, despite my American family's preoccupation with more healthy foods.

⁂ ⁂ ⁂

Because we were forbidden to travel, and due to her heavy workload on the farm, Mother had been unable to join Aunt Anča and her sisters, Růžena and Máňa, the first two times I visited their cabin in the mountains. Now, with Mother working only part-time, she decided that we would defy the Germans' prohibition against our travel and that we would visit Aunt, who was spending a few days of vacation in the cabin. Although the offense was punishable by death, we boarded a train without our yellow *Jude* stars attached to our outer clothing.

The train was packed with passengers leaving the Prague area for the weekend. Each second-class compartment was crammed with twelve people on its two wooden benches and the passageways were filled with people standing or sitting on the floor. I slept on Mother's lap in one of the compartments. When I woke up, I had to go to the bathroom. Seeing that making my way to the toilet would be impossible, I held on for more than an hour, hoping the urge would go away. Instead, it got worse and soon I was in agony.

"Mother, I really have to go," I said, finally. "I can't hold it anymore."

Mother looked around and surveyed the situation. She turned to the hefty stranger sitting between her and the window.

"My son has to tinkle," she said. "Do you think there's any way we can make our way to the toilet?"

"No, that would be impossible," he answered. "It's just too crowded out there."

He leaned across the aisle and whispered something to the man sitting across from him. Then he turned to me.

"Stand up and pull down your pants," he commanded.

I did as I was instructed, and he stood and picked me up, while his partner on the opposite side opened the window. As the train hurtled through the countryside, I relieved myself into the rushing airstream. After I finished, I pulled up my pants and buttoned my fly; our fellow compartment occupants applauded the effort. My savior pointed to a small white sign below the window, written in several languages. With an exaggerated accent, he read the Italian version:

"*Non sputare de la finestra,*" and everyone, including Mother, broke into uproarious laughter. I had no idea what was so funny, and I was too embarrassed to ask. It would be a few years before I would ask Mother about it. She explained that the sign had warned: "Don't spit out of the window," but that it had said nothing about peeing.

※ ※ ※

During the entire war, it was extremely difficult for Czechs to track the progress of the fighting. The propaganda spouted on domestic stations had the Germans winning battles on the eastern and western fronts at all times, with the Allies on the run. In order to keep Czechs from knowing the truth, the Germans tried to jam British broadcasts. It did not work. Then they ordered all radios to be taken to shops in order to be gutted such that they could receive only Nazi-controlled domestic stations. This surgery consisted of taking out one small part from each shortwave radio. In every household, the radio was required to have a paper certificate issued by the shop, signifying that the radio had been gutted. It hung from the volume knob and read:

"*Pamatuj. Pamatuj. Že poslouchání zahraničního rozhlasu je zakázáno a trestá se kazníci nebo i smrti.*" ("Remember. Remember. That listening to a foreign broadcast is forbidden and is punishable by imprisonment or even death.")

But Czechs are known for hording parts for everything: cars, bicycles, clocks – and radios. Everyone seemed to have a spare of that little coil which had been removed. Called *Čurčílek* ("Little Churchill"), it could be slipped in and out of a radio in a minute in order to restore short-wave capability. Listening to the BBC out of London every evening became Czechs' only connection to the outside world. At first, when my various hosts listened to evening broadcasts, I sneaked around corners and listened through closed doors. But, later in the war, Mother decided that I had passed the test and was no longer a security risk. I was allowed to sit with the adults and listen to the broadcasts, which constituted the highlights of each day, despite the fact that listening to them was punishable by death at the hands of the occupiers.

To this day, a chill runs up my spine when I hear the first four dramatic notes of Beethoven's Fifth Symphony: boom-boom-boom-BOOM! These announced the start of every eagerly-awaited Czech-language BBC broadcast, followed by "*Volá Londýn*" ("London calling"). With the help of an atlas, I followed the progress of the war. I learned the location of

Stalingrad during the Russians' heroic stand. I traced the path of V-1 and V-2 rockets fired from Germany and raining destruction upon London. I memorized the names of German cities – Dresden, Bremen, Cologne, Essen, Hamburg – and I cheered silently whenever I heard about American and RAF bombing raids destroying these enclaves of our captors. I had no idea where in my atlas I could place my father, but my imagination had him killing Germans on all fronts.

* * *

On October 15, 1944, Mother received notice that she was to report to the slave labor camp, Hagibor, in Prague. A camp for Christian spouses of Czech Jews, it was a facility manufacturing windshields for German warplanes. For the first month, the Nazis allowed her to live outside the camp. So that she could be with me each night, she commuted from Kojetice, leaving home each morning at 4:20 and returning at six in the evening, seven days a week. Then, on the 20th of November, one day before her 29th birthday, the Gestapo informed Mother that she was going to be imprisoned in Hagibor and would be unable to leave the premises any longer. She was told to bring nothing more than one set of clothing and items for personal hygiene. She was heartbroken and nearly hysterical. What would happen to me? Would the Germans find me and take me away?

I went to the Kojetice train station to see her off, along with our friends who had stood by us throughout the war: Aunt Anča, the Tůmas, and the families Beran, Opelt, Suchý, and Svoboda. I stood on the platform, praying that the RAF had bombed the tracks and made it impossible for the train to reach Kojetice. I was crestfallen when I saw smoke in the distance, followed by the huffing and puffing of the locomotive's steam engine.

Before she boarded the train, Mother told me to be respectful of Vladimír Tůma and Marie Tůmová, our farmer friends who had promised her that they would hide and look out for me, to avoid Germans, and to do whatever I was told. Then she turned to Aunt Marie.

"I am leaving you my most prized possession. Please take care of him," she said.

The solemnity of her voice and the anxiety in her eyes hit me hard. *"This is the last time I'll see Mother,"* I thought, and I made life even more difficult for her by crying hysterically as she boarded the train. When the caboose disappeared around the bend, my knees buckled and Mr. Tůma had to pick me up and carry me away from the station.

With the exception of fifty days in the hospital with scarlet fever, this was the first time I was totally alone, without any family. Until then, Mother was always there to allay my fears. Her beautiful brown eyes would mist over, shine and focus on me, as she would assure me that soon things would be better. Now, I was overwhelmed by loneliness and a feeling of powerlessness and loss of control. Even more devastating was my conviction that I would never see Mother again. I would be forever totally dependent on strangers and a pawn of external events.

By now, the Tůmas had lost their farm to the Germans and had taken jobs in the fields of Mr. Vávra, the estate owner, who moved them and a number of his workers into that large, brick chateau – the Castle. I was going to live in that mysterious place which I had admired from the time I could first speak! Soon, I found out that there was no princess in the tower and that life in the Castle was not exactly the life of royalty.

We were not starving, but there was very little food. Moreover, we were under the constant watch of people whom Mrs. Tůmová identified as Czech collaborators and who occupied the outbuildings of the estate. But, despite the loneliness which overwhelmed me mostly during the night, life was not all bad. There were other children living in the Castle, and, for the first time since the war began, I had playmates. We borrowed a wooden tub used for washing clothes, converted it into a boat, and took turns rowing it across the estate's pond. We played cowboys and Indians in the woods.

One day, while I was playing outside, Mrs. Tůmová ran out, grabbed me, pulled me inside the building, and pushed me into a broom closet.

She ordered me not to move or speak until she came back for me. I did not know what was going on, but I knew that I was in danger. After a frightening half hour in the pitch-black closet, she came back for me and told me that the Gestapo had been looking for me. She said she told them that she had not seen me in many weeks, and they seemed to have believed her. For the next few days, I would have to stay out of sight of everyone, in case the Germans would question our neighbors. After a week of solitary confinement, I ventured out again.

Whenever Allied bombers hit nearby Neratovice, a few boys and I climbed up on top of the estate wall and watched the fireworks less than two miles away. On one such occasion, a stray bomb landed in the field not far from our perch. A microsecond after being deafened by the noise of the explosion, we were blown backwards and off the wall by the concussion. I landed in a bush and, besides a few scratches, I was unhurt. But, it became quite clear to me that bombing was not pure entertainment.

Mother's work at the slave camp consisted of peeling mica, in preparation for the windshield assembly line. The labor was hard and the days were long. But, mostly, she worried about me. Once, she managed to arrange to borrow an identity card of a prisoner who lived in Prague and who was allowed to commute to the camp from home. She sent word to Aunt Anča, who brought me to the city by train. Together, Anča and I sat in a pub down the street from Hagibor until Mother came in. She did not wear her yellow star – otherwise she would not have been permitted inside the bar – and we had to hide our joy over seeing each other in order not to be detected. We were able to spend two wonderful hours together – laughing, crying, telling stories – the only time we would see each other during her imprisonment.

* * *

While Mother was in Hagibor and I was being hidden out in Kojetice, one of my former nannies, Zdeňka Věchtová, and her husband, a glamorous former cavalryman in the pre-war Czechoslovak army,

73

occasionally sneaked me out of the Castle and brought me to their home for a few days. The Věchets lived in Roztoky, a small town located a few kilometers from Prague, high on a bank overlooking the Vltava river, in a pretty little house surrounded by flowers and fruit trees. Whenever I visited, I spent much of my time walking on the ridge above the Vltava with the Věchets' collie, Rin, named for the pre-war American movie-star dog, Rin-Tin-Tin.

One day in the early spring of 1945, with Mrs. Věchtová along on my walk with Rin, we observed a strange and miraculous sight. In the sky above Roztoky, an airplane was performing a variety of maneuvers – inside loops, outside loops, vertical climbs, and rapid dives. Not only was it unusual to see an aircraft performing air-show tricks in a sky which was often filled with silver British and American bombers, but this one was flying at speeds far exceeding any I had ever witnessed and making a sound which I had never heard. The plane was black, so we knew that it was German. Knowing that, we did not have to be concerned about an attack. So, Mrs. Věchtová and I sat down in the grass and watched the amazing show while Rin romped around. At the bottom of one his loops, the pilot flew close enough for us to see details.

"Look, Mrs. Věchtová!" I shouted. "He doesn't have any propellers!"

"You're right, Oto," she said. "But, that's impossible. We'll have to ask my husband what this is all about."

That evening at dinner, Mr. Věchet told us that he had heard that the Germans had built an airplane powered by some kind of air-sucking turbine which would make it fly at least twice as fast as propeller-driven aircraft. He said that the rumor was that the Aero aircraft factory in Prague was making modifications to the plane and that we must have witnessed its flight tests.

He was correct. After the war ended, I would read that the Germans had developed the first jet aircraft, the Messerschmitt Me-262, as one of their last efforts to stave off defeat. Fortunately, they were too late and their new weapon saw only minimal combat.

All that is necessary for the triumph of evil
is for good men to do nothing.
Edmund Burke

CHAPTER 7

Catholics and Nazis

Several months before my mother passed away in 2006, I overcame my reluctance to bring up a subject which she had avoided throughout her life in America.

"Mother, we were both Catholics," I said. "Did the Church help us at all during the war when you were fighting so hard to save our lives?"

Mother waited a long time to answer. She had remained a devout Catholic throughout her life, and undoubtedly she must have given this question a great deal of thought when she sat through years of sermons on morality during Mass.

"Do you remember Father Erhard?" she asked finally.

"Sure. He was the priest in Kojetice, and our next-door neighbor."

"Well, he was a very nice man," she said. "He told me that he couldn't explain, and that he was sorry about all our troubles, but he could do nothing to help us. Just the facts that he was nice to me and that he didn't denounce us to the Germans made him a good man. But, that was the extent of the help we got from the Catholic Church."

On the one hand, I considered this a confirmation of the fact that I had made the correct decision to leave the Roman Catholic Church – and, in fact, all organized religion – many years ago and to honor God my own, private way. At the same time, I was puzzled. I had read conflicting stories about the behavior of the Vatican, Catholic churches and priests, as well as laypersons during the war. I wanted to know more about the church in our village, one which Mother and I were helping to restore at that very moment, and to try to understand why it failed to assist us. I asked my Czech friend, Vladimír Svoboda, to help me uncover stories of the Church's actions on behalf of converts from Judaism or those, like Mother and I, from mixed marriages. Like everyone else whom I had asked to find instances of the Czech Church's help for converts and "hybrids," Vlád'a was unable to find any such instances. However, he was able to solve the puzzle of "good man" Father Erhard. Speaking with the historian of our village, Kojetice – Jaroslav Kučera – he discovered that there was a reason for the priest's inability to help us.

"Father Erhard was an anti-fascist," Kučera explained to Vlád'a. "He had an Austrian cook from Vienna, also an anti-fascist. But, in the village, there were four German farmers, one of whom was an ardent Nazi. All four of them attended church regularly, only so they could spy on the priest and follow him around. They kept the priest, the cook, and St. Vitus church from doing anything to help anyone."

For Mother and me, no help was forthcoming because of fear of denunciations by Germans and by collaborators in our town. Others – Jews as well as those of mixed blood who were branded Jews by the Nürnberg Laws – were left friendless and defenseless by a combination of the same fear and passivity by the majority of Czech *Švejks*. The Irish-English author, Edmund Burke, once said that "all that is necessary for the triumph of evil is for good men to do nothing." This was, for the most part, the situation in the Protectorate.

In the early years of Nazism, German Roman Catholic and Protestant churches enthusiastically supported their new regime. They had a common cause with the Nazis: ridding the world of godless communism. Moreover, Hitler convinced them that his anti-Jewish policies were based on principles set forth, and followed since, by the Catholic Church. In November 1938, two cardinals in Breslau congratulated the Führer on his escape from an assassination attempt. They celebrated the event in a Munich cathedral, where they thanked God for saving Hitler's life. Little did they know that the leader had no intention of allowing Christianity to be the religion of the new Reich. The truth was that he, Göbbels, Himmler, and Bormann were fanatical anti-Christians.

Alfred Rosenberg, the leading "intellectual" of the Nazi movement, structured a plan to replace the Catholic Church within Germany and its present and future colonies with a Reich Church, outside the control of the Vatican, and under the leadership of the Führer. The government would confiscate all Catholic Church property and replace crosses in, and on, churches with swastikas. Priests would be removed in favor of Nazi officials. While God would be recognized, bibles would be burned, with *Mein Kampf* becoming the word of a new "god."

Although Germany's successes as conquerors grew, the plan to introduce a new religion never got off the ground. The Nazis came to realize that the traditions and influence of the Catholic Church were too strong, both in their own Bavarian region and in the conquered nations. Instead of Rosenberg's drastic measures, they decided on a more workable approach: weaning youth away from the Church by closing parochial schools and banning the teaching of religion in public schools, along with using the Vatican and its proxies to help eradicate communists and Jews.

Throughout centuries, as Jews have been victimized by pogroms and inquisitions, many have sought safety by converting to Christianity, usually Roman Catholicism. The period leading up to the Second World War was no exception. As Nazi persecution became increasingly clear in the 1930s, hundreds of Czechoslovak Jews converted. Those who were partners in mixed marriages, like my father, thought that they, their Christian spouses, and their children were safe. Early on, the Catholic Church encouraged conversions, considering them its missionary duty. But, barely a year into the occupation, the Germans made it clear that they did not recognize such desperate, last-minute, switches. Czech priests and bishops could have falsified the conversion dates in order to protect the former Jews; instead, they permitted the Nazis to examine records of baptisms, making it easy for the Germans to hunt down Jews who had converted recently.

Recognizing that conversions would not help save the Jews and that the institutional Church would do nothing, individual members of the Catholic clergy, as well as many lay persons in their congregations, turned to hiding Jews in homes, parish houses, and monasteries. No statistics are available on the number of people saved this way in the Protectorate, but the number was small when compared to the multitudes of Jews deported. Most of those hidden were children. Because a sympathetic Christian family generally could not hide more than one person, invariably the stowaway would be a child whose parents hoped that their offspring might survive the war in hiding, even as they resigned themselves to a less fortunate fate. This was dangerous business. In the early years of the war, hundreds of Christians were turned in to the authorities by Czech fascists and collaborators. They and their hidden Jews were shot or hanged. After the war, those of us who were hidden and survived would become known as "Hidden Children."

While the official Church hierarchy in the former Czechoslovakia did little to distinguish itself, the wartime actions of the Vatican are awash in controversy to this day. Prior to the war, Pope Pius XI spoke out strongly against the Nazis, condemning them in an entire encyclical. His secretary of state, Cardinal Pacelli, was a particularly outspoken critic of the Germans. According to former Israeli diplomat and rabbi, Pinchas Lapide, Pius XI "had good reason to make Pacelli the architect of his anti-Nazi policy. Of the forty-five speeches which the Nuncio Pacelli had made on German soil between 1917 and 1929, at least forty contained attacks on Nazism or condemnation of Hitler's doctrines."

Consequently, the Germans were not very pleased when, upon the death of Pius XI, Pacelli was elected Pope Pius XII. However, the new pope surprised them. Upon assuming the papacy, he became silent, despite the fact that he was aware by now of the fact that the extermination of an entire people was at stake. The British ambassador to the Vatican,

Sir Francis d'Arcy Osborne, stated in December 1942: "I am revolted by Hitler's massacre of the Jewish race on the one hand and, on the other, the Vatican's apparently exclusive preoccupation with the effects of the war on Italy and the possibilities of the bombardment of Rome. The whole outfit seems to have become Italian." What remains a question is whether the Pope's silence was a deliberate, scandalous attempt to save the Catholic Church by appeasing Hitler, a selfish regard only for the safety of the Vatican and its occupants, or a strategy intended to save lives.

Those who defend the Vatican today claim that it was the latter. They say that, once the deportations of Jews began, the new pope played a game of chance with the Nazis. When Hitler promised not to interfere with the Catholic Church, Pius XII agreed not to speak out against Nazi activities and atrocities. He was saving his church from destruction while, at the same time, secretly pledging to help the Jews because he had determined that pronouncements and condemnations were bringing them more harm than good. When his archbishops and bishops had tried such public criticisms in their respective countries, the results were even greater retaliations against Jews. Instead, while appearing neutral, Pius XII chose to work secretly to save as many lives as possible from extermination. Even while the United States and Great Britain turned their backs on Jewish refugees seeking asylum, the Vatican printed thousands of falsified documents which allowed Jews to pass as Christians, provided financial aid to Jewish organizations, and opened up churches, parish houses, and monasteries as hiding places. At war's end, Rabbi Lapide estimated that Pius XII's efforts saved more than 800,000 lives.

Despite this, critics of the Vatican maintain that this was a time when quiet diplomacy may have been strategically correct, but morally wrong. They claim that, whatever the practical effect might have been, a Church which preached morality acted hypocritically and immorally. It needed to cry out in moral outrage at the Germans' crimes against humanity.

When compared to the assistance provided to Jews in other occupied countries, help extended by the Church in the Protectorate of Bohemia and Moravia was nearly nonexistent. When an innocent group of people is being deprived of its rights, abused and beaten in the streets, robbed of property, and eventually subjected to mass murder, one has every right to expect expressions of outrage from those who supposedly represent God and Christ on earth. By 1941, nearly everyone in Europe, even small children, was aware of the death camps. Yet the Archdiocese of the Protectorate remained silent. In the most complete history on the subject, Livia Rothkirchen writes in *The Jews of Bohemia and Moravia: Facing the Holocaust*:

"There is no evidence that the Catholic Cardinal of Prague, Karel Kašpar, protested…against the intention of promulgating anti-Jewish legislation…"

Looking back at the behavior of the Catholic Church in the former Czechoslovakia, it is necessary to distinguish between the western part, the Czech lands, and the eastern portion, Slovakia, because anti-Semitism in the rural east was historic and institutionalized. In the late 1800s, a Catholic priest named Andrej Hlinka had founded the Slovak anti-liberal and anti-Semitic People's Party. The party, known as the Ľudaks, opposed the union with the Czechs and, even as Czechoslovakia was emerging as the most liberal and democratic of all nations in Europe, the Ľudaks ranted against the influence of Jews. The great majority of pre-war 137,000 Slovak Jews belonged to upper and middle classes and occupied a disproportionate number of positions in business, finance, medicine, law, and academia. While constituting only about 3.5 percent of the total population, Jewish citizens owned nearly one-half of the wealth of Slovakia.

The day before the Germans marched into Prague, the Slovak parliament, controlled by the Ľudaks, declared its independence as a fascist state. Its president was another Catholic priest, Jozef Tiso, and the Church assumed control over the state as one-fourth of the seats in parliament came to be occupied by Catholic clergy. The Catholic-controlled government enthusiastically signed on to the Nürnberg Laws and enacted its own anti-Jewish legislation.

The Ľudaks were a Roman Catholic political party with primary support coming from the peasant population. The party formed its own paramilitary militia, called Hlinka Guards, to act as its security arm. The Hlinkas actually had been preceded by a group called Rodobrana, a paramilitary band formed in the 1920s. Styled after the German SA (*Sturm Abteilung*) and Italian Black Shirts, its members were united by a common desire to separate Slovakia from the First Republic of Czechoslovakia and by their hatred of Jews, whom they blamed for the economic hardships suffered by ordinary Slovaks. Although the Czechoslovak government shut down Rodobrana for publishing and distributing subversive and anti-Semitic literature, the Hlinkas took up their cause a few years later.

Encouraged by Tiso, the Hlinka Guards were trained in SS camps in Germany to take charge of the deportation of Slovak Jews to Auschwitz. The Germans promised the Slovak government that, if the Hlinkas would direct the identification and rounding up of Jews for deportation and the confiscation of the victims' properties, and if the Slovaks would pay 500 Reichsmark for every Jew removed from their country, none of the Slovak Jews would ever be returned to their native land. Slovakia would be totally free of these Jews who had dominated the country's professions and culture. The Nazis told Tiso that the Jews of Slovakia would be transferred to an area of occupied Poland, bounded by the Vistula and Bug rivers. There, in a territory designated as a "Jewish reservation," they would live in a near-autonomous, self-governed, state, where all of Europe's Jews would be settled permanently.

In the summer of 1942, the Czechoslovak government in exile approached the Catholic bishop of London to seek his influence with the Vatican in order to stop the Catholic-run deportation of Jews from Slovakia. A memorandum was given to the bishop for delivery to Cardinal Hinsley of Westminster, requesting intervention by the Holy See. It cited the case of 48,000 Slovak Jews who had already been deported in contravention of the "principals of Christian ethics," and an act which was "an outrage upon humanity." The request was ignored and the transports continued.

By October 1942, 80,000 Slovak Jews had been deported. Then, almost overnight, the transports stopped. Leaders of the Protestant community had become extremely vocal in their protests over the treatment of Jews, once they became aware of the fact that Jews were not being resettled on a "reservation." When the Protestants presented leaders of the Slovak Catholic Church with evidence that Slovak Jews were being murdered systematically in concentration camps, the Catholic hierarchy, with encouragement from the Vatican, backed away from its support of deportations. For a short time, a country which had been most cooperative in their removal now became something of a haven for Jews, and several hundred Czechs and Poles crossed the border into Slovakia in search of safety.

But Adolf Eichman did not allow this momentary lack of cooperation by Tiso and his government to deter him for long. He brought in Nazi troops who, with fanatical support from the Hlinkas, deported an additional 13,500 Jews to Terezín, Auschwitz, and Sachsenhausen, and imprisoned an additional 5,000. Deaths in the ghettos of Poland, mass murders in concentration camps, and post-war emigration of survivors would reduce a Slovak Jewish population which once numbered 137,000 to a mere 3,000 today.

While a certain amount of anti-Semitism existed in the Czech lands, and the Czechs' famous indifference and passivity toward conquerors which has come to be known as *Švejkism* brought about a general failure to intervene, this situation was totally different. While the Protectorate had its own version of Hlinkas, an extremist party based on Nazi ideology and known as *Vlajka* (Flag), the group was relatively small. No doubt as a result of the culture of tolerance and equality introduced by Jan Hus and nurtured by Tomáš Garrigue Masaryk, Czechs and Moravians, with the notable exceptions of members of Vlajka, did not demonstrate any of the vicious behavior and atrocities exhibited by Catholics and other Gentiles in Slovakia and in the countries of Eastern Europe.

But any acts of kindness were not sponsored or supported by the Czech Church; they were actions of individuals, assisting on their own. In Prague, Monsignor Josef Beran, Privy Chamberlain of His Holiness, made arrangements for Jews to hide in the homes of members of the Church. For this, he was arrested and sent first to Terezín and then to Dachau. He would survive and later would speak out against the communist regime after its takeover. For this, he would be imprisoned again, this time for fourteen years. After his release in 1965, Pope Paul VI would name him Cardinal.

In late 1944, a special German-Czech court sentenced a Czech Catholic priest to death for having held Mass for a man condemned by the Nazis and for having made public statements about torture and maltreatment of Jews at Terezín. The Nazis beheaded the priest by guillotine in Peček Palace, the site of Mother's many interrogations and tortures.

After the war, Gentiles who risked their lives to save Jews would be recognized by the State of Israel as "Righteous among Nations" and honored at a place called Yad Vashem. The great majority of Czechoslovaks so honored were Roman Catholics. Unjustly, those Christians who tried to help but were caught and murdered for their efforts are not recognized, since the Jews whom they had hidden were killed along with them. Neither are those who may have received even small amounts of remuneration to cover some of their expenses for hiding and feeding Jews. One of the latter was a Czech hero named Dr. Rudolf Štursa, nephew of famous Czech sculptor, Jan Štursa. After enlisting the assistance of a priest to help a Jewish friend escape by having a Roman Catholic baptism certificate forged for him, Štursa found his niche. He handed out more than 1,500 such certificates to Jews. The latter were able to find refuge in Australia, New Zealand, and Africa, countries which had restrictions against Jewish immigrants, but were able to accept these "converted Christians." Štursa asked for no money, but, when it was offered, he took it in order to finance his life-saving activities. Because of this, he is not officially one of the Righteous.

Whatever the flaws in recognition may be, the statistics at Yad Vashem serve to emphasize the indifference of Gentile Czechs toward their fellow citizens of the Jewish faith during the war. The numbers of Righteous honored at Yad Vashem, by country, are:

Poland	-	5,941
Netherlands	-	4,726
France	-	2,646

Denmark stands near the bottom among European nations with 21. This is terribly misleading; the small kingdom should be in *first* place. The Danish Underground, which numbered in the thousands, helped to save nearly all of the nation's Jews. But, it requested that all its members be counted as <u>one</u> at Yad Vashem. The Czech Republic? It sits in fifteenth place among European countries, with only 115 Righteous. 77,297 dead Jews – 115 Christian heroes in my native land.

We are going to have peace
even if we have to fight for it.
Dwight D. Eisenhower

CHAPTER 8

Papa's War

While Mother and I were surviving in occupied Czechoslovakia, my father was fighting on various fronts in the war. After enlisting in Jaffa in today's Israel, he was sent with the newly-formed Czechoslovak 11th Infantry Battalion-Eastern to Jericho, one of the world's oldest continuously-inhabited cities, located on the West Bank. The purpose of this initial deployment was acclimatization to the tropical climate of the region. The battalion was led by Lieutenant Colonel Karel Klapálek, who would become a highly-decorated general a couple of years later.

"It was hot like an oven, 120 degrees Fahrenheit every day," my father would tell us years later. "We had no equipment, no uniforms, and the Arabs stole from us every chance they got. We learned to stand guard at night, not against the Germans, but against Arab thieves."

After several weeks of this, the unit was shipped to Alexandria, Egypt, where the soldiers were issued uniforms and numbers. My father was number 588; since the numbers started with 200, it meant that he was the 388th Czech volunteer to join the British Army. Many of the early signees were Jews; eventually, about 1,200 of them would be part of the Czechoslovak Division.

Fighting had broken out in Syria, and the division was shipped there for its first taste of combat. After a few small victories, they were advancing through Lebanon toward Beirut, when a truce was declared. The unit was brought back to a base in Aleppo, Syria. There, Papa fell ill. Boils developed on his left arm and soon there were more than fifty all over his body. He was in pain and terrible discomfort in his bunk when, to add to his suffering, he was bitten in the right arm by a scorpion. He was taken to a French hospital, where the doctors were too baffled by his condition to treat it. At last, they transferred him to an Australian hospital in Lebanon, where doctors cleaned the boils with purified hot water and placed him on a special diet. The treatment worked, and, four weeks later, he was on his way back to Alexandria, where his unit was assigned to guard German and Italian prisoners of war. Undetected at the time, and discovered only after we came to America, Papa had also contracted malaria. Many years later, this would prove to be the cause of heart disease which, ultimately, would lead to his death.

My father's unit was packed into British torpedo ships which sailed toward Tobruk, a Lybian city totally surrounded by the German army. Although strafed by Nazi aircraft and shot at by artillery on shore, the ship made it through. In Tobruk, the Czechs, along with the Polish Carpathian Brigade, replaced Australian and South African troops which had been helping to defend the city for many weeks.

The siege of the critical ocean port of Tobruk had begun on April 10, 1941, when Allied forces, under the command of British Lieutenant General Leslie Morshead, were attacked by Lieutenant General Edwin Rommel's Afrika Korps and their Italian cohorts. It was necessary for the Brits to hold Tobruk because its port was the only one on the Mediterranean coast between Tripoli and Alexandria. If the Germans gained control of the port, their supply lines would be shortened drastically and Rommel's advance toward Cairo would be made possible.

Although Morshead had been asked to hold Tobruk for eight weeks, the siege went on for eight months. My father's unit suffered great losses, more from exploding mines than from open battle. There was little food and very little drinking water. Many soldiers became seriously ill from thirst. Occasionally, a British supply ship broke through the blockade.

Father would recall one such episode, when a ship made it into the harbor, only to be sunk by German artillery before reaching the dock.

"We spent hours in the water. I was able to grab several small boxes of food and even a floating can of orange juice. I thought I was in seventh heaven. Amazingly, some of my comrades were too busy grabbing floating packs of cigarettes and ignoring the food and drink. I was glad I wasn't a serious smoker."

Finally, after months of suffering, the Czechoslovak troops were relieved. Regulations called for one month behind the lines after every six months of combat, so they were sent back to Haifa to guard a refinery. But, after that respite, they returned to Tobruk, where they helped Field Marshal "Monty" Montgomery and his troops make history by stopping the German Blitzkrieg and surviving the longest siege in British military history. Unfortunately, in a second offensive in 1942, the Afrika Korps finally managed to capture Tobruk. But, by then, the 11th Battalion was on the high seas. My father had served directly under Colonel Klapálek, and he developed a great rapport with, and even greater respect for, the Czech leader. Years later, Papa would be asked to contribute a short chapter to a book, in Czech, titled, *The Man Who Led Men: Life Story of Army General Karel Klapálek*, a tribute to the man who became a hero in post-war Czechoslovakia. To show that humor was found even in war, my father wrote:

> "During the siege of Tobruk, when we were totally surrounded, only the most seriously wounded were evacuated to Cairo or Alexandria. One of them was Private Puliček, who had dental problems so serious that he could not eat. After several weeks, he returned onboard the 'Warsaw.' It was the same ship which had brought us from Messina to Haifa in 1940. Now, she was part of a convoy of ships which were bringing Christmas gifts from our countrymen. But, the 'Warsaw' was torpedoed and sunk. Puliček was rescued. Proudly, he reported to Klapálek and informed him that he had lost all his personal belongings in the sinking, but he

had managed to save an envelope (which had been entrusted to him) with important information for Klapálek. (It turned out that) inside the envelope was a request to punish Puliček for having spent evenings off-limits and for disturbance of the peace and drunkenness..."

After more fighting alongside Monty's armored corps, the Czechs received great news. They were being relieved and sent to England! My father was elated when he boarded the *Mauretania* in Suez. The ship sailed south and around Africa, to Madagascar, Cape Town, Sierra Leone. Along the way, she was attacked several times by German submarines and aircraft, but with minimal damage. Seven weeks after her August 11, 1943, departure, the *Mauretania* tied up in Liverpool. In England, the unit was merged with a Czechoslovak brigade from France. When they had formed originally in Alexandria, Papa's outfit started life as infantry; in Tobruk, they became anti-aircraft artillery. Now, the merged units became an armored brigade. They trained in a number of places in Britain: Colchester, Northampton, and the Scottish Highlands. Then, in preparation for the invasion, they were shipped to London.

Papa's first step onto the land of continental Europe, after a four-year adventure, came on June 6, 1944, "D-Day." He was in the second wave of the great Allied invasion which landed on French shores. While disembarking trucks and jeeps in stormy seas, Papa's small ship broke loose and, with a few men and two trucks on board, wallowed in the chop. Eventually, the soldiers made it to shore, but far from the original landing spot, near the town of Caen. Once on land, they were lost. It took them five days and many miles of walking, under the weight of the equipment on their backs, to find their unit.

Acting primarily as a motorcycle advance scout and courier, Papa fought in bloody battles with American and British infantry and tank units in heavily-fortified Dunkirk and in other parts of France, encircling the Germans. In the middle of December 1944, the Germans launched a desperate counteroffensive in the Ardennes, an area covering parts of

France, Belgium, and Luxembourg. The Allied armies of the invasion were bogged down in one of the bloodiest and costliest, in terms of casualties on both sides, fights of the war, one which became known as the Battle of the Bulge.

Amazingly, in the midst of this fierce battle, both sides stopped to celebrate Christmas. While Mother spent Christmas Eve in the Hagibor barracks with her fellow inmates and I tried to get into the spirit of Christmas with my protectors in Kojetice, my father celebrated with his fellow soldiers in the Ardennes.

It may have seemed strange to his comrades that this Jewish soldier searched the battlefield for "chafe," the tinfoil dropped from aircraft to confuse enemy radar, to decorate his platoon's make-shift Christmas tree. It may have appeared stranger still that he knew the words to "Silent Night," and that he led its singing in Czech, English, and even German. But, as a secular person who had embraced Mother's and my Catholic traditions, he had come to consider Christmas Eve the holiest night of the year. He prayed that both of us were alive and that we would be reunited soon.

"I prayed for you and your mother," he would tell me a few years later when describing our last Christmas apart. "At midnight, I celebrated by drinking a cup of French tea. And then it was time for me to go on watch. On Christmas Day, the fighting started all over again."

Finally, they defeated the enemy and entered Germany, crossing the Rhine River on a Czechoslovak holiday, the birthday of late President Masaryk, March 7, 1945. There, along with 139 other Czechoslovaks, Papa was selected by Montgomery to accompany General George S. Patton's Third Army as it headed toward the western border of Czechoslovakia.

❋ ❋ ❋

As it neared the border, the 2nd Cavalry Group encountered stiff resistance before it crossed the border into the westernmost Czech city of Aš, located inside the "ear" (so called because of the shape of the Czech-

German border) of the former Sudetenland. Just west of the border, the 90th Infantry Division liberated one of the lesser-known concentration camps, Floessenburg, where the soldiers found emaciated prisoners left to die and heard the horror stories of murders and deaths which were spreading among Allied armies as they pushed into the center of Europe.

"We caught up with Patton almost at the Czech border," my father would explain when recounting the last days of the war. "There was fighting everywhere. And, to make things more difficult, we had to supervise the liberated concentration-camp prisoners so they wouldn't die from overeating, after starving for so long."

Seeing these prisoners and hearing stories from other soldiers about liberated concentration camps elsewhere terrified my father. He wondered about the fate of his family. But, there was little time for contemplation because he and his comrades were busy rounding up Gestapo men who were fleeing west from Prague with their families and (mostly stolen) belongings.

"The Americans were at a loss as to what to do with these bastards," Papa would recall. "They gave us *carte blanche* to deal with the Germans at our discretion. But, soon they disapproved of our methods. We simply chased the Nazis from their cars and trucks, made them abandon all their belongings, and then we forced them to march on foot, straight to prison camps. The Americans just didn't hate the Germans the way we did."

As Patton's army approached Czechoslovakia, Papa and two other Czech-speaking soldiers were assigned to the Office of Strategic Services (OSS, the predecessor of the CIA). For the moment, the Americans were being held back from the border because of a rumor of the Nazis' upcoming last stand in the Alps and thus a possible drive south, rather than east toward Prague.

Finally, on May 4, 1945, General Dwight D. Eisenhower gave Patton permission to drive into Czechoslovakia. He was to move out the next morning and advance to a line drawn from Karlový Vary to Pilsen to

České Budějovice, and no further east. Czech partisans in Pilsen had already begun to fight the Germans in an attempt to liberate the city. But, the Germans feared the Czechs as much as they did the Russians, knowing that they would be subject to brutal revenge if captured by Czechs, so their commander gave the order to fight and to surrender only to the Americans. The fight was in full force until Patton's troops entered the city, at which time the Germans hoisted the white flag.

Czechs living in the western part of the country had been subjected to the tyrannical rule of the Germans for more than six years, longer than any other people who had been enslaved by the Nazis. They greeted the Americans' entrance into Pilsen and surrounding towns with such unbridled joy and enthusiasm that the soldiers were shocked. An American sergeant wrote home that the experience was "like a hero in a great football game, carried off the field on the shoulders of the spectators." Colonel Charles H. Noble, who led the troops, was hailed as the "Liberator of Pilsen." And when they saw the word "Czechoslovakia" on the shoulder patch of my father's Eisenhower jacket, the Pilsners went crazy, pushing flowers and bottles of beer into his hands. But, Papa had mixed feelings. On the one hand, he was ecstatic. The war was nearly over, and he was a liberator of his native country. But, fear of the unknown – the fate of his family – weighed heavily upon him. He had not had any news about us for five years, and, by now, he was well aware of the unspeakable atrocities committed by the Germans.

General Patton was anxious to push on to Prague. But, unbeknownst to his soldiers or the Czech citizenry, he was under strict orders from Eisenhower to stop in Pilsen and to go no further east. Patton bombarded his immediate superior, General Omar Bradley, with messages, begging permission to push eastward. He had received reports that an uprising was taking place in Prague and wanted to provide assistance to the Czech fighters. In order to strengthen his case, he dispatched a small group led by Lt. Eugene Fodor and three Czech soldiers assigned to the OSS, including my father, to ride the fifty miles to Prague on motorcycles. After passing through German lines undetected at night, the soldiers arrived in Prague in the middle of a violent revolution.

"There were barricades made up of overturned street cars, cobblestones, furniture, and trash cans," Papa would recall years later. "Czechs were shooting at Germans with rifles, pistols, and *panzerfausts* (German recoilless rifles, similar to American Bazookas). Czechs were dying for nothing because we could have driven out the Germans in a day."

When the scouts returned to Pilsen, they found the Americans at headquarters listening to a broadcast from a Prague radio station. In broken English, revolutionaries were begging the Americans to come to save them. Patton called Bradley again.

"For God's sake, Brad," he screamed. "Those patriots in the city need our help!"

Bradley agreed with Patton, and tried to change Ike's mind. But, the Supreme Commander ordered Bradley to inform Patton that he was not permitted to cross the demarcation line. Observing this, my father did not realize at the time that he was living history, for this was another crucial moment in the sad saga of my native land.

Papa was distraught. For more than five years, he had fought on two continents with one objective driving him through times of horror, uncertainty, and boredom – the liberation of his country. Now, after Tobruk, Dunkirk, D-Day, and the Battle of the Bulge, he was a mere 60 miles from home and unable to finish the job. He decided to take matters into his own hands.

"We have to get to Prague to help our countrymen," he announced to several Czech soldiers who had gathered around him upon his return.

They stole a U. S. Army truck and loaded it with weapons and ammunition. With my father at the wheel, they sped east on the highway toward Prague. Czech citizens, seeing the white star painted on the door of the green vehicle, cheered madly as they passed through town after town. Everything went smoothly until they reached the small city of Beroun, less than twenty miles from Prague. There, they were stopped by a barricade across the road, manned by armed soldiers of the Red Army, apparently an advance unit of the Soviet division heading south from Berlin. Papa and his friends argued in Czech, and their Russian allies responded in their own language, each group understanding perhaps a tenth of the other's words. But, the Czechs did not have to comprehend the verbiage to realize that their so-called allies were serious. There was no way that they would be permitted to continue.

After an hour of fruitless attempts to convince, and even bribe, the Reds, they turned back. Now, having accomplished nothing, they would have to face the Americans for not only having disobeyed orders, but also for having stolen Army property.

As soon as they arrived back in Pilsen, Papa sought out a lieutenant colonel whom he had befriended. My father explained what had taken place, admitted that he had been the instigator, and apologized.

"Good try," said the colonel. "I'm sorry you didn't make it through. Just return the truck where you found it. We'll forget the whole incident."

While the misadventure could be forgotten, the events which led up to it, on a global level, could not. We know that an agreement had been struck between the Soviets and the Americans that the Red Army would be the liberators of Czechoslovakia. Some American historians have claimed that, at the Yalta Conference in February 1945, Josef Stalin insisted on liberating Prague "in payment for the great suffering of the Soviet people," and that President Franklin D. Roosevelt acquiesced. This is not true.

While Yalta included specifics regarding the post-war division of Germany, and even a gift of the easternmost region of Czechoslovakia to the USSR, it did not include details regarding the liberation of the capital, Prague. In fact, Czechoslovakia was not even mentioned in the official Yalta agreement, nor was it included in any agreements among the allies regarding the status of post-war Europe. On April 23, 1945, General Eisenhower sent a message to Winston Churchill:

"I had never conceived of Prague as a military, still less as a political, objective."

It was Ike and Soviet General Alexei Antonov who made the handshake deal that would bring about this travesty. Eisenhower was concerned about getting his troops out of Europe as quickly as possible in order to fight the continuing war against Japan, and he was eager to please his Soviet counterparts who would be left to maintain peace in Europe. Although Winston Churchill begged Harry S Truman to overrule his general, the president who had succeeded FDR upon the latter's death considered this a military matter to be settled by military leaders. On April 30, Truman informed General George Marshall that Churchill had requested that the Third Army of Patton liberate Prague ahead of the Soviets. Misunderstanding the magnitude of the situation, Marshall supported Ike and told him that he "would be loath to hazard American lives for purely political purposes."

America, that bastion of liberty and justice, and the nation which deserves so much credit for the annihilation of the Nazi tyrants, shares a large part of the blame for the fate that befell the fifteen million people of Czechoslovakia. The Americans' naïve decision to stop in Pilsen not only caused hundreds of Czechs to die while awaiting the Red Army to arrive from Berlin in May 1945, but it provided Czech communists with the opportunity they needed to establish themselves in a partnership with our so-called "liberators." This horrible miscalculation helped to bring about 41 years of subjugation of the Czech and Slovak people and a near-total devastation of what had once been one of the world's most vibrant democracies and economies. Once again, the decisions of foreigners would have a profound effect not only on my native country, but on the fate of my family.

I would harbor resentment toward Dwight D. Eisenhower for a long time, well past his military career and his presidency of the United States. But, I would forgive him when, many years later, I would read the words of the order he gave to his soldiers while liberating one of the Nazi concentration camps. Like many people, I had considered Ike a man of limited intellectual capacity. I changed my mind in an instant when I discovered his prediction of the coming of Holocaust deniers long after his death.

"Get it on record now," he ordered in 1945. "Get the films, get the witnesses. Because somewhere down the track of history, some son of a bitch will get up and say this never happened." How true; how sad! And it <u>is</u> on record and on film, and there have been thousands of witnesses.

CHAPTER 9

Revenge and Liberation

The turning point of the war had been the battle of Stalingrad. Lasting 199 days and ending in February 1943, it was the bloodiest battle in world history, with nearly two million dead on both sides. With 1.5 million of their troops killed, wounded or captured, the Germans were stopped on the eastern front and the Soviets went on the offensive. With the western Allies also gaining the upper hand, the Germans began to retreat on all fronts. Now, it was simply a matter of time before the war would be won.

By the first of May 1945, the Germans knew the end was near. Rumors were swarming around us like gnats: the Red Army had taken Berlin; Hitler had died in a bunker; there were Americans on the western border of Czechoslovakia. I was interested in only one thing: when are my parents coming home?

Many of the Nazi soldiers who had been guarding the Hagibor slave labor camp where Mother was imprisoned ran off toward the west. Those who stayed were in a drunken stupor. Along with four other women, Mother escaped from camp, hid in Prague for three days, and then came home to Kojetice. We held a tearful reunion after which Mother moved in with us at the Castle.

On May 8, a mysterious band of soldiers entered Prague in the middle of fierce fighting between Czechs who had begun the uprising and Germans who were trying to escape to the west. Prague citizens knew that Americans and Russians wore green uniforms. So who were these men dressed in black? Could they be the SS? Fear gripped the city until it became clear that these were "General Vlasov's Men." Vlasov was once a Soviet hero who had obtained the rank of general in the Red Army. Then he and his soldiers were taken prisoner by the Germans after a major battle on the eastern front. While imprisoned, he came to the conclusion that Stalin was as ruthless as Hitler and decided to switch sides. The Germans allowed Vlasov to command his two divisions and provided him with arms and transportation. He and his men fought valiantly alongside the Nazis.

Now, they had entered Prague, and the Czech streetfighters were terrified that Vlasov was there to decimate them. But, the General had seen the handwriting on the wall, and once again decided to switch sides in order to redeem himself and his troops. He had heard the Czechs' pleas for help on the radio. Not bound by any agreement like the Americans, he came to help the patriots rid themselves of the Germans. Although this would not appear in the history books once the communists took control of Czechoslovakia, it was actually General Vlasov's army – and not the Red Army – which liberated Prague on that day. Postscipt: the Soviets would capture Vlasov in Czechoslovakia, and he would be brought to Moscow and executed as a traitor.

On May 9, the Red Army's First Ukrainian Front, led by Marshal Ivan Konev, arrived in Prague from Berlin, to be hailed as our official liberators. The city had been spared major damage during the war, until this very end, although there had been hundreds of times during which Prague's citizens had been sent to bomb shelters.

Prague's historic district sustained nearly all its physical losses during the few days of fighting in May 1945 and during the Germans' retreat. As they rolled west out of Prague, the Nazis blasted the neo-Gothic wing of ancient Old Town Hall and shot up the world-renown astronomical clock. Before they retreated, the Germans killed hundreds of Czech patriots during the uprising. Visitors to Prague today wonder about the many plaques, small silver wreaths, and flowers on building walls throughout the city. These mark the places where Czechs died heroically on the barricades that first week of May 1945.

Today's tourists rarely venture outside of Prague, and they are under the impression that all of Czechoslovakia was spared from bombing during the war. This is a fallacy. Our neighboring town of Neratovice, with its chemical plant and German railroad depot, was hit repeatedly. Nazi ordnance factories and other strategic targets were dispersed throughout the country, and they were bombed regularly by American B-17 Flying Fortresses and B-24 Liberators, as well as British Wellingtons. It was easy to distinguish the good guys from the bad guys in the sky. The aluminum fuselages and wings of Allied airplanes were a glittery silver, while the Nazi aircraft were painted a dull black. Watching the show in the sky presented me with a dilemma. I cheered for the silver planes, while fearing their bombs. I hated the black birds, but I knew that they would not harm me. British and American bombers generally flew on cloudless days. For many years after the war, in the safe sanctuary of the United States, I would unconsciously search a brilliant blue sky in fear of silver aircraft coming to deliver their deadly cargo. It would take me many years to rid myself of the initial fear I would feel on such sunny days.

* * *

During that first week of May 1945, retreating German occupiers – soldiers and civilians, men, women, and children – filled every north- and westbound road out of Prague, hoping to be captured by civilized Americans, rather than the brutal Soviets. Although our village of Kojetice was two kilometers from the highway between Prague and the city of Mělník, German soldiers and workers had been passing through for several days on their way north. A few found temporary lodging before continuing; injured soldiers fleeing the front were treated in a make-shift infirmary in the elementary school. Two boys I met when I ventured out of the dark corner room in which I had been hiding told me that some

Wermacht deserters had taken refuge in the outbuildings of the Vávra estate where we were living.

Like most Czechs, I found it difficult to believe that our hated oppressors were really running away. Now, my new friends and I decided to observe the exodus. We exited the estate surrounding the Castle, a one-time residence of the region's major landowner, but now a dormitory for farm workers, through a rear gate, and we walked out to the highway. The Nazis were gone by the time we arrived. But, wanting to be unarmed when captured, the soldiers had been throwing away their military equipment along the way. In the ditch by the road, we found a treasure trove. There were gas masks, bayonets, helmets, binoculars, clips with bullets – and guns! I picked up a black Walther pistol. It was heavy and cold, but it gave me an unexpected jolt of power.

"I'm going to shoot a German," I announced to my companions matter-of-factly, as I stuck the loaded pistol inside my belt. I remembered the boys' comment about Germans hiding inside the estate courtyard and thus, in a flight of fancy and without consideration of the consequences, I knew my target. We headed back to the village, each of us with his favorite piece of loot. Along the way, the boys laughed at my bravado and teased me about having read too many Karl May cowboy and Indian novels.

We returned to the Castle by climbing over a wall surrounding the large estate. Once inside, we sneaked into the woods and to the edge of the courtyard. We crawled through thick brush to watch several men and women load boxes onto two gray trucks. A short distance away from us, a tall, blond, Aryan – a poster child for a Nazi propaganda billboard – was carrying a small table through a door and toward a truck. The man was dressed in dark trousers and leather boots, was hatless and wore a white undershirt and dark green suspenders. The boy named Pepík pulled his newly-obtained gas mask away from his face.

"Well, are you gonna do it?" he whispered.

I stared at him for a long moment, taking his dare as a signal that the man was one of the escaping Germans, and wondering if I had the courage to back up my boast. Finally, I swallowed hard and carefully drew the Walther from my belt. Getting on my feet, cocking the pistol, and assuming a two-handed pose I had seen in American cowboy movies before the war, I aimed at the blond-haired man's chest. I squeezed the trigger. Bam! The noise was ear-shattering. The pistol recoiled and flew out of my hand, and I was propelled into the bushes.

"You got him!" screamed Pepík.

I crawled out of the brush and looked. The man was lying on the ground, while a woman was screaming in German from the doorway. Leaving the gun behind, I took off running as fast as I could toward the Castle, while my two companions scattered in different directions. I hid behind the brick building which had been my hideaway and waited for what seemed like hours, with my heart pounding wildly. Amazingly, no one had followed. After an initial crush of fear, I experienced an adrenaline rush unlike any I had ever felt before – or since.

"*I killed a German,*" I screamed silently. "*I killed a German!*"

I did not know if I had really killed the man, but I hoped that I had. In that splendid moment, I felt as if I had singlehandedly won the war. For most of my young life, I had been running and hiding. Now, finally, I had struck back. I had taken revenge for everything the Nazis had done – for taking my family from me, for stealing our home and all our possessions, for forcing me to hide like an animal, for desecrating my beloved Czechoslovakia. I was nine years old.

The initial jubilation over my victory soon turned into trauma. Night after night, I dreamed about the incident, often being caught and shot by German soldiers, at other times being dragged off to a concentration camp by the Gestapo. I decided that I had to erase the experience from my mind, so that I could experience the joy of the war's end unimpeded by its memory. I hoped that the boys who had been with me would return to their own villages and keep their silence. I vowed not tell anyone – even my parents.

I would keep that promise to myself for many years. I would never tell my father and would not confess to my mother until two years before her death, only because I would feel that I would have to reveal everything important when writing my life story. Later still, I would describe my adventure to Jaroslav Kučera, the town historian. He would shock me with his response. After having lived with both the pride and the trauma caused by the shooting, I would be told by Kučera that my victim may not have been a German soldier after all. More likely, he was a Czech Nazi collaborator. And he had not died; the word in the village after war had been that a man had been wounded by someone. After initial astonishment, I would be simultaneously disappointed and relieved, though more the former than the latter.

* * *

After her return from the Hagibor camp, Mother, along with everyone in the village, celebrated the end of the war. But it was a muted celebration. Mother was filled with fear of the unknown: what happened to Papa and the rest of our family? Later, she wrote in her journal:

> *"During the revolution, when I was back in Kojetice and all of us were celebrating the end of German tyranny, I knew that for me the worst period was about to come, waiting to find out who from our family will return home."*

Josef Hollman, the Sudeten German who had been sent by the Nazis to take over all of our family's properties, somehow managed to get his wife and daughter out of Kojetice. However, he was not so lucky. Before he could escape, he was arrested by a group of townspeople and, since Kojetice did not have a jail, he was being held prisoner in the mayor's office. On May 9, liberation day, it was my godfather, blacksmith Karel Šubrt, who was guarding Hollman. He had taken a *panzerfaust*, a German recoilless rifle, from the escaping Wermacht, and had it trained on Hollman as the two sat next to the mayor's desk. Suddenly, the weapon went off. Karel Šubrt was killed instantly by the recoil blast from the rear of the tube, another innocent victim of the Nazis.

Hollman was not seriously injured from the explosion, and he was imprisoned. During the summer of 1945, he was brought before a commission investigating war crimes. During the hearing, he asked to be allowed to go to the toilet. There, he swallowed a poison pill and died instantly, like many of his fellow master-race "heroes." He is buried in the Kojetice cemetery. My only post-war encounter with a member of his family would be an indirect one. It would come after the 1989 Velvet Revolution when Hollman's granddaughter would have the audacity to come to Kojetice from Germany to claim our factory as her own through the restitution process. No doubt, she inherited much of her grandfather's Nazi arrogance. I would have been happy to supply her with a poison pill, but the Czechs threw her out before I had a chance to meet her.

Two days after liberation, on May 11, Patton ordered a group of Czech soldiers to proceed to Prague. My father was in the group. On the way from Pilsen to Prague, Czech citizens nearly went berserk when they saw Czech-speaking men in American uniforms and British berets passing through their towns and villages. In Prague, Papa and his colleagues got the same reception from the locals. However, they were not welcomed by their Russian allies, who told them in no uncertain terms to leave Prague and to return to the demarcation line. Since it was late in the evening, the Red Army granted the Czech soldiers permission to spend the night in the city and to proceed west in the morning.

Of course, Mother and I were unaware of the fact that Papa was only ten miles away from us. We did not even know that he was alive. We could only hope. Throughout the war, Mother had been strong and brave. Even when all seemed bleak and hopeless, she never stopped fighting and urging me to look forward to a better day. But now that it was over, there was nothing and no one to fight. She felt lost because she had no control over events. Then, suddenly, there was cautious hope. Mother wrote in her journal:

> *"11 May 1945 was the happiest day of my life. It was the first day that trains ran to Prague and I went there. On Wenceslas Square, I saw several soldiers in American uniforms with*

'Czechoslovakia' emblems. That evening when I returned home, a neighbor lady was waiting for me with the news that she had seen Rudy in an American uniform on Wenceslas Square. This made me very angry because the only news I had about Rudy came in 1942, that he was in a prisoner of war camp in Germany (a false rumor). After hearing my neighbor, I decided that it would be best to say nothing to Ota.'

Despite being watched closely by the Russians, my father defied orders, sneaked away, and borrowed a motorcycle from a Czech civilian. He raced out of Prague, onto the Mělník highway, toward Kojetice. Just as Mother and I knew nothing about his fate, he did not know whether we were alive or dead. As he neared our village, many of the people who were outside celebrating their newly-found freedom recognized him, and the telephone wires began to buzz with the news: Rudy Heller made it through the war, and now he's heading home, dressed in an American uniform!

František Volt, the man who had risked his life to be my secret teacher during the occupation, came running to our door just as we sat down to dinner in the Castle. Someone had called the municipal building to say that my father was approaching Kojetice on the highway.

Then someone told us that Papa had just ridden his bike through the gate of the estate and was heading for the Castle. Mother and I took off running down the path in the direction of the courtyard where, just a couple of days ago and unbeknownst to Mother, I had shot the Nazi. I heard the sound of the motorcycle seconds before Papa roared around a curve toward us. When he saw us, he screeched to a halt, with the bike flying away onto its side, and ran to meet us. I tackled him and held on to his leg as tightly as I could, while he and Mother hugged and kissed. I was not about to let go – ever again. My war-hero father, my courageous mother who had loved me irrevocably, unconditionally and had protected me throughout the war, and I were reunited after all!

"I still didn't believe it, but within a few minutes, Rudy was home. It was the happiest day of my life. (Mother had every right to repeat it in her

journal!) *Ota's favorite game during the war had been to play soldier, and to my great horror, to tell everyone that 'I'm a soldier like my Papa and I'm shooting Germans!' Now, when he saw his father, he could not stop admiring him. Not only was he happy that his father had returned, but he was proud that he came in an American uniform and on a motorcycle!"*

✳ ✳ ✳

For me, the end of the war in Europe was pure euphoria. I was totally unaware of the fact that another war still raged on in a strange part of the world. Incredibly, despite often having listened behind doors while my various hosts monitored the progress of the war – secretly and unlawfully – on the BBC, I had no idea that America was fighting against Japan in the Pacific. Moreover, because my parents decided on a code of silence in my presence regarding the fate of our family, I was unaware until much later that we had lost at least fifteen family members and that the three of us were the only survivors. I did not know that our family tree had been destroyed until only a very small stump remained. I had no idea that I was the single root protruding from that stump.

Actually, there were <u>four</u> of us who survived, but I did not recognize this at the time because perhaps saddest of all is the fact that my parents' silence allowed no discussion of my maternal grandmother, Marie Kozuschniková. It would not be until years later, in the waiting room of a New Jersey hospital where my father was undergoing surgery, that Mother would tell me what this wonderful lady had done for the two of us – risked her own life to save ours. Since she was a Sudeten German living in Czechoslovakia, I wonder today if she was among the 2.5 million ethnic Germans who were deported after the war. I hope and pray that she was not, and that my father was able to use his influence as a war hero and that my mother was able to testify as to Grandma's anti-fascist activities, so that she could remain in Ostrava with her family. Sadly, I have been unable to learn her fate.

Another distressing aftermath of the post-war weeks concerned my wartime protectors, the Tůmas. The German army traveled with its own mobile brothels, with prostitutes of various nationalities serving at the pleasure of Nazi officers. As our former occupiers ran before the Red Army toward the west, their whores ran with them. I was told that Mr. Tůma became acquainted with one of the escaping prostitutes and fell in love with her. He saved her from prosecution, divorced his wife, and married the German woman. My parents and all our friends were enraged by this, and all of us helped and protected Mrs. Tůmová, who was one of the special ladies whom I called "Aunt." Mr. Tůma and his new wife moved to the town of Kladno, and we shunned him. Just as in the case of my Sudeten German grandmother, I am truly sorry today that I participated in this, even when I became an adult and visited Czechoslovakia while both Tůmas were still alive. I am very grateful for everything Vladimír Tůma did for Mother and me during the war, and I wish I had given myself the opportunity to tell him that. But, it is too late now. He passed away many years ago.

In our own way, we helped to make Marie Kozuschniková and Vladimír Tůma victims of that horrible war, too.

My great-grandfather Gustav Neumann (*"Dědeček"*), founder of the clothing manufacturing firm – Gustav Neumann/Labor – standing in front of the factory's retail store in Kojetice [circa 1930].

Left to right: my great-grandfather Gustav Neumann (*"Dědeček"*), my grandfather Artur Neumann (*"Děda"*), and my mother Ilona Neumannová (*"Maminka"*), vacationing on the Riviera [1932].

Wedding of my parents, Ilona and Rudolph Heller, at City Hall in Old Town Square, Prague; young Tom Eisner, whose family would sponsor our immigration to America in 1949, stands on the right [16 December 1934].

My mother, Ilona, with me at the age of four, one year after the German occupation of Czechoslovakia [1940].

My father, Rudolph Heller, a soldier in the artillery of the Czechoslovak Division of the British Army, pauses during the siege of Tobruk, Libya [1941].

First portrait of the Heller family after our post-war reunion in May 1945; my father is still in his British army uniform.

Dinner on the evening of our first day in America.
Sitting left to right: Robert Eisner, Ilona Heller,
Mitzi Eisner, Tom Eisner. I am standing to the left
of Steve Eisner [30 May 1949].

Our first Christmas Eve in America, Morristown, New
Jersey [24 December 1949]. Note that I am wearing the
same shirt I wore our first day in the U.S.

In New Jersey, I discover basketball, a sport which opens doors for me and becomes an important part of my life [1953].

On June 3, 1959, I marry my high-school sweetheart, Susan ("Sue") Holsten, at the First Methodist Church in Morristown, New Jersey. Our friends throw rice at us outside the church.

Following near death at birth and a harrowing first month of his life in the hospital, Sue and I, along with my parents, celebrate the arrival of our son David Arthur at our home in Annapolis, Maryland [May 1964].

Sue and I learned to sail at the U.S. Naval Academy in Annapolis in 1965 and David began sailing as a small child. For the next 30 years, we are seldom happier than onboard one of our racing sailboats. This is "Pistol Pete" under spinnaker.

Our family's former factory Gustav Neumann/Labor in Kojetice, in sad shape when we got it back through restitution three years after Czechoslovakia's Velvet Revolution [1993].

Our office building in Prague, shortly after it is returned to us after a court settlement with the Czechoslovakia's Communist Party [1994].

My mother, Ilona (center), expresses her joy at the wedding of her only grandson David to Elizabeth ("Bobbi") Bass [26 October 1994].

Sue and I are standing at our favorite spot in the Czech Republic – the Mělník castle; the mountain, Říp, which is important in the history of the nation, as well as that of my family, is in the background. [2003]

The entire Heller family gathers for the celebration of my mother's 90th (and last) birthday; left to right: me, daughter-in-law Bobbi, grandson Sam, granddaughter Caroline, Mother, granddaughter Sarah, son David, and Sue [21 November 2005].

Freedom suppressed and again regained
bites with keener fangs than freedom never endangered.
Cicero

CHAPTER 10

Short-Lived Freedom

For me, many emotional moments followed the end of the war. One of the first came the day President Beneš and his government in exile returned to Prague. With my parents, I stood in the courtyard of Hradčany Castle along with hundreds of jubilant Czechs, looking up at the window from which the president would address us. Finally, the window opened and the man who had spent the war in London working to free Czechoslovakia from Nazi oppression and to protect the nation from a post-war Soviet take-over, stood there and waved to us. The roar of the crowd was deafening. When he finished his uplifting speech, it was even louder. Finally, a military band played the national anthem, *Kde domov můj?* ("Where Is My Home?"), and tears flowed freely and unashamedly from every eye, including mine.

Holding a small red-white-and-blue Czechoslovak flag in my hand, I walked with Papa and Mother down the narrow streets from the Castle and toward the center of Prague. We crossed the Charles Bridge and made our way to Wenceslas Square. Along the way, we savored the sight of large, blank spaces on shop windows and over doors, indicating hasty paint jobs covering up German words which had identified bakeries, laundries, barber shops, and others in a language I hated. We saw flowers on sidewalks and Papa explained that they commemorated the deaths of Czech patriots on those spots during the first week in May. Sometimes, we saw blood spattered on the walls. When we reached the top of Wenceslas Square, I was startled by the sight of debris strewn everywhere on the nation's most famous street and the destruction of the corner building to the left of the statue of Charles IV. Amazingly, the good king, as well as the ladies and gentlemen of stone behind him on the terrace of the National Museum, stood undamaged and seemingly bemused by the defeat of yet another conqueror in the long history of their country.

A few weeks later, I saw and heard the president again, this time in the village of Lidice, which had been wiped out by the Nazis in retaliation for the assassination of the Butcher of Prague, Reinhardt Heydrich. Returning soldiers and their families were given special seating, and I sat proudly next to my father – in his treasured green Eisenhower jacket with ribbons on his chest and "Czechoslovakia" on his sleeve, a green beret with the emblem of the Czech two-tailed lion on his head – as the president dedicated a memorial to the victims of Lidice. The stark, simple cross and crown of thorns affected me deeply, as it does each time I visit that sacred place to this day.

* * *

It did not take long for the euphoria of having been "liberated" by the Soviets to wear off. Most of the simple, uneducated – and brutal – Russian soldiers were totally unaware of the fact that the Czechs had been on their side during the war. They thought they had conquered us, just as they had conquered the Germans. They staggered down the streets of our cities and villages with bottles of vodka in their hands, picking fights with, and sometimes shooting, civilians. They stole valuables and scarce food supplies. Worst of all, they craved Czech girls and women. I was too young to understand and wondered why men did not allow their mothers, wives, and daughters to leave home alone. Later, I would learn of thousands of rapes committed by these Red Army brutes.

I did understand, and laughed along with my fellow Czechs, at these simple characters' love for watches. How many timepieces a Soviet soldier could buy or steal, and wear simultaneously on his forearms, seemed to be a measure of success among the primitive enlisted men.

"What time is it?" they would ask a Czech in the street. If the unsuspecting pedestrian looked at his watch to give the Russian the time, he could kiss his timepiece goodbye. If he was lucky, the soldier paid for it. In most cases, he simply took it.

Vladimír Tůma returned to his farm a few days after the end of the war. One evening, while he was eating dinner, someone knocked on the door. He opened it to find two Russian soldiers standing there, along with one of Mr. Tůma's cows. They had stolen the animal from the barn and now they wanted to trade it for the farmer's watch.

"Davaj časy, suda! ('Give me your watch, quickly!')" one said in Russian. Mr. Tůma was prepared for such an incident and wore a cheap watch on his wrist. He handed it over, while his gold Omega remained hidden in a drawer. The Russians left the cow and walked out the gate, happy with their latest trinket.

* * *

In Prague, thousands of Germans who had moved into the capital and had not escaped back to Germany were rounded up and thrown into make-shift prisons. More than 5,000 of them were held at the Strahov football stadium, where Red Army soldiers raped the German women on a daily basis. The former Nazis' clothes were painted with huge white swastikas, and men, women, and children were formed into gangs to clean up the barricades and other remnants of the uprising.

Prior to the war, and soon after its start, most Sudeten Germans had become enthusiastic Nazis. When the war ended, they incurred the wrath of the long-oppressed Czech people. Thirty thousand were killed or seriously injured by revenge-seeking citizens. President Beneš recommended that all those Sudetens who had been Nazi sympathizers be deported to Germany. But, when it was determined that the selection process would be too difficult, he reversed the proposition: all but those who were proven anti-Nazis would be expelled. Known as the "Beneš Decrees," the result was that only 10,000 Sudeten Germans were allowed to stay; close to three million were exiled to Germany. The Sudeten lands were nearly emptied, as they awaited colonization by ethnic Czechoslovaks. To this day, Germans resent this act of revenge and even some Czechs, certainly none who had suffered at the hands of the Nazis, speak out against Beneš's expulsion orders.

"*Tatínku,* is it true that our people are treating the Germans as badly as the Germans treated us?" I asked my father at dinner one evening. I had heard stories of atrocities and savage behavior on the radio, and I was confused. I had thought that we Czechs were more civilized than Germans.

"I'm afraid it is," he said. "I don't condone this kind of behavior, but you have to realize that these Sudetens brought it on themselves. They swore loyalty to our country and then they betrayed us. They elected Nazi politicians; they invited and welcomed Hitler. Now, they're paying for it."

There had been thousands of open and secret Czech Nazi collaborators, as well. The former had belonged to such organizations as the Czech Association for Collaboration with Germans and the Anti-Jewish League. During the war, many claimed their German origins and changed their Slavic names to those with Germanic spelling (for example, a man named Šubrt became Schubert; in Czech, both are pronounced the same). They became petty chieftains as foremen in factories, editors of fascist newspapers and magazines, interpreters for the Gestapo, and black-market operatives. Those who collaborated secretly denounced their neighbors anonymously for having expressed a negative opinion about the Third Reich, for having listened to a BBC radio broadcast, for having spoken kindly about Masaryk or Beneš, or for having had contact with a Jew and thus having earned the label of "Jew-lover." They used their denunciations both for financial gain and to settle old scores with neighbors, acquaintances, and even relatives.

Some collaborators were hanged and many were imprisoned after the war, ironically hundreds of them in Hagibor, the former slave labor camp where Mother had spent the last part of the war. But, most collaborators covered their tracks and were never punished. Many cowards who had denounced their fellow citizens in order to gain the Germans' favor were able to meld into society and pretend to have been secret patriots. Hundreds of unscrupulous and unprincipled Czechs who had looted the homes of Jews who had been sent to the camps, kept the properties and other valuable belongings, often even after survivors came back and tried to reclaim them.

One of thousands of notorious Czech fascists was a man named Václav Píša, a pre-war petty criminal who became an editor of a weekly anti-Semitic tabloid called *Árijský boj* ("Aryan Struggle"). The paper's major objective was to expose "Jew-lovers, Benešites, and the like." While its articles demonized Jews and spoke out enthusiastically in favor of the Germans' measures against them, its main service to its masters was "The Floodlight," a weekly column featuring exposés of Czechs, Jewish and Christian, those who had been disloyal to the German state and those who had broken any of the many anti-Semitic laws. The input for the column came from citizen readers, who, on good weeks, swamped the paper with 500 denunciations of friends, neighbors, and family members. Píša was tried and hanged after the war, and many of his confederates were jailed. But, there were so many traitors that it was impossible to punish them all.

Perhaps the worst collaborator of all was a former colonel in the pre-war Czech army named Emmanuel Moravec, who had been appointed Minister of Education and National Enlightenment. As such, he was the Nazis' head of propaganda in the Protectorate. He cleansed schools of patriotic Czech teachers, transformed education into training grounds for future workers in the German World Order, and he directed a campaign to persuade Czechs to be loyal to the Nazi regime. Known as the "Czech Quisling," the cowardly and morally corrupt Moravec committed suicide in order to avoid the gallows.

Post-war Slovakia had much greater problems dealing with collaborators than did the Czech lands. Many citizens of this easternmost part of post-war Czechoslovakia continued to support Josef Tiso, the anti-Semitic fascist priest who had been its president, even after the war. When leaders of the Hlinka party were tried and convicted in 1946, many Slovaks protested by going on a rampage during which they murdered some of the Jews who had managed to survive the war.

I was too young to realize how difficult it must have been for my parents to return to Kojetice. The village, like all communities throughout Czechoslovakia, had its collaborators. While there were many citizens who had helped us, there were just as many who had treated our family shabbily during the war. Ilona Hellerová, who had been effectively a single mother during the war, had received no sympathy or help from many who had benefitted from the generosity of her family in the past and who had been her friends before the Germans arrived. Now that the war was over, these same people went out of their way to curry the Heller family's favor. Suddenly, they remembered how *Starý Pán* ("The Old Gentleman," as *Dědeček* had been called respectfully by nearly everyone) created jobs during the depression so that their families could survive. They recalled how his sons, my grandfather and great-uncle, provided the entire region with free cultural and sports events and how my family donated its properties for public use. They reminded my parents that they had been friends of theirs before the war.

Just beyond the walls of St. Vitus church in Kojetice stood a monument honoring local citizens who had died in World War I. When my great-uncle, Ota, participated in the selection of a rock outcropping in the Skalky forest beyond the village, and provided financial assistance in its move to town, he had not dreamed that one day his own name would appear on the monument. It was added, along with those of fifteen others, when the town fathers decided to attach to the boulder a black marble plate listing those who had perished in the recent war. Beneath the words *Nezapomene vašeho utrpení, 1939-1945,* ("We will not forget your suffering, 1939-1945") were engraved the names of the local victims:

Ladislav Bobek, Václav Linek, Václav Moravec – three blue-collar workers, aged 45, 47, and 35, respectively, who were murdered in the Mauthausen concentration camp.

Jaroslav Řezníček – a 30-year-old salesman, who was put to death in Dachau.

Gustav Neumann – my great-grandfather who, at 82, perished in Treblinka.

Ota and Artur Neumann – my great-uncle (55) and grandfather (52), respectively, who were murdered by the Germans in Yugoslavia.

Karel Šubrt – my godfather and local blacksmith, who died from an accidental explosion while guarding the Nazi thief of our properties, on May 6, 1945.

Antonín Bat'ha – a laborer, age 38, who died in a German prison camp after being denounced by a local German for insulting Hitler.

Rudolf Korálek – the brother of Alice Fischerová, who was murdered in a concentration camp.

Oskar and Jan Fischer; Adéla, Marie, and *Alice Fischerová* – an entire Jewish family wiped out by the Germans in the Polish camp, Malý Trostinec, at ages 61, 25, 53, 22, and 18, respectively.

Václav Kozelka – who died at the age of 31 in a German prison camp, only four months before the end of the war.

If one measures damage using quantifiable factors – deaths, destruction of infrastructure and property – Czechoslovakia suffered less than many European neighbors. While many strategic German targets within the country were bombed and destroyed, Prague escaped nearly unscathed. And, from a population of fifteen million, "only" about 300,000 – two-thirds of them Jews – died. Kojetice, a village of only 800, gave up sixteen of its citizens.

* * *

My father had been away fighting a war, and now he was busy trying to rebuild the business; he managed to hide his feelings about those neighbors and so-called friends who had betrayed or, at the very least, abandoned his family during the past six years. Conversely, my mother, who had been subjected to considerable maltreatment by these people, neither forgot nor forgave.

After having protected and nurtured me throughout the war, Mother continued to shield me from the post-liberation trauma. Although I certainly remembered being stoned the day I had ventured outside of Tůmas' farm and I overheard a few of my parents' quiet conversations about the behavior of some of the citizens of Kojetice, Mother made every effort to minimize the aftereffects of the war on my psyche and my life. Even the loss of fifteen members of our family was not discussed in my presence. My parents' reaction to the incredible hardship and loss they had suffered was silence. While they attempted to isolate and keep me from being traumatized by the events of the past six years, I tried to keep from them the fact that I was scarred by the war and the Holocaust. I had nightmares, and I was in constant fear of Papa leaving us to go fight the Germans all over again.

Having been hidden or sequestered all that time, and sworn to silence, I was dealing with an unfamiliar world. I was terribly sad that I had such a small family. During the war, I had fantasized about a reunion of all the Hellers and Neumanns once the Germans were driven out. Now, I had no great-grandfather, no great-uncle, no grandfather, no grandmothers. Although I called several ladies "aunt" and one man "uncle," I had not a single real aunt or uncle, nor did I have any cousins. There were not even any graves to visit. Going forward, it would be just the three of us. I was a voracious reader, and, unbeknownst to my parents, I began reading and learning about the Holocaust, and I suspected that there might be an association between it and the fact that no one else from our family had returned. Yet, I failed to make the direct connection between religion and our own tragedy. I was struck by guilt because I had not suffered as much as the rest of my family, and I felt that I did not measure up to the courage of my parents.

Nevertheless, partly to make my parents happy, and mostly because I could now consider myself a normal nine-year-old boy, I began to enjoy my new-found freedom. We moved into our spacious apartment on the second floor of the building in front of our factory. For the first time, I was able to attend school, completing the last three weeks of second grade across the street at the Kojetice elementary school. Since I had missed nearly three years while my fellow students had been receiving a formal education, I was concerned about being able to compete. But, Mr. Volt's secret wartime tutoring paid off and I found myself ahead of the others in reading and arithmetic, and on an equal basis in geography and history. Only art and handwriting gave me trouble. All Czechoslovak students were required to have one hour of Roman Catholic religion studies each week and, despite the fact that I was, once again, a devout and churchgoing Catholic, I had trouble memorizing the strange names in the Bible. Nevertheless, the teacher gave me a "1" (an "A") in religion.

Looking back on it later, I would realize the hypocrisy of children who had shunned me during the war, no doubt upon orders from their parents, now wanting to be friends of the richest kid in town. But none of this entered my mind at the time because, for the first time in many years, I had playmates. The German army had stored uniforms, gas masks, and other equipment in our factory. I invited my friends over and, day after day, we ran around the flat roof wearing Wermacht helmets and gas masks, with bayonets hanging from our belts. We divided ourselves into good guys and bad guys, and we hid behind skylights as we fought epic battles. As the host, I was always the leader of the American army, albeit one wearing a German uniform, leading charges against the Nazis.

At other times, we played cowboys and Indians. During the war, I had borrowed and read the books of the American West by the German author, Karl May. The hero of May's books was Vinnetou, an Indian who teamed up with Old Shatterhand to fight against white outlaws. A few years later in America, I would find that American boys played the same game as we did. But there was one major difference. Americans wanted to be cowboys. Because of Karl May, Czech boys wanted to be Indians. As the leader of the "tribe," I was not only an Indian; I was Vinnetou.

Although the war was over, the American army faced a dilemma. In the last days of the war, the U. S. and the U.S.S.R. had agreed that, in Czechoslovakia, all Germans to the west of the demarcation line at 12:01 am on May 9 would be prisoners of the Americans and those to the east of the line would be prisoners of the Soviets. For the U. S., this presented a huge problem because thousands of German soldiers and civilians had made a mad, desperate dash to the western side. Dealing with these hordes of surrendering Germans was an enormous undertaking, made more difficult by the fact that many high-ranking SS and Gestapo officers were disguised and hiding among the throngs, attempting to escape justice. Additionally, some high-level Nazi officers were forming guerilla groups in various parts of Bohemia, hoping to continue fighting against the liberators. Papa had to remain in the army and help round up hundreds of these Germans who were concealed in the Czech countryside. Finally, late in the summer of 1945, with the job completed, he was discharged. He had entered the British army a lowly private and came out a decorated major – in my eyes, the greatest warrior of them all.

Now, my parents started the long, tedious process of getting back our various properties which had been stolen by the Germans. Bureaucracy and the intervention of communist revolutionary squads which were beginning to make inroads into Czechoslovak industry, made the task difficult and frustrating. The facts that my father came home a war hero, and that our family had suffered greatly at the hands of the Nazis, made little difference. But, in time, obstacles were cleared and, with the assistance of able and well-connected lawyers, my parents managed to retrieve most of our assets.

Of course, there was the factory; also, there were several single-family homes and some undeveloped land in Kojetice; there was a house in Papa's home town of Kralupy; and there was the seven-story apartment building in Prague. Located in the district of Libeň, and not far from the river Vltava, the building had been built by my grandfather Artur and his brother Ota in 1934. In the early 1930s, the two bachelors had been spending a great deal of time in Prague on business and, according to my mother, "drinking and chasing women," while always staying at the beautiful Hotel Esplanade, managed by their friend and Kojetice neighbor, Mr. Opelt. Soon they realized that they could save a great deal of money by constructing their own building in Prague, keeping an apartment there, and renting out the rest of the flats. After the occupation, the apartment building, like the factory and our other properties, had been given by the Nazis to their man, Josef Hollman. Now, it was returned to us.

The school year 1945-1946 marked the first full year of my formal education. Perhaps because I had been prevented from attending school, I enjoyed the classroom experience more than my jaded friends did. I finished third grade with a report card full of "1's" ("A's"), with only one exception – a "2" ("B") in art. It was becoming obvious that I would not become a great painter.

During the summer of 1946, my parents decided that I needed to attend a better school than the one in rural Kojetice. With plans to move into our Prague apartment building eventually, they registered me at the Palmovka elementary school in the same district. In September 1946, at the age of ten, I began commuting from Kojetice to Prague five times a week. I got up early each morning, dressed and ate breakfast, slung my leather backpack over my shoulders, and walked the length of the village to the train station. After a half-hour train ride, I got off at the Libeň station and walked ten minutes to the two-story school on Palmovka Street. In the afternoon, I reversed the process.

It was there, in the fourth grade, that I met a boy who would become my best friend. His name was Vladimír "Vláďa" Svoboda. Vláďa's last name is quite common, meaning "freedom" in Czech. Because of my commuting, he and I were unable to spend much time together on school days that first year. So, quite often, my father picked up Vlád'a and brought him to Kojetice on weekends, and we romped around the factory property and in the woods called Skalky, above the village.

One day after I returned home from Prague, Mother and I placed flowers inside the fence of the monument honoring victims of the two world wars. Then, she took my hand and said:

"Let's walk. I want to show you something."

We set out past the monument on the unpaved back road toward the neighboring town of Neratovice. When we came near the Kojetice cemetery, Mother turned right and walked into an opening among the birch trees. I followed as she approached a large rock outcropping. She pointed at a small plaque embedded in the rock. The bronze plate was nearly black and unreadable.

"Look, it has the date of your birthday on it, 25 January 1936," she said. "This land belonged to Uncle Ota, and he dedicated a park to you here on the day you were born."

Another secret uncovered. I had lived in Kojetice for nearly ten years, and I had not been aware that this was "my" park. Perhaps Mother had kept it from me for the same reason she had shielded me from any knowledge of my Jewish heritage. Probably, she had been afraid that I would try to claim the park as my own while the Germans occupied the village.

My father set about rebuilding the Labor factory with great energy. He hired highly-skilled people, purchased modern equipment, and began to develop sales both domestically and internationally. Soon the firm employed several hundred people and once again became the largest manufacturer of men's work clothes and women's dresses in Central Europe. Labor was one of the fastest-growing post-war companies in Czechoslovakia, and Papa was hailed as a major industrialist.

* * *

Following the initial trauma of learning to be free, I found living in Kojetice that first year after the war an exhilarating experience. After having been restricted and in hiding for six of my nine years, every day was a new adventure. One day, Papa came home with a surprise – a dog. We had had two dogs prior to the war. Jerry had been a totally undisciplined, crazy, white terrier with whom I had played when I was a baby. After he passed away, we got an Airedale named Argus, who was rambunctious and barked constantly. Argus and I did not get along, and I was in constant fear of him. Despite the fact that only two or three cars a day passed through the village in the pre-war days, Argus managed to run under one and get killed. Now, Papa introduced us to Alma, a beautiful black and tan German shepherd, who had been in the Wermacht canine corps. Although she never hurt anyone, Alma was trained to growl at strangers; she became the scourge of Kojetice. I got a huge kick out of walking her down the street and easing out the leash such that she could come up to a villager and growl. It became a family joke that Alma was the town's military commander; everyone she confronted stopped and came to attention. Only the salute was missing.

Papa and I became reacquainted by taking frequent long walks with Alma in the woods above the village. Our conversations were about the history of the Czech nation, about sports, about the nature surrounding us, about his hopes for my future. The subject of the war never came up. One such walk had a lasting effect on my attitude toward all living things of a lower order. I was walking on a narrow path following Alma, with Papa a few steps behind. Suddenly, a cricket jumped across the trail. I moved quickly toward him, stepped on him and squashed him. Just as suddenly, I was on the ground, wondering what had hit me.

"Don't you ever do that again!" Papa shouted. Then, his voice became calm and gentle as he continued: "Every bug, every bird, every animal has just as much right to live on this earth as you do. You must be kind to all living things."

This seemingly minor incident forever affected the way I feel. I despise hunting as a "sport," and I have no interest in fishing. I simply cannot kill anything other than a fly or a mosquito. This, despite the fact that, until recently, I thought without regret that I had shot and killed a man. In my mind, an insect's life was worth more than that of a Nazi.

By early 1947, Papa felt that his management team in Kojetice was able to function without his everyday supervision, and he and Mother decided that it was time to move to the big city. They did not want me to spend another semester commuting to school, and they wanted to be closer to the center of culture and sports, and to their friends. Also, my father wanted to open a Prague sales office for the company. But, more than anything, life in Kojetice was a constant reminder of family members irretrievably lost in the war. It was time to get away from that, as well as from the few people in town who, having been infected by communist propaganda, resented the fact that my capitalist parents had been given back their property and were prospering once again. So, we left our flat in Kojetice and took over the entire third floor of our apartment building in Prague 8, Libeň. From the small window in my room, I looked across the street at the movie house, *Svět* ("World"), and the large steel globe on its roof. From our living room window, we looked out over the Rokytka creek. The view was dominated by *Libeňský zámek* (Libeň castle), a beautiful Rococo mansion on a site once occupied by a real castle, one in which Emperor Rudolf II signed a historic peace treaty in 1608.

But, things were not as lovely as they appeared at 16 Blanická Street. Because the building had been taken from our family by the Germans, in the tumult following the war's end, the communists considered it confiscated Nazi property and established their regional headquarters there. Even when my parents managed to work their way through the legal process and the building was returned to them, the Reds refused to vacate the two floors below our apartment. As time went on, they became bolder and eventually affixed a red neon star on the building's façade, below our living room window. Each evening, Mother drew closed the heavy curtains, yet an ugly pink glow came through to remind us of our unfriendly neighbors.

Nevertheless, I was ecstatic about my new home, mainly because my friend Vláďa Svoboda lived on the opposite side of the square. We became inseparable buddies, playing street hockey, swimming in the filthy water of the Vltava river, and riding streetcars all over Prague. In the winter, we skied and sledded on the hill above Libeň, with *Koule* (Ball), a huge sphere used to store gas, at its summit. Together, Vláďa and I graduated from Palmovka elementary school and made plans to attend the Libeň gymnasium, located next to the little castle up the hill from our building. "Gymnasium" was a term for a high school (beginning with the sixth grade and ending with the twelfth) which prepared students for university studies, whereas "Realka" was the slang term for a high school for students who intended to enter the trades after graduation.

To be admitted to gymnasium, we were required to take a full day of entrance exams, written in the morning and oral in the afternoon. My father tried to play the role of the typical, strict, European father, who seldom compliments his child. But, he could not hide his pleasure and pride when I came home from the exams at noon one Saturday and told him that I had done so well on the written portion that I had been excused from the orals. Vláďa, too, had no trouble passing the tests.

Throughout my life, my parents never argued with one another in my presence. As an adult, I would realize that, in every marriage, there are tensions between the partners. However, Mother and Papa adhered to a hard and fast rule: never have a confrontation in front of your child. They came close when it came to discussing my struggles with music. They had given up hope of my becoming a violinist, so they decided that I needed to learn to play other instruments. After all, they believed in the rich tradition of music in the Czech lands, expressed through an age-old saying, *"co Čech, to muzikant"* ("every Czech is a musician"); I was not about to be an exception. First, they purchased an accordion and hired a teacher to help me master it. I enjoyed pressing the various buttons and squeezing loud noises out of the contraption, but I showed no knack for making real music. Mother, who had been an accomplished pianist before the war, and who was regaining her skills after a six-year hiatus, had purchased a beautiful, black, Steinway grand piano which occupied the corner of our large living room. Papa hired a piano teacher, who came to our apartment twice a week to work with me. Finally, my parents had found an instrument with which I seemed to be compatible. I learned quickly, and soon I was playing well enough for Mother to ask me to demonstrate my skills to their visiting friends. But, then Papa discovered that my teacher was a communist. The next time the poor fellow came through our front door, my father was waiting for him. He confronted him, called him a "commie bastard," and fired him on the spot. Thus ended my musical training.

Two things which America will never match are Czech bread and beer. Both are staples of the Czech diet and both are world-famous for their unique tastes. Although we had a large refrigerator in our Prague apartment, neither bread nor beer was kept there. Bread had to be fresh from the oven, and beer had to be fresh from the tap. Each evening before dinner, I was sent to the pub across the street with a pitcher and, on Saturday mornings, Mother gave me a shopping net and dispatched me to the bakery on the other side of the square for bread and *rohlíky* (elongated rolls with salt and caraway seeds on top). If my parents noticed that the beer pitcher was never quite full when I brought it home, they never let on. Like any Czech boy, I learned to love the national drink at an early age. And I am sure that Mother must have known that the bread I brought home had nibbles taken out of both heels and that, often, a dozen purchased *rohlíky* added up to eleven when I delivered them. The bewitching aroma of freshly-baked warm bread and rolls was just too difficult to resist.

We truly enjoyed life in those two-and-a-half post-war years of freedom. My parents were great athletes and sports fans, and we attended hockey games at the Winter Stadium, motorcycle races at Strahov Stadium, and we had choice seats at the games of Prague's two major-league *fotbal* (soccer) teams, Sparta and Slavia. Both were located in Prague and they dominated the sport. Praguers were divided into two camps: those who rooted for the maroon-clad Sparta and those who were for red and white

Slavia. The division existed even in our family, with Papa rooting for Sparta and Mother and me for Slavia. The latter's stiker, Pepi Bican, was my first sports hero.

In the winter, we had season tickets to Prague's two major-league hockey teams, LTC and ČLTK. The "LT" in both clubs' names stood for "Lawn Tennis," and on summer Sunday mornings, I took tennis lessons near the hockey rink. On several occasions, I was given the honor of being a ballboy for the club's most preeminent member, Jaroslav Drobný, one of the top tennis players in the world, a future Wimbledon champion who also played hockey at the highest level.

Most often, we were accompanied by my parents' closest friends, Viktor Hahn and Aša Hahnová. Aunt Aša had been Mother's best pal for many years. Uncle Viktor was the only relative on the Heller side to survive the war. Even that relationship was a bit of a stretch because he was a distant uncle of my father. He was a Holocaust survivor and a well-known persona in Prague. Viktor had been an inmate at three of the worst concentration camps: Auschwitz, Dachau, and Sachsenhausen. In order to prolong his own life, he volunteered to carry corpses from the crematorium at Auschwitz. Eventually, the Germans uncovered one of Viktor's hidden talents – as a counterfeiter. They sent him to the Sachsenhausen camp near Melk, Austria, where a team of skilled Jews made false American passports and British pounds sterling. The counterfeiting of western currencies was part of the Germans' Operation Bernhard, intended to destabilize the British, and later American, economies by creating and putting into circulation millions of falsified banknotes. Fortunately for the Allies, distribution of any significant amount of the money never took place.

After the war, according to his daughter Sylvia, Viktor walked into a Prague bank and told the manager that he wanted to exchange some Czech crowns for British pounds. When the banker brought out a stack of pound notes, Viktor examined them closely and said:

"I made these. They're all false." And he walked out.

Aunt Aša, a Catholic, no doubt would have accompanied Mother to the Hagibor slave labor camp for Christian wives of Jewish men. But, although they fell in love before the war, Aša and Viktor wisely decided to wait to marry in order to spare her from the Nazis' wrath. They were married in 1945. Uncle Viktor told his war stories on Czechoslovak radio, and they were reported in newspapers. After the communist takeover of the country, he defied the Reds at every opportunity. He figured that, as a survivor of three death camps, he could take anything the comrades threw at him. No compliant *Švejk* was Viktor.

On many Sunday afternoons, Mother dragged me off to the opera at the National Theater, one of the nation's most hallowed sites, affectionately called *Zlatá kaplička* (Golden Chapel) because of its golden roof which can be seen from everywhere throughout central Prague. I saw *"Prodaná nevěsta"* ("The Bartered Bride"), the Czech national opera by Bedřich Smetana, so many times that I knew every word by heart. However, I would have much preferred to be playing or watching soccer or hockey. After opera, Mother and I always walked along Narodní ulice to Nad Příkopech, where we climbed the stairs up to the Pelikán restaurant. There, we found my father engaged in his Sunday-afternoon, big-money game of *mariáš*, a card game similar to bridge, with Uncle Viktor and their friends.

One day, we were given a private tour of one of Europe's oldest and most prominent movie studios, located on a plateau above the Vltava River in Prague. Barrandov was founded in 1931 by the father and uncle of Václav Havel, who was the same age as I and would become Czechoslovakia's president many years later. After a guided tour of the large complex by the studio's general manager, we were brought to the set of a movie in production and given the opportunity to observe its filming. In the scene, a family was sitting inside a mountain cabin during a snowstorm. A boy who had been lost in the storm came upon the cabin. He walked up to a lighted window and scratched the frost off the glass in order to look in.

"Mother, windows have frost on the inside, not on the outside," I whispered.

"I don't know about that, but don't say anything," she replied.

But, my father overheard the conversation, and, after the shooting was completed, he told the director what I had said.

"You have a smart kid there," the director told Papa. "But, other people won't notice, and we'll keep the scene that way."

I told all my friends and alerted them, so that they would look for my great discovery when the movie came out. But, much to my chagrin, the film must have died in the can and never made it to the theaters.

In the summer, we hiked in Slovakia's spectacular Tatra mountains. In the winter, we made frequent ski trips to the Krkonoše mountains, in the northern part of Bohemia, usually with Uncle Viktor and Aunt Aša along. Skiing in the late 1940s was quite different from skiing today. First, there was the equipment. I had actually begun skiing in Kojetice, on an old pair of skis which my father had discarded. They had "bear-trap" bindings made up of two leather straps – one across the toe of the boot and the other tightened around the heel. My skis were very long for a small boy, around 175 cm, and were made of hickory. The poles were bamboo, with huge baskets keeping them from sinking into deep snow. The boots were made of leather, with leather laces. For our vacation trips, I received a pair of new, shorter, skis, but the technology, such as it was, was unchanged. The other way in which alpine skiing differed from that of today was the absence of lifts to whisk skiers up mountains. Our typical day would consist of spending the morning climbing from our hotel up a trail leading to a mountaintop lodge. There, we would grab lunch and then spend the next couple of hours making short runs on nearby slopes, each time climbing back to the top. In mid-afternoon, we would ski back down the mountain to our hotel, following the same trail we had taken up in the morning.

While I enjoyed skiing with other kids on the hills near the mountaintop lodge, I hated the trip up the mountain to get there. I was always last, falling further and further behind as I got cold and tired. As the trail became steeper, generally I fell so far behind that I lost sight of the others. Now, in addition to freezing and being sore, I was scared. I imagined bears, wild pigs, and other beasts jumping out of the dark forest and attacking me. I whimpered and cried all the way to the lodge. Skiing down to the resort at the end of the day was a little easier, but still not much fun. My parents, Uncle Viktor, and Aunt Aša took off and soon were out of sight. In an attempt to control my speed, I placed my skis in the v-shaped snowplow position and, using my crotch as a fulcrum, applied the poles as a brake between my legs. I was happy when the ordeal was over each vacation day. It is hard to believe that, with such an inauspicious start, I would become an avid, accomplished skier – and even a skiwriter – as an adult.

Uncle Viktor and Aunt Aša lived at 36 Dobrovského Street in the Letná section of the city, not far from the Sparta football stadium. I spent many hours at their apartment, accompanying my parents there for lunch, which was followed by the adults' games of cards, with lubrication provided by beer and that wonderful Czech liqueur, Becherovka. I got a lot of reading done, and became very familiar with the neighborhood on my many solitary walks, while the adults were entertaining themselves. On many such hikes, I wandered over to the stadium and, staring out at the green playing field through the fence, I imagined myself someday playing there for my favorite team, Slavia, against the hated Sparta maroons.

* * *

During this time, in Nürnberg, Germany, a trial of 22 leading Nazis, conducted by an international military tribunal of American, British, French, and Russian judges, held everyone's attention. Twelve of the criminals were sentenced to death. Among the latter were: Martin Bormann, secretary of the Nazi party; Herman Göring, head of the Luftwaffe and high-level SS murderer; Wilhelm Frick, author of the Nürnberg race laws and the Reichsprotektor of Czechs in the final years of the war; Julius Steicher, who incited hatred of Jews through his newspaper; and Ernst Kaltenbrunner, SS leader and commandant of death camps. My parents followed the trial very closely, and it was the main subject of dinner conversation every evening for several weeks. Mother was concerned that the American judges would show mercy toward these murdering scumbags because the United States had suffered relatively minor losses in the war and thus she feared that Americans did not appreciate the extent of German atrocities. She was wrong. Death penalties and long imprisonments were handed out, and many trials of less prominent Nazis followed this show trial. Regrettably, the coward Göring was able to swallow a poison pill the day before he was to be hanged.

Throughout their country, Germans were proclaiming that they had had no idea of what had been taking place in concentration camps during the war. This was very curious, since it turned out that every one of our Czech friends had known. The Germans considered all Slavs inferior people, so how was it possible that members of the Master Race had not known at least as much as the lowly Czechs?

In the aftermath of the war, there was a movement to the left throughout Europe. In Czechoslovakia, despite atrocities committed by individual soldiers of the Red Army, and although there existed a feeling of gratitude toward the U.S. whose belated entry swung the war in favor of the Allies, the general populace felt an attraction to the Soviet Union. After all, the nation had been liberated by the Soviets. Moreover, Czechoslovaks remembered the treachery committed by England and France at Munich, with the United States giving its tacit approval.

During the war, as many Czechoslovaks had escaped to the east to fight alongside the Red Army as had gone over to the west, where they joined either the Royal Air Force or the British army. My father, having been assigned to a small special unit attached to General Patton, was one of very few early returnees among the western fighting men. By design (some thought that Stalin had dictated this to Beneš when the latter was ordered to stop in Moscow before returning to Prague from his London exile), the eastern-front soldiers came home first. By the time the soldiers and airmen returned from the west, Czechoslovak members of the eastern army, the majority of whom were communists, had received most of the glory, the best housing, and the plush jobs. Because we owned a factory and various properties, our family was not affected by this directly. However, my father spoke out publicly against this injustice committed toward his fellow patriots from the west.

* * *

The nation's first post-war elections were held in May of 1946, exactly one year after the end of the war. There were four political parties: the Communist Party consisted of a few idealistic intellectuals, but primarily of ne'er-do-wells, former Nazi collaborators, and other riff-raff. The party received 38% of the vote. The National Socialist Party was made up of centrists who were mainly businesspersons and intellectuals. It came in second with 26%. The Catholic People's Party was centrist as well, and its main support came from Catholic farmers. It received 20% of the total. The Social Democrats were moderate leftists, who came in last with 16%. My parents were National Socialists, as were nearly all their friends.

To its everlasting shame, Czechoslovakia became the only country of what was to become the Soviet Bloc, in which the communists won in a free election, although they did not receive a majority of the total vote. Most Czechoslovaks thought that the communists had won only because the liberals, centrists, and rightists had been fragmented. They were convinced that, come the 1948 elections, the anti-communists would combine forces and that the Reds would become a minority party in Parliament. Little did they know that there would be no more free elections.

In 1947, the United States initiated one of the greatest rescue missions in the history of the world. The Marshall Plan was designed to rebuild war-ravaged Europe through massive economic and technical assistance. Politically, the Truman administration hoped to build a strong foundation which would help to keep communism from spreading throughout the continent. The Soviets, of course, rejected the plan and called it "dollar imperialism."

The government of Czechoslovakia signed on to the Marshall Plan, after Foreign Minister Jan Masaryk convinced the cabinet to approve its acceptance by unanimous vote. Czechs celebrated in Wenceslas Square. But, this did not sit well with our Soviet "liberators," who summoned Masaryk and other Czechoslovak leaders to Moscow, where they informed them that accepting assistance from the U.S. would be regarded as a hostile act against the USSR. Threats of retaliation resulted in President Beneš and his government backing off, and it marked the first major step toward total Soviet domination which, except for a brief respite in 1968, would last for 41 years.

"I went to Moscow as the foreign minister of a sovereign state," Masaryk said upon his return. "I came back a stooge of Stalin."

Despite this, Beneš continued to act under the delusion that Stalin would keep his word and give Czechoslovakia autonomy. Too late, Beneš would admit:

"My major error was that, until the very end, I refused to believe that even Stalin cold-bloodedly and cynically lied to me in 1935 and likewise later, and that the assurances which he gave me and [Jan] Masaryk were an intentional and deliberate deception."

By the time the president came to realize this, it was too late. Klement Gottwald, a communist thug, had been working hard behind Beneš's back to infiltrate all government agencies and the police force with his comrades. By early 1948, Gottwald and his cohorts were able to manipulate all governmental actions to suit their Soviet masters.

In February 1948, in a desperate attempt, twelve members of the cabinet representing the three non-communist parties resigned, hoping to force a constitutional crisis which would cause a dissolution of the entire government and thus a new election. However, the strategy backfired as Gottwald, directed by Soviet deputy foreign minister Valerian Zorin who came to Prague, quickly moved his hand-picked communists into the vacant positions. He presented the new cabinet, which, for the sake of appearances, included Foreign Minister, patriot and son of the "father" of the country, Jan Masaryk, to Beneš. Simultaneously, the communists used their armed People's Militia to intimidate citizens into signing a petition urging the president to approve the new government. Beneš refused.

Thousands of People's Militia members were trucked to Prague from various parts of the country. They were issued guns and ammunition and ordered to seal off the President from the people. Recovering from a recent stroke, Beneš became a prisoner in Hradčany Castle. When thousands of protesting students marched through Prague to the Castle in order to show Beneš their support for him and the cabinet members who had resigned, they were beaten and shot by the militiamen.

The President asked his Defense Minister, Ludvik Svoboda, if he could count on the army to defend the Czechoslovak Republic against the communists. Svoboda, who had hidden his communist leanings and who would become the nation's president many years later, told Beneš that he could not.

"I will never order the army to go against the people," he told him and proceeded to confine his anti-communist officers to quarters.

With no real support remaining, on February 25, 1948, Beneš signed the papers legitimizing the communist-led government. At that point, the man who had been president prior to the war and who had led the government in exile, became a mere figurehead. He would resign in June and die in September.

* * *

Immediately after their putsch, the communists began nationalizing (translation: "stealing") private enterprises throughout the country. Less than three years after a period during which the Germans had decimated Czechoslovakia, Czechs and Slovaks became the oppressors of their own nation. Among the early firms to be nationalized was my family's company. On March 4, 1948, the Reds sent a memorandum to all of my father's employees under the letterhead "Labor, Manufacturer of Work Clothes, Gustav Neumann, Kojetice u Prahy." It read:

> Mr. Rudolf Heller was employed by the firm, Gustav Neumann, in Kojetice from March 1932. In 1934, he established his own business, "textile finishing," which became a sister company of Gustav Neumann. In 1934, he became part of the management of the firm, Gustav Neumann – manufacturer of aprons, dresses and work clothes – together with the owners, Messrs. Ota and Artur Neumann.
>
> In February 1940, he escaped out of the country, joined the Czechoslovak Army abroad, and returned to Czechoslovakia with that army in 1945.
>
> In July 1945, he was appointed national manager of the firm Josef Hollman in Kojetice, a company which was the "aryanized" firm, Gustav Neumann. In February 1946, this firm was restitutioned and Mr. Heller took over its management in the position of managing director. He holds this position today.
>
> Since the conditions for nationalization of the firm applied, it has been necessary to place the firm under national management. Upon the recommendation of the Action Committee and the Factory Council, in the meeting of all the employees, and in the presence of representatives of the URO, Mr. Rudolf Heller was unanimously elected national manager. The action itself demonstrates that Mr. Heller enjoyed the trust of all employees, and that he managed the firm well and, from the social point of view, proved his positive attitude toward employees and society.
>
> The firm, Gustav Neumann, was placed under the administration of the National Enterprise OP Prostějov, and this organization appointed its own representative to the firm. Mr. R. Heller turned over management of the firm to this representative in an orderly manner, and – based entirely upon his own decision – he will leave the firm at his own request.

The letter was signed by three communists: Žežulka, representative of the National Enterprise OP Prostějov; Marie Nováková, for the Factory Council of Gustav Neumann; and Hovorka, on behalf of the Action Committee. Years later, Papa would explain to me that "action committee" was actually a communist cell of the labor union, "factory council" was the union representing workers at our factory, and "URO" was the national organization of labor unions. As to the "transfer in an orderly manner," my father would tell me later:

"I simply told the communists to go to hell and walked out."

In addition to being despised by the communists for being a bourgeois capitalist, and for having served in the western (rather than eastern) forces during the war, Papa had tangled with the comrades on many occasions. In meetings with his employees and management team, he had lectured on the evils of communism. On Victory Day in May 1947, he had refused to fly the Soviet flag alongside that of Czechoslovakia; he flew the Stars and Stripes and the Union Jack, instead. The Reds were furious.

Twelve years later in the United States, on Papa's fiftieth birthday, his friends would compile a three-volume tribute to him called "This Is Your Life," in the style of a popular TV show of the same name. In it, our family's friend Frank Cífka would write about the take-over of the Labor factory:

"...*The local communists, now rabid – thanks to Soviet propaganda – forgot you had fought for the liberation of the country; they forgot that your family had paid the price for your service to the homeland; they forgot all that your family – and the Neumanns – had done for the community and the people of Kojetice. They simply confiscated your property – your family fortune – and drove you out...*

"*There was no option – either you become a communist – sell out the beliefs you held dear... forget democracy... bend your spine... pollute your character – or you had to flee abroad once again. You were not at great pains to make the choice. Masaryk's*

*ideals of democracy and humanism, the tenets of humaneness
and justice that had been your lode star all your life – they
asserted themselves!"*

Although some of the people of Kojetice and the surrounding
region who had benefitted both from employment at Labor, and from
the hundreds of good deeds performed by the Heller/Neumann family
for the community, treated our family badly under the Nazis and now
under the communists, there had been many isolated acts of kindness and
courage. Several friends had sheltered us, and some had hidden me from
the Germans, during the war. It took almost as much courage to help us
after the communist putsch as it had during the occupation.

One such example was Papa's receiving advance word of the factory
take-over while it was being planned in secret at the office of the communist
party. The wife of the local party chairman, Marie Červinková, a long-time
employee of Labor Gustav Neumann, walked four kilometers along the
highway to a place she knew Papa would be traveling in order to inform
and warn him. This took courage.

A few days after the company was nationalized, a delegation of
employees traveled to Prague and met with Papa. They told him that, when
the Factory Council came to take over the company, supervisors arranged
a meeting of all employees. A vote was taken, and it was unanimous.
All 200-plus employees voted to retain my father as general manager.
But, they said, their vote was ignored by the communists. The delegation
begged Papa to come back and said they were prepared to go on strike in
order to accomplish his reinstatement. Because he knew that this would
be an exercise in futility, and because he recognized that the potential
consequences to the workers were horrific, Papa spent more than two
hours convincing them that their best course of action was to go back and
go along with the current situation. These workers, too, were brave under
the circumstances.

❊ ❊ ❊

Unbeknownst to me, my parents began to plan our escape from Czechoslovakia almost immediately after Papa returned to Prague from Kojetice. Had I known, I would have been extremely upset because I was waiting for something much more important than any communist revolution. As my major Christmas present in 1947, I had received a photo of a motorized kick scooter, one with a small motor that would produce speeds of twenty miles per hour. The manufacturers had promised Papa pre-Christmas delivery, but then they informed him that the new, revolutionary product would not be ready until spring. Every day, as I waited impatiently, I stared at the photo and imagined myself riding my sleek, black, motorized scooter to and from school, with my classmates looking on with envy. Little did I know that such a vehicle would not be built for another fifty years and that Papa had been defrauded.

I found gymnasium considerably more challenging than elementary school. The subjects were more difficult, and our school hours were 8:00 am to 4:00 pm on weekdays and 8:00 am to noon on Saturdays. In sixth grade, I was introduced to zoology, and I devoured chapters about exotic animals in Africa and Asia. I did quite well in all the other subjects, with the exception of religion and handwriting, including my first foreign language, Russian, which was not an elective. My favorite course was geography, and I continued to hold on to my wartime dreams of traveling the world over. Then my education was terminated once more, and I became a world traveler much sooner than I had expected.

As my life was about to take another drastic turn, I had completed only three weeks of third grade, the entire fourth and fifth grades, and six months of sixth grade – a mere two-and-a-half years of formal schooling – and I was already twelve years old!

CHAPTER 11

Escape

The opportunity for our escape presented itself sooner than my parents had expected. On March 10, 1948, Jan Masaryk, the lone democrat in the president's cabinet and son of the revered first president, was found dead on the street below his office in the Foreign Ministry building. Gottwald and his lackeys claimed that he had committed suicide and even showed off a stool which they claimed Masaryk had placed in the bathtub in order to climb to a window prior to his jump. But, most Czechoslovaks were convinced that he had been pushed and murdered by the communists.

My father calculated that Masaryk's funeral in Prague would bring about protests and major clashes. He concluded that the government would attempt to quell the riots by reinforcing the Prague police force with army units, including some of those guarding the border. Wisely, he thought that the day of the funeral would be the optimal day for us to escape from the country. He filled two suitcases with our clothing and hid them in the trunk of our 1938 Ford sedan. In order that nothing would appear out of the ordinary, he parked the car in front of our building on Blanická Street.

The next morning, March 11, we carried two additional suitcases and a small bundle of blankets down to the car, pretending that we were going away on a short vacation. Otherwise, the communists, with their offices on the floors below us, would suspect something more sinister and would stop us. I, too, was told that we were going on vacation. I was surprised because my parents seldom took me out of school to go on holiday. But Czech kids did not question their parents, and I was no exception.

After loading the car, we drove to the Letná section of Prague, where we spent the rest of the day and the next night in the Hahns' apartment. The following morning, we headed west out of Prague. When we reached Pilsen, we checked into a hotel. After dinner, my father finally explained to me what was taking place.

"We are leaving the country," he said. "The communists, who are very bad people, have taken away our factory and they would harm us in other ways if we stayed. So, we're going to start a new life, hopefully in America. You'll have the chance to be whatever you want to be there because America is known as the land of the free. But, first, you have to be brave because we're going to cross the border tomorrow night, and it's going to be dangerous. The communists may even try to shoot us."

I was worried, but I was not scared. After all, I was with my father who had fought and defeated the Germans! He would never let harm come to Mother and me. As I lay in bed that night, I was more upset about the fact that I had left without saying goodbye to my friend Vlád'a. If I had only known, I would have given him my bike and my prized stamp collection, and I would have asked to have the motorized scooter delivered to him. Of course, such generosity may have given us away, and this was exactly why my parents had not let me in on their plans. No one other than Uncle Viktor and Aunt Aša could be told.

The next day, Saturday, March 13, was the day of Jan Masaryk's funeral in Prague. We got back in the car and drove out into the countryside. There, with no one in sight, Papa drove the Ford into a field. We took out our baggage, abandoned the car, and walked back to a small village we had passed. Mother went to a bus stop, while Papa and I walked to the other side of town. We went into a tavern and had a snack. My father whispered to me that we were taking separate busses in order not to arouse suspicion. An hour or so later, he and I went back to the stop, and we caught the next bus to the town of Aš, the westernmost large city in the country, located in Bohemia's geographic "ear," and the same town through which my father had entered Czechoslovakia with the U.S. army less than three years before.

On the bus, I asked Papa why we had not taken our car.

"Because it was a partial payment to the people who are helping us escape," he whispered. "They'll pick it up later from the field."

We met Mother in Aš, and we walked to the railroad station. Papa bought third-class tickets to Rossbach, a village near the German border. The train, belching white smoke from the stack of the coal-fired locomotive, arrived a few minutes later, and we rode it, without incident, to Rossbach. The village station was tiny, and there was no one in sight. But, a few minutes later, a horse-drawn wagon pulled up near the tracks.

"Mr. Heller?" asked the driver. "Come with me."

We piled our belongings into the wagon and hopped in behind the driver. He cracked his whip, and the two horses began to trot out of town. We rode for some time until we came upon a farm at the edge of a thick forest. The farmer motioned us inside.

"Make yourselves comfortable," he said. "You'll stay here till midnight."

I noticed that he never introduced himself, nor did we ever hear the name of his wife, who served us dinner. None of us realized that this would be our last decent meal for some time. I dozed off in a chair, while my parents sat quietly and spoke to one another only occasionally. A grandfather clock in the corner seemed to be in slow motion as its little hand crawled toward twelve. Finally, the clock announced that it was midnight.

"Get your things, and let's go," we were ordered.

Sleepily, I put on my jacket and shoes and headed out the door. Just then, I heard my father yell at the farmer.

"Where is our suitcase?"

It turned out that our host had stolen one of our bags while we were sitting in his living room. He proclaimed his innocence, but how else could one-fifth of our worldly possessions have disappeared inside his house?

There was nothing to do but to go on, considerably poorer than we had been when we arrived.

We walked outside, where we were greeted by a spectacular, starry but moonless, sky. The farmer motioned for us to follow him, with Mother carrying one suitcase and Papa having two bags strapped together, one in the front and the other in the back. I carried a bundle of blankets which, I found out later, contained valuable jewelry that would constitute our major assets in exile. We walked across a field to the edge of the forest. There, the farmer stopped and pointed into the woods.

"Walk a few kilometers in that direction and, if you're lucky and the border guards don't shoot you, you'll run into American soldiers. Good luck."

With that, he turned and sauntered off to the farmhouse. We began walking in the direction he had indicated, avoiding footpaths in order not to be detected. It was dark and scary in the woods, and I imagined being attacked by wild animals. My bundle was getting heavier with each step, and I stopped every few minutes to rest. Papa urged me to keep going. I kept tripping over roots, stumbling and falling, all the time frightened that I was making so much noise that I would give us away. I expected to hear gun shots at any moment, and my heart was beating wildly. The night was cold, but I was sweating profusely. I was totally exhausted when, after three hours, we reached the end of the forest.

Suddenly, out of the darkness, there appeared two men in uniform, shining flashlights into our eyes. One was holding a rifle.

"*Oh, my God!*" I thought. "*They've caught us. Now, they'll take my parents away from me, just like the Germans.*"

The soldiers came closer. They and my father began to speak in a strange language. Papa did not seem worried.

"These are American soldiers," he finally announced to us. "We're in the U.S. Zone of Germany. We're free!"

I have loved justice and hated iniquity;
therefore I die in exile.
Pope Gregory VII

CHAPTER 12

Refugees

We spent the night in an American army barracks near the border. The next day, after my father was interviewed by the authorities, we were trucked to a World War II prisoner of war camp, now called a "refugee distribution camp," outside the small German town of Moschendorf. Ironically, the date of our arrival in our first "home" as refugees was March 15, 1948 – the ninth anniversary of the day that Germany, now our new and unwilling host country, occupied Czechoslovakia. We were assigned to one of the wooden barracks, already filled with about 50 other Czechoslovak refugees. My parents and I were able to find three beds next to one another in the dingy, stinking room without electricity and with the only light provided during the day by several small windows near the ceiling. Men's and women's toilets were located in a nearby building. The place was revolting and chaotic. Everyone there had just recently left a comfortable home in his or her native country, and living like a POW was a new and unaccustomed experience. My parents had not envisioned finding pleasant conditions on the western side of the Czech border, but they had not expected such horrible living quarters and the near-starvation diet which followed.

In a matter of days, we had undergone a metamorphosis – from wealthy citizens of Czechoslovakia to dirt-poor, hungry refugees without a country. The United Nations called us "displaced persons," or "DPs." I preferred the term "exiles," because it had a romantic ring reminding me of my Czech heroes, Jan Masaryk and Eduard Beneš. My parents and the other adults truly were political exiles, unlike the mostly economic immigrants of later years.

Our fellow exiles were people who had been, or would have been, persecuted by the communist regime for their political beliefs, for having spoken out for democracy, for having fought in the west during the war, for believing in private enterprise. They had been businessmen, politicians, teachers, engineers, lawyers, doctors, and students in Czechoslovakia. Beside their disdain for the communists, they had one other thing in common: they had left everything behind – material possessions, families, friends, and their homes. While they looked forward to freedom and opportunity in the countries where they would land eventually – the U.S., Great Britain, Canada, and Australia were the most likely – they knew that they would be starting from zero. Some of them were luckier than others. Engineers, scientists, and physicians had directly-transferrable educations and skills. But others – lawyers, businessmen, salesmen – had capabilities unique to their native country and would have to begin at the lowest rungs. My parents were in the latter group and were well aware of the difficulties which lay ahead.

Fortunately, we stayed in Moschendorf only a few weeks before being transferred to a better camp for Czechoslovak refugees. Located a few kilometers south of Nürnberg, and outside the town of Schwabach, our new home was also a former POW camp, but with somewhat better accommodations. My father guessed – correctly, it turned out – that Moschendorf had been a Nazi camp for Soviet prisoners, while Schwabach had been for Americans and Brits. Thus the difference in quality.

The rooms in the one-story wooden barracks were smaller, just large enough for 14 double-decker beds. Mother took a lower bunk, while I moved into the one above her. Papa staked out a lower bunk just a few steps from ours. There was a wood-burning stove near the center of the room. There were no closets, wardrobes, chairs or tables. Everyone's belongings were stored in suitcases under the beds. Unlike the previous camp, Schwabach provided toilets and washrooms inside each building.

Privacy was something all of us had left behind in Czechoslovakia. In order to have a conversation we did not want heard, we went outside. The nights were terrible. A light sleeper, I dreaded going to bed. Soon after the lights went out, the cacophony of snoring and farting began. Frequently, someone cried out in the middle of a nightmare, perhaps dreaming about experiences of a very recent past. Most mornings, I rose feeling more tired and sleepy than I had been when I had gone to bed.

The food was barely edible. Three times a day, we stood in line outside a mess hall, waiting for our so-called "meal." Each of us was issued an empty pineapple-juice can as our only "dish," into which a dour German worker poured one ladleful of slop. My father found some wire and made us handles, so that we could carry the cans more easily once they were filled. We had no utensils, so Papa carved spoons out of wood for the three of us. The meals were the same every day, three times a day. It was a sort of stew: a light brown gravy, with pieces of potato and small lumps of meat floating on top. The meat chunks had suspicious-looking small tails which, I told everyone, meant that we were being served the mice which had coexisted with us in the barracks.

But, things were not all bad. Our twenty-five roommates were, for the most part, very nice people, many of whom became our good friends for years to come. Among my parents' closest companions were Jan and Hana Tůma, who arrived a few weeks after us. Jan had been a well-known structural engineer and academic in Prague. Since I was being deprived of formal schooling once again, Jan volunteered, much to my chagrin, to tutor me in mathematics. He was a tough taskmaster who insisted not only on accurate answers to the problems, but also on neatness and organization. While I did not appreciate it at the time, his insistence on clear thinking and orderly presentation would benefit me tremendously throughout my life.

František (later, Frank) Cífka and his wife, Anna, were among our favorites and both would remain our very close friends for the rest of their lives in Forest Hills on Long Island after their immigration. The other roommates with whom my parents struck up friendships were the Kubát and Červinka families, both of whom had children younger than I. The two families would eventually follow us to the U. S. and settle in New York City, where Mr. Kubát would resume his practice as a barber and Mr. Červinka would become a head waiter. Vladimír and Anna Vacek, too, became our mates. Vladimír would Americanize his first name to Harry, and become a supervisor for a firm provisioning airplanes at one of New York's airports.

On the other side of the unpaved street which ran through the center of the camp lived a boy my age. Jirka (later, George) Rosenkranc had escaped from Prague with his mother, Nan. Like we, they were applying for immigration to the U. S. Since it was nearly impossible for a single mother and her child to get a visa to America, Nan and a handsome bachelor in camp, Zdeněk Ryšavý (later Sidney Ryshawy), entered into a marriage of convenience, so that they could apply as a family. George and I became fast friends. The blond-haired George was taller than I and, although he was not the sports fanatic that I was, we had a great deal in common. Both of us were voracious readers (when we could get our hands on books). We had a passionate interest in geography and spent hours drawing maps and imagining ourselves in glamorous places around the world, especially the United States of America. My interest in geography may have had its roots in the fact that, while growing up during World War II, I was unable to venture beyond the confines of our village. I had spent my free time reading books by and about Roald Amundsen, the great Norwegian explorer of the polar regions, and the tropical adventures of Daniel Defoe's Robinson Crusoe. I had dreamed about someday traveling around the world and exploring the unknown.

The camp was located in the rural countryside, and we were free to walk anywhere we wished. This was somewhat limited by the fact that the Germans who lived in the surrounding area hated us, were not too pleased with our presence, and had no qualms about letting us know that we Czechs were an inferior race, as they had been taught by their Führer. But, George and I ignored the hateful stares and name-calling (which he understood, but I did not). We swam in a nearby river, and we tramped through the forests in search of mushrooms. One day, we came upon a German army ammunition dump, where we found unexploded shells, Wermacht helmets, and other great toys. When we showed up back in camp with the shells, the adults gave us hell and immediately disposed of our loot.

But, our booty was not always declared unacceptable by our elders. On one of our treks, George and I found an old leather briefcase in a dank, dark culvert. We had visions of finding secret war documents inside, but instead we found the case filled with potatoes, probably hidden there by another refugee who had stolen them in a nearby field. Any food other than the slop served to us in camp created excitement. We brought the potatoes to our families and all of us enjoyed a feast, as we baked them in the ashes of an open fire. George and I hid the empty briefcase for future use, since it was obvious from its initial content that there had to be a potato field somewhere in the area. We spent several days scouting the countryside around Schwabach until we found it. We made two raids in the darkness, each time coming back with the briefcase filled with potatoes. We were heroes, as our families invited others to share in our booty. But, after the second raid, my father put his foot down.

"You've done really well," he said. "But, the Germans would like nothing better than to catch a couple of Czech boys stealing from them. This is it. You won't take anymore chances." We returned the empty briefcase to the culvert.

As more and more Czechs escaped from their homeland, the communist regime sought to stop the flow. It fortified the border and began punishing the refugees' relatives who had stayed behind. In order to obtain names of Czech escapees, the communists sent spies across the border to infiltrate the refugee camps. The Americans, who were managing the displaced persons camps on behalf of the United Nations, were aware of this, and they set out to catch the spies by tightening the refugee screening process. In order to accomplish this, they needed Czech speakers whom they could trust and with whom they could converse in English.

Enter Rudolf Heller, my father. Because he had been a decorated member of the British army, and since he spoke Czech as well as English, the U. S. commander named Papa the chief of the Schwabach Counter Intelligence Corps (CIC). As such, he was responsible for the interrogation of hundreds of Czech and Slovak refugees, all of whom were now passing through Schwabach. He and his staff uncovered a number of communist spies and turned them over to the U. S. authorities for imprisonment. But, my father's work went far beyond screening. For most escapees, exile was a terribly traumatic experience. Many had trouble coping with the fact that they had left their families behind and with the uncertainty of the future. Papa listened to their problems, advised them, helped them with their immigration issues, comforted them, and was a calming influence on them.

His new exulted position brought more than fame and respect. He was paid for his services. While his salary was minimal, it brought us advantages which our fellow refugees did not enjoy. He reported to his American superiors in nearby Nürnberg, where, occasionally, he was able to purchase small presents for Mother and me.

Because of the Germans' hatred for Czechs, we avoided population centers as much as possible. One of the few times I left the confines of Schwabach came when the Americans offered to take several DPs to Nürnberg on a sightseeing tour. My parents made a particular point of wanting me to go on this trip because they knew that the sight would stay with me for the remainder of my life. They were correct. About thirty of us jumped aboard olive-drab, two-and-a-half-ton, military trucks for the half-hour trip to the center of the city. The trucks were covered with canvas and we were unable to see out until we jumped to the ground in what passed for the central square.

My first sight of what had once been a great city of knowledge and culture took my breath away. In every direction, there was nothing but rubble, with the exception of a single church steeple. Allied raids had leveled every building except that steeple, which stood there almost in defiance of man-made destruction and death. For a few moments, I forgot my feelings toward the Germans and was moved, almost to tears. Here it was, nearly three years after the end of the war, and these people still had no real homes, no shops, no schools, no theaters, nothing. My father sensed my despair and brought me back to reality.

"Cities all over Europe look like this," he told me. "Prague was lucky and was mostly spared. The Germans did this to London, and we gave it back to them. They brought it on themselves."

We took a short walk through Nürnberg. Our feet kicked up dust, and there was a strange acrid smell coming from the piles of bricks and concrete. Papa told me that battlefields during the war had smelled like that. He explained that it was a combination of rotted flesh and mold, and he expressed surprise that it had hung over the city so many months after the last bombs fell. As we walked along with our American soldier hosts, we were the subjects of hateful stares from German inhabitants who were sweeping the streets with homemade brooms made of tree twigs and clearing the rubble with their bare hands. Obviously, it was hard and seemingly hopeless work, and I found it difficult not to feel at least a little pity for these Germans.

When our group of sullen Czechs began to board the trucks for a return trip to camp, my father held us back.

"Stay here," he said to Mother and me. "I have a surprise for you."

He walked over and spoke to the American officer in charge, who had come by car. Papa motioned for us to follow as he walked with the officer toward the auto. The three of us piled into the back seat, and the officer sat down in the front passenger seat. He gave his driver instructions. We rode through the bombed-out city in silence until we came to the outskirts, where the damage was nearly nonexistent. The car stopped in front of a small restaurant. The officer spoke to my father in English.

"This is your surprise," Papa told us. "We're going to have dinner in a restaurant. The soldiers will pick us up later."

Mother and I were in shock. A real restaurant! We had not eaten a decent meal in more than three months. The officer entered the dining area with us and ordered the maitre d' to seat us. The fact that the German's smile disappeared as soon as the American departed and the hateful looks on the customers' faces did not faze us a bit. We were going to eat restaurant food!

Mother was nearly fluent in German, and she translated the menu for us. I ordered soup and then some sausages with potato salad. I practically swallowed my meal. I had never enjoyed dinner so much. An hour later, when we went outside to await the American soldiers, I hugged Papa.

"Thank you, *Tatínku*," I said. "Those were the best sausages I've ever tasted."

"Really?" he laughed. "I didn't know you were so fond of horsemeat!"

As the local head of the CIC, my father recruited three other Czechs to assist him with interrogations of newly-arrived exiles: Jan Tůma and two men named Obst and Schafus. One day, the four apprehended a communist spy who, after a bit of rough handling, no doubt in violation of some international treaty or convention, confessed that the assignment given him by his bosses in Prague was to ascertain the names of his interviewers and to bring the list back to the communists.

"Suddenly, I realized that this work had an element of danger," Papa told us later. "I went to the CIC to ask if, in case the Russians crossed into the U.S. Zone, as was then rumored, the Americans would protect and evacuate us. He said 'no.' So, I gave up my career as an intelligence officer after six months. I quit on the spot."

The Soviets did not cross and, in August 1948, we packed up our meager belongings. Along with many of the other occupants of the Schwabach camp, we boarded cattle cars of a freight train for a ride to Stuttgart. I found the trip traumatic. I stared at the red wooden walls of the cattle car, at the straw on the filthy floor, at the huge iron bar across the sliding door, and I imagined that the train was really a transport taking us to Auschwitz or Treblinka. By now, I had read a number of books about the death camps, and I was convinced that Germans, despite the near-total destruction of their country, were on a mission to send all Czechs to the ovens. But, we made it to Stuttgart and, instead of Dr. Mengele and the SS, we were met by a U. S. Army truck convoy, which transported us a few kilometers north to the town of Ludwigsburg. We had been told that we would be moving to much more comfortable quarters in a new camp, and it turned out to be true.

We were brought into a courtyard surrounded by dark gray, four-story, brick buildings that had once been German army barracks called *Jägerhof Kaserne*, and now were known simply as "DP Camp #643." My parents and I moved into a one-room private apartment on the second floor. The bathroom was at the end of the hall and was shared by several families. We were overwhelmed by the incredible luxury and excited to have an element of privacy after so many weeks of communal living. We still had to stand in line three times a day for our meals, but the rations now provided us with 1,200 calories per day. A growing boy, I continued to be cross-eyed with hunger every day, but my father occasionally managed to supplement our diet with food received from the officers with whom he worked in his new job, as immigration advisor to the International Relief Organization (IRO). Even better, all of us were discovered by American charities, via UNRRA (United Nations Relief and Rehabilitation Administration), which began delivering occasional CARE packages to us.

Much later, in the U.S., I would be amazed by the fact that the term "CARE package" was something of a joke to the natives. I would hear my well-fed college classmates use it to describe food packages from home. To our family and to our friends in the DP camps, CARE packages were life-savers. "CARE" stood for Cooperative for American Remittances to Europe and was created during the first Thanksgiving after the end of the war. It was made possible by a consortium of 22 charities for the purpose of funneling food from private American citizens to friends and relatives in Europe. At first, packages made up of Army ration packs were purchased for $15 and designated by the buyers to specific recipients. But, when one such donor designated a package "for a hungry person in Europe," CARE's mission was changed. From that time on, the packages were sent to thousands of needy anonymous Europeans like us. Once the Army food supply was depleted, CARE prepared its own content.

It was in the first of these packages that I discovered the eighth wonder of the world. One day, my father brought home a cardboard box with the markings of the United Nations and those magical capital letters, "C-A-R-E," stenciled on the outside. Enthusiastically, my parents and I tore into the box and began to examine its contents. There was a can of pineapple juice, a cylindrical can containing a fruitcake, a small pack of Pall Mall cigarettes, cocoa, Nescafé, dried milk, sugar, crackers, and chewing gum. All of this was exciting and wonderful, but the real treasure was at the bottom. It was contained in a blue, rectangular can with rounded edges, adorned by a photo of a pink slice of meat and the word "SPAM."

Mother was not quite sure how to prepare the meat inside the can that evening and, since we did not have a stove in our barracks room, she simply shook it out of the can, placed it on a piece of wood which passed for a cutting board, and cut three slices for each of us. With the first bite, I thought that I had died and gone to heaven. To spoiled Americans who love to make fun of Spam, it may be a mishmash of ham, pork, and some sugar and salt. To me, it was filet mignon, caviar, and lobster – all in one can. After having eaten mostly slop and subsisting on a minimum amount of calories each day for months, a miracle had taken place. From that moment on, I waited anxiously for the next CARE package delivery, ignoring its other contents and wishing only to tackle that new-found pinkish delicacy. For me, it was love at first bite, a love affair with Spam that continues to this day, much to the amusement of family and friends.

The United Nations Refugee Relief Agency provided training for DPs who wished to learn various trades. My father, ever the practical one, had read that the highest-paid blue-collar workers in America were welders.

In order to have a back-up skill in case his plans to return to clothing manufacturing would not pan out, he signed up for welding training. There were no academic schools for refugee children in the camp, so he decided that I, too, should attend trade school. I would learn to be a carpenter.

Each morning, he and I walked to the town of Ludwigsburg, to an old munitions factory which had been converted to a training center. When we met at the end of each day, Papa told me of his progress as a welder. He seemed to be enjoying the experience. On the other hand, I was having a difficult time. The problem began with my teacher, a local German. He treated all the students as if the Nazis had won the war. He was arrogant and nasty. I seemed to be a special target for him, perhaps because I was the only child in the class, and because I did not speak his language.

One morning, I came to my assigned space and found that my plane was missing. I told one of the other students who translated for the instructor. He went berserk, screaming at me in German and accusing me of having stolen the tool. He filed a written report of my theft with the UNRRA. My father assured the American representatives that I had not taken the plane and told them that "the Nazi teacher no doubt stole it and now blames it on my son." To no avail. We hunted throughout Ludwigsburg until we were able to buy a replacement plane with Papa's hard-earned money. We brought it to the UNRRA office, and, on our way out the door, my father turned around.

"I won't have my son cheated by a Nazi," he said. "He's finished with your training."

While my training as a carpenter was over, Papa completed his course and received a certificate as a welder. Fortunately, he would not find it necessary to use his new skills in the United States. On the other hand, I would try my hand at a few carpentry projects around the house, but with little success.

An activity I enjoyed immensely in the Ludwigsburg camp was scouting. A couple of university students from Prague formed a

Boy Scout troop and about a dozen of us, aged 12 to 15, signed on. Scouting had a long tradition in Czechoslovakia. Like the gymnastics organization, Sokol, Boy Scouts were a patriotic group that had worked in the underground during World War II. Called *Junák*, the national organization had been banned by the Nazis in 1940 and again by the communists in 1948. Our Ludwigsburg troop had no uniforms. But, each of us was issued a maroon kerchief; I wore mine proudly, identifying myself as a scout. We met weekly and studied from the single Boy Scout handbook owned by one of the troop leaders. We hiked and camped in the countryside outside of Stuttgart and Ludwigsburg. Sitting by the campfire in the evening and singing was my favorite time as a scout. I particularly enjoyed a song about a river which I hoped to see someday:

Smutně hučí Niagara,
Smutně hučí do noci...

"Sadly roars Niagara, sadly she roars into the night..." Scouting was a wonderful diversion from life in the DP camp and my first experience as a member of an organized group.

* * *

After nearly eight months in the camps, my parents managed to get me into a United Nations-sponsored program which sent kids to various YMCA camps around Europe. My best friend, George Rosenkranc, and I, along with about twenty-five other Czech children, were designated for the beautiful alpine town of Davos, Switzerland. We took a passenger train out of Stuttgart, bound for Geneva, and then Zurich. During the night, one of the counselors came into the compartment in which eight of us were sleeping. She woke us up.

"Children, look out the window," she said. "We're passing through France."

As if the excitement of seeing the lights of another country, especially one that was not Germany, was not enough, the counselor came back

157

to our compartment after we pulled out from the only stop we made in France. In her hand, she held a strange, greenish bottle containing a dark liquid.

"This is Coca-Cola," she announced and passed a bottle to one of the kids. "I bought six bottles at the station. This one is for all of you in this compartment. Share it."

Like most post-war European children, I had heard of Coca-Cola, but I had never had the opportunity to taste it. Finally, my turn came. I took a huge swig and swished the liquid around. The bubbles tickled the roof of my mouth as I nurtured and slowly swallowed the sweet-tasting liquid. It was wonderful, partly due to its unique taste, but mainly because it was American. I could identify with movie stars whom I had seen sipping Coke on movie screens in Prague.

The next day, a train from Zurich took us through the spectacular Alps to the famous resort town of Davos. I knew that my parents had vacationed and skied there, and I had heard their stories of glamorous people who frequented the town's hotels and night clubs. But, we had little time to sightsee because we were picked up at the train station and driven to the opposite side of the lake to Davos Wolfgang, a small and sparsely populated village a few kilometers from the resort.

We were brought to a two-story, brown and white, alpine cottage with an A-frame roof and balconies with heart cut-outs. The pretty house was surrounded by a large grass lot with a swing set, a clothes line, and bordered by a split-rail fence. After months in ugly and primitive German camps, I could not contain my excitement about spending the next two months in this paradise.

All the boys slept in a single dormitory room, containing about fifteen single beds. Three of us, George and I and a fellow named Jožka, were the oldest and thus became the *de facto* leaders of the male contingent. We did not always live up to our exalted positions and often behaved badly. One of the younger boys, a nine-year-old whom I will call Pavel, became a target of our worst misdeeds. Pavel was thoroughly disliked by the other boys because he cried at the slightest provocation, complained constantly, and ratted on others to the adults. His tattling brought frequent punishment to other boys and girls. Our trio made a joint decision to make his life miserable and to invite the wrath of the counselors on him. After noticing that Pavel occasionally wet his bed, we decided to make his nighttime misadventures a *cause célèbre*.

Because the toilet was located downstairs and our dorm was upstairs, a chamber-pot was placed under each child's bed for nighttime use. Jožka came up with a brilliant idea:

"Every night after everybody goes to sleep, let's all pee into one pot. Then we'll take turns. Each night, one of us will pour all the piss into Pavel's bed. The counselors will go crazy in the morning."

George and I thought this would be a great way to punish the kid and to bring his brown-nosing of the counselors to an end. We began our nightly ritual. All three of us peed into a pot and hid it under the bed of the boy whose turn it was to do the pouring that night. That boy stayed awake until everyone was asleep, quietly sneaked to Pavel's bed, lifted up the covers, and poured the pot's content all around his body. Every third night, when my turn came, I tiptoed carefully in the darkness, fearful that I might trip and wake someone or, worse yet, spill the pee. When I came to Pavel's bed, I pulled off his covers very slowly and poured quickly on each side, stopping each time he moved as he felt the liquid engulf him. Amazingly, the boy never woke up.

Each morning, poor Pavel woke up in a pool of urine. Pretending to notice nothing, we washed up, brushed our teeth, and went to breakfast. When we returned, Pavel's yellow-stained sheets were draped across the headboard, drying. The other kids laughed, Pavel cried, and the three of us pretended not to notice. Every day at breakfast, we observed the counselors huddling and quietly discussing the situation. After a couple of weeks of this, Jožka overheard them saying that they did not believe that one small child could produce so much urine, especially after they had reduced his evening liquid intake to nearly nothing. It was obvious that they were beginning to suspect foul play. We stopped abruptly. Pavel, too, must have suspected that he was not producing a prodigious volume of pee every night and that, perhaps, he was being sent a message. He stopped tattling, whining, and crying, and became a decent kid, sleeping in a dry bed. We were not particularly proud of our methods, but we were happy with the results.

Living in a large mountain chalet with other boys and girls, eating good food, hiking in the mountains, and going on trips throughout Switzerland was a dramatic change from the life we had come to know in the displaced-persons camps. I had little time to be homesick because we were busy every day. It was autumn, snow had not yet fallen, and I particularly enjoyed our hikes on ski slopes such as the Jakobhorn. We had fun on trips into the town of Davos, where we window-shopped, watched polo matches, and admired the beautiful people vacationing there. But, most of all, I loved a daredevil sport George, Jožka, and I invented.

At the chalet, they had a small, wooden, four-wheel cart used for moving firewood and other items. After first pulling one another around the yard in the cart, the three of us decided that it would be much more exciting to ride it down a short ski slope near the cottage. We enjoyed the spills and thrills for a few days, but, after mastering the slope, we decided that we needed to go faster. We pulled the wagon up the steep two-lane highway leading down into Davos-Wolfgang. George, Jožka, and I took turns blasting down the hill, often ending up in a high-speed, end-over-end, crash in a ditch. We thought this was great fun, despite the fact that we came home with bumps, bruises, and bloody knees and elbows nearly every evening.

More than thrilling rides, great food, spectacular surroundings, and friendly treatment by the Swiss, what stood out for me from this experience was one beautiful girl. Her name was Lucy Baca. She was eighteen years old, hailed from Vienna, and she worked at the camp as a combination counselor, cook, and general helping hand.

I fell madly in love with this gorgeous creature. But, there were several problems with trying to further this one-way relationship. One, of course, was the age difference: I was a kid and she was a woman. Second, she spoke German and did not speak Czech, while I spoke Czech and did not speak German. Third, I was so shy that, even if we could have found a common language, I would have been too scared to tell her how I felt. Finally, every boy in camp, including the male counselors, seemed to be in love with Lucy, so the competition was stiff.

Despite these seemingly insurmountable problems, I thought I was making progress. During free time, when Lucy was cooking, I found an excuse to go to the kitchen to help out; Lucy seemed to appreciate my assistance. When she was working in the garden, I sat on the fence and watched. She simply looked up and smiled at me. When she was cleaning, I grabbed a broom and made myself useful. Again, Lucy's smile told me that she enjoyed my company and my help. By now, I had learned some German and gotten up the courage to speak to her on occasion. I was convinced that she was falling in love with me. In my dreams, I saw Lucy coming to America with us and marrying me.

I lived in this fantasy world for four weeks until, one morning, I came to the kitchen to help, but Lucy was not there.

"Lucy got a letter from her father informing her that her mother is seriously ill," I was told by the Swiss cook. "Mr. Baca wants her to come home to Vienna. She's leaving this morning." I was stunned and heartbroken.

Word of Lucy's impending departure spread like wildfire among the campers. Everyone stood outside while Lucy finished packing and a car waited to take her to the railroad station. Finally, she came out the door carrying a suitcase. She waved to the group of gathered children.

As she waved, her eyes were searching for something, or someone, in the crowd. Finally, she stopped scanning. Lucy had been looking for me! She spied me off on the side, put down her suitcase, and briskly walked over to me. As I stood there, with tears in my eyes, she hugged me and, in front of my stunned fellow campers, kissed me on the lips.

"Auf wiedersehn," she whispered. *"Ich liebe dich."*

It was my first kiss from my first love. I have often wondered what happened to this Viennese angel.

Lucy's departure created a void in my life, but only for a short time. I received a package from America. In it was a Kodak Baby Brownie camera with film, sent to me by our friend, Mr. Robert Eisner, who was sponsoring our immigration to the U.S. As the only kid in camp with a camera, I became something of a hero.

Then one day, I came back from one of our hikes with a large blister on my foot. Within a couple of days, the blister became infected. Two or three days later, a large boil, about two inches in diameter, appeared under the skin of my right thigh. The nurse determined that the infection had traveled from my foot, up my leg, and into my thigh. It was time for a doctor to examine me. I was driven to Davos and to the emergency room of the hospital. There, the physician on duty decided that the boil would have to be removed surgically. I was checked into the hospital where, after surgery, I remained for five days. At first, I was petrified. I was alone, without my parents or my friends, and among people who spoke only German or French. But, the Swiss nurses were extremely nice to me, and we managed to communicate quite well. When I returned for the last couple of weeks of camp, my ability to speak and understand Swiss-Deutsch was quite decent.

* * *

I returned to Ludwigsburg in November 1948 to spend a cold and uncomfortable winter in the camp. I have a photo of Christmas Eve in our barracks room. My parents and I, Mr. and Mrs. Cífka, Mr. and Mrs. Tůma, and a man whose name I have forgotten are seated around a small table, on which stands a very small Christmas tree. The tree is decorated with aluminum chafe, which had been used by Allied bombers to confuse German radar and which was plentiful in the German countryside even three years after the end of the war. Just as he had done at Christmas

1944 as a soldier in the British army, my father collected the chafe from fields around Ludwigsburg. It made for great *faux* icicles. Instead of the traditional Czech Christmas dinner of breaded carp, the eight of us shared three herrings in cream. In place of Czech Christmas cake, *vánočka*, we had a few rolls from our regular camp rations. But, it was Christmas, we were among friends, and we were free. My present was a German world atlas. Titled *Weltatlas*, I treasure it today as much as I did then.

In the early spring, word came that a new DP camp, with "first-class" facilities and amenities, was being opened somewhere in the north part of the U.S. Zone of Germany. Refugees interested in transferring there were encouraged to sign up. My parents and several of our friends, along with several hundred others, jumped on the opportunity. Papa told me that the decision was based on two factors: one, of course, the promised better conditions, and two, the fact that the new camp would be considerably closer to the port of Bremen, the German city from which we hoped to depart by ship as soon as our immigration to America would be approved. I hated to leave my friends, but I understood the rationale.

Once again, we boarded a freight train. We traveled for a full day and, as before, I was certain that we were being taken to a concentration camp. When the train stopped in the middle of nowhere for no apparent reason, I feared that we were going to be herded out and shot by Germans. We were permitted to go outside to relieve ourselves in the fields. While stopped, we observed conversations taking place near the locomotives between an American officer and some civilians. We waited to be told to reboard the train in order to continue on to our destination. But nothing happened. After an hour or so, a Czech who appeared to be in charge left the discussion and began walking back, stopping at each car with news. Finally, he came to ours.

"Ladies and gentlemen," he said solemnly. "There is no new camp. It simply doesn't exist. Someone gave us false information. We have no choice but to go back to Ludwigsburg."

With that, he turned on his heel and continued to give the bad news as he headed down the line. We returned to our old camp. Luckily, since we had been gone only one day, our old rooms had not been given away, so we moved back into our quarters and our friends to theirs, and all of us continued to wait. Because of my father's service in the British army during the war, we could have received visas to immigrate to Great Britain immediately upon leaving Czechoslovakia. But, my parents were determined to start our new lives in the United States of America. So, we waited for our sponsor, Robert Eisner in New York, to work through the bureaucratic immigration process in order to secure our visa. Each day, we hoped for good news.

Finally, an envelope arrived in the mail from the Eisners. It contained an affidavit for entry to America. After a mad scramble to locate and fill out all necessary documents, we were done. We had our visas! On May 11, 1949, we set out for the Ludwigsburg train station, accompanied by many of our friends. Wishing us *"na shledanou"* and *mnoho štěstí* ("goodbye" and "good luck") were the Tůmas, Cífkas, Nan and George Rosenkranc, Zdeněk Ryšavý, Cyril Holásek, an old friend from Kojetice – Vrát'a Böhm – and many others. It was a melancholy moment for everyone. We were elated to be going to the U.S., but sad to leave them. Our friends were happy for us, but wondering when their own moment would come. All of us wondered if we would ever see each other again.

A passenger train, not a freight train this time, took us to Bremen. We checked into a small hotel – a real hotel! – and took a walk around town. As we neared the port, I could see shells littering the streets. Oyster shells, clam shells, the hard skins of shrimp – all novelties to me. Then, for the first time in my life, I saw and smelled the ocean. From a sidewalk at the edge of the harbor, I saw blue water in every direction. It was beautiful. And there, past the western horizon, must be America.

* * *

On May 20, 1949, an overcast and breezy day in Bremenhaven, we boarded the *General M. B. Stewart*, a 523-foot World War II army transport ship with a capacity of 3,100. On this day, 816 refugees from eleven countries boarded the ship, bound for New York City. As we climbed aboard, the women were separated from the men, with females being shown into quarters in the center of the ship and males occupying the fore and aft portions. After Mother disappeared down a passageway near the bridge, Papa and I were sent forward. We descended down several ladders to the very bottom of the steel hull, where we were pointed forward to the bow by a uniformed sailor. In a steel, gray, triangular area, we found canvas bunks, four deep, located just aft of rows of open toilets reaching into the very pointy end of the ship. Papa took a bottom bunk, and I threw my belongings in the one above him.

Soon, hundreds of other men and boys arrived and all bunks were filled, including the two above mine. My father and I climbed back out on deck where we met Mother, just in time to watch the ship pull away from the dock. We stood there for a long time, looking back toward Germany, each with his and her own private thoughts. The next day, my father pointed out to me the white cliffs of Dover and told me about his travails during the invasion. He told me to say goodbye to Europe and explained that the next time I would see land, I would be seeing America. The whole experience was almost too overwhelming to comprehend.

Once we reached the open ocean, the passage became difficult. It did not take long for us to find out why the men were in the ends of the ship and the women in the center. The Atlantic Ocean in the spring can be rough. It was that in May 1949. As the ship began to encounter large waves, it started to pitch and heave. Of course, when a ship pitches, it rotates vertically around its center of gravity and, the points furthest from that center, the bow and stern, pitch the most. So it was in our cabin, which slammed up and down at an alarming rate. The refugees, the great majority of whom had never been at sea before, began to get seasick the second day out. Men were throwing up in the sleeping areas, in the heads, and over the rails on deck. Although things were not as bad in Mother's area, seasickness prevailed there as well.

By the third day, the stink in the bow area became unbearable. There was the open head, with its smell of urine and solid waste. Added to that was the stink of vomit on the decks, bunks, and even ladders. My father and I hung in there and did not get sick throughout the ten-day passage. In fact, the situation was something of a bonanza for us. After fifteen months of living on a low-calorie diet, suddenly we were on an American ship with a galley loaded with every type of food imaginable. For breakfast, there were fruit, eggs, bacon, sausage, and rolls. For lunch and dinner, we had choices of chicken, beef, ham, potatoes, salads, and vegetables. There were milk, lemonade, and real cocoa. And the best news: hardly anyone was eating. Being among the few who did not succumb to seasickness, Papa and I had the run of the ship. We explored the engine room, the supply area, and once the captain invited us to watch the action on the bridge.

On May 26, at 11:27 am, the ship received a radiogram, via the Radiomarine Corporation of America. It was addressed to "Rudolph Heller, USAT General M B Stewart," and the message read:

"Welcome in (sic) America," and it was signed "Robert and Mitzi" – our friends, the Eisners. But, we were not "in America" – not just yet.

Each day, the captain posted our progress on a bulletin board. Most passengers were too ill to care, but I, the budding geographer, was very interested, and I plotted our journey across the Atlantic in my journal. When I did so, I was unaware of the historical fact that another thirteen-year-old Czech boy had left his native country only to become one of America's most preeminent geographers 331 years earlier. In 1618, two years prior to the Battle of White Mountain near Prague, a family named Heřman left Bohemia and settled in The Netherlands. Their thirteen-year-old son, Augustine, apprenticed as a surveyor and went to work for the Dutch West India Company. A few years later, the firm sent him across the Atlantic to New Amsterdam (today, New York). There, he became a successful fur trader and the largest tobacco exporter on the continent. In 1659, he was called upon to use his expertise as a surveyor and mapmaker to help settle a border dispute between the Dutch and the English in Maryland. In exchange for 13,000 acres of land on today's Delmarva Peninsula, he produced the first map of Maryland and Virginia, including that of the Chesapeake Bay, culminating ten years of painstaking survey and chart work.

Ironically and totally coincidentally, the Czech boy who followed him across the sea, Ota Karel Heller, also would eventually settle in Maryland. Moreover, during our many years of sailing on the Chesapeake Bay, our family would discover Augustine Heřman's Bohemia Manor, the estate built by this First Czech-American on a river he named Bohemia.

There are no limits to what is possible in America.
Hillary Rodham Clinton

CHAPTER 13

America, the Beautiful

On May 30, 1949, at six o'clock in the morning, my father shook me awake in my bunk in the bow of the *General M. B. Stewart*.

"Get dressed in a hurry! I want you to see something very important."

I threw on my clothes and we climbed up a steel ladder to the ship's deck, where I was surprised to see several passengers standing near the rail at such early hour. I was even more astounded to see lights on both sides of the ship after ten days at sea, during which time we had seen nothing but water. The air had a strong fishy smell. Papa took my hand and we walked to the starboard side, where we leaned against the rail. I knew from the daily calculations in my log that we must be entering New York harbor, but my father said nothing. He seemed to be waiting for something. Suddenly, he pointed forward.

"There she is!" he said excitedly.

As the ship slipped quietly through the water, "she" came into view through the mist. She was beautiful. The lady seemed to be about fifty meters tall, standing on a pedestal, wearing a flowing robe and a spiked crown, holding a book in her left hand and a torch in her raised right hand. She appeared to be stepping toward us with her left foot, as if to welcome us.

"That's the Statue of Liberty," said Papa. "Remember this moment for the rest of your life. That lady is a symbol of everything your mother and I want for you in America – happiness and freedom to be whatever you want to be."

I knew that this must be a sacred moment in our lives and the beginning of a new, and scary, adventure in a strange land. Simultaneously, I was excited and frightened.

The ship docked and soon the refugees began to walk down the gangplank, carrying their total belongings into the New World. The three of us hauled two suitcases and a wooden footlocker which my father had built in the refugee camp. As soon as we touched the ground, we were embraced by our dear friends, the Eisners. There was Robert, a short, balding, smiling man with rimless glasses, whom I had met three years earlier when he visited Prague and brought me a transparent belt made of a substance totally foreign to us Czechs, nylon, and a small plastic radio which began playing whenever I flipped open its top. When I was in Switzerland, he had made me a hero among the Czech campers with a gift of a Kodak Baby Brownie. Hugging my mother was his wife, Mitzi, a lovely lady with reddish hair who spoke Czech with a German accent. Standing behind them were their two sons, Tom and Steve. Tom was eighteen, tall, handsome, dark-haired, wearing horn-rimmed glasses, and with a perpetual bemused smile on his face. Steve was seventeen, also good-looking but slightly shorter than his brother, and with thin, black hair. Tom spoke a few words of Czech, but Steve did not, so our introductions were brief.

We piled our belongings into the Eisners' car, while Mr. Eisner hailed a taxi to carry the overflow to their home on Talbot Street in Long Island's Kew Gardens. As he drove us slowly through Manhattan, I was mesmerized. I had read about New York, and seen photos, but I was not ready for its enormity. The buildings were gigantic, appearing to reach the sky. They were so tall that, on this beautiful, sunny day, the streets were completely dark in their shadows. Everywhere there were stores, displaying more products than I had ever seen: clothes, glassware, books, sporting goods. There were more cars in the streets than I had ever seen in Prague. The people on the sidewalks were dressed in clothes much more colorful and gay than those worn by Europeans. And everywhere I looked, there were American flags waving in the light breeze. Could these be in honor of our arrival? I nudged Mother and whispered the question to her.

"Robert, why all the flags?" she asked.

"It's Decoration Day," he answered. "It's a holiday which commemorates Americans who have died in wars."

I did not have time to be disappointed by the fact that New York was not celebrating our landing because Mr. Eisner was giving us a tour of sights which, to me, were among the wonders of the world: the Empire State Building, Rockefeller Center, and Macy's department store.

When we arrived at Eisners' two-story home, my parents moved their belongings into a guest room upstairs, and I moved in with Steve. The rest of the day was a blur. I spoke two words of English – "sank you" – so I could converse with Steve only through an interpreter, either his father or mine. Tom relished trying his Czech on me, and occasionally we were able to connect. That evening, we enjoyed our first American dinner from Mitzi Eisner's kitchen. It was a festive occasion, with the adults toasting our families' good fortunes long into the night.

"We're going to stay with Eisners for a few weeks," Papa told me the next morning. "My job is in New Jersey, which is a state on the other side of the river from New York. After I start working, I'll find us an apartment there, and we'll move into it."

The Eisner family story was similar to ours. Robert was a Jew who had married Mitzi, a Christian. Like me, both children, Tom and Steve, were baptized and brought up as Roman Catholics. And like my father, Robert was mobilized as an officer in the Czechoslovak army in 1938, in preparation for the defense of the country against the Germans. But, the two men's lives diverged at that point because, when the army was about to be dissolved without firing a shot and Jewish soldiers were given 24-hours' advance notice in order to have the opportunity to flee the country, Robert took the advice and left for London. My father chose to come home to Kojetice, only to have to escape later.

Because war between Germany and England had not yet been declared, Mitzi was able to obtain a visa, but only for herself, and not for her sons. She pretended to have left the boys behind as she boarded a train out of Prague. But, actually, Tom and Steve were on the same train, hidden in the kitchen of the dining car.

"Sometime before the Gestapo came through, the dining car was scheduled to be uncoupled in the freight yard and then re-coupled when the train to Holland was assembled," Steve would explain many years later. "Somehow, it worked out and we crossed the Channel, but without passports or visas. Eventually, all of us got on the train to London. It was the first and only time I saw my father cry."

The Eisners got their visas in London and came to America in the spring of 1941, on board a blockade runner out of Glasgow. They began life in the new world in Grand Rapids, Michigan, where the boys attended St. Thomas, a Catholic school. Eventually, they moved east and settled on New York's Long Island.

Robert's parents, Heinrich and Hortense, sold their Prague jewelry business, including a substantial collection of garnets, in order to obtain enough money to pay off German officials who provided them with visas to get out of the occupied country. They spent some time in Lisbon before obtaining passage to Havana, from which they hoped to get to the United States. But, they became stuck in Cuba, speaking neither Spanish nor English. It was 1941. In Europe, Africa and elsewhere, the war was in full fury, but the U.S. was still in a state of denial about thousands of innocent people fleeing from the Germans and seeking safety through asylum. State Department officials stonewalled the elder Eisners.

Then Hortense decided to take matters into her own hands. She purchased a Czech-English dictionary and, using it, she wrote a letter addressed to "Mrs. Eleanor Roosevelt, White House, Washington, USA." She explained that she and her eighty-nine-year-old husband had three sons and six grandchildren in the U.S. and that the two senior citizens would be no burden on the country. The First Lady not only read the letter, but she took immediate action. Within a few weeks, Heinrich and Hortense arrived in New York.

"One day, after FDR's death," recalls Steve, "about fifteen of us paid a visit to Eleanor Roosevelt at 25 Washington Square Park. We had a charming visit with her."

* * *

My first couple of weeks in America consisted of one discovery after another. At the home of Mr. Eisner's brother Paul, I saw television for the first time. On a local elementary school playground, Steve taught me to play stickball, New York City's version of baseball. At Silver Point Beach on Long Island, I had my first swim in the ocean. Interspersed among the rush of activities and discoveries were English lessons from Tommy. By the end of the second week, I could manage a few sentences in my newly-adopted language. After much early trepidation, I was beginning to enjoy this new life, one full of excitement and devoid of danger and fear.

During week three, there arrived a moment which would distance me further from my former life. One evening, Mr. Eisner and Papa told me that they had something important to discuss with me.

"Your name, Ota, is a Czech name, and Americans would have a hard time with it," said Mr. Eisner in Czech. "Your father and I have talked about it and we think you need to Americanize it."

"How? I won't ever be Otto. That's German!" I said.

"Well, your full name is Ota Karel Heller. Robert thinks we should translate your middle name into English and then reverse your first and middle names," my father said.

"What does that mean?"

"It means that your American name would be Charles Ota Heller," said Mr. Eisner. "People would call you Charlie."

I had heard the name, Charlie, used in American movies, and I had seen Charlie Chaplin in "The Great Dictator." It sounded o.k. to me. But, I had been Ota for thirteen years, and I liked my name. I realized that a new name would be something with which I would have to live for the rest of my life. As I contemplated the momentous impact of this decision, I came to the conclusion that Mr. Eisner knew much better than I what would be best for me in America, and becoming an American was the most important thing in the world to me. Moreover, I was determined to leave all memories behind. I may as well leave my name, too.

"All right, let's do it," I said.

"Great," said Mr. Eisner. "You'll use your new name in school and elsewhere, but it won't become official until you get your U.S. citizenship five years from now."

With that, Mr. Eisner instructed everyone in his family and ours to begin calling me Charlie immediately. It was very strange at first. People would call out, "Charlie!" and I would not respond. But, my transition from the Czech boy, Ota, to the American boy, Charlie, had begun, and it was not long before it became natural.

* * *

One of the requirements for immigration to America was that the head of the family had to have a job guaranteed prior to arrival in the New World. Finding such a job for the émigré was the job of the American sponsor. Mr. Eisner had found work for my father with McGregor Sportswear, at that time the largest sportswear manufacturer in the world. This was quite appropriate for the former owner and head of Central Europe's largest workmen's and ladies' clothing factory and one of the leading industrialists in Czechoslovakia. However, there was a difference between my father's former position and that in America: here, he started at the lowest possible rung, as a pattern-cutter in the design department, at a weekly salary of $37.50. Father's job was at McGregor's then-headquarters in Dover, New Jersey. The first few weeks, he stayed in a boarding house in Dover during the week and came back to Kew

Gardens on weekends. In late June, after returning from a week of work, Papa hit me with a bombshell.

"Tommy is going away for three weeks to be a counselor in a summer camp in a place called North Carolina. That's in the southern U.S.," he announced. "He's been able to work things out so that you can go with him as a camper."

"But, father, I can't speak English. How can I do this?"

"That's the whole idea. You won't be able to speak Czech. Being around nobody but American kids for three weeks will help you learn English fast. By the time summer is over, you'll be ready for school."

I was upset and scared out of my wits. But, obediently, I accompanied Tommy to High Valley Camp near Canton, North Carolina. Papa had decided to teach me English the same way he had taught me to swim back in Czechoslovakia. There, he had thrown me into the middle of a river and then waited for me to dog-paddle back to him. It worked. Now, he was throwing me into a tank of English-speaking sharks! Once again, my wise father had made the correct call. Three weeks later, when we returned to New York, I not only spoke passable English, but I chastised my parents whenever they spoke Czech to me.

While I was at summer camp, Papa and Mother had not found the blue-collar town of Dover, New Jersey, where McGregor's plant was located, appealing as a place for us to live. They had decided that, despite our near-poverty situation, we would live in the nearby upscale town of Morristown. In August of 1949, we settled there into our first permanent home in the U.S., a two-bedroom apartment in Franklin Village. I was thrilled. After living in refugee camps for 18 months, it was great to have my own room again and a place I could call home. There were no Nazis from whom to hide. There was no neon red star lighting up our living room at night.

Morristown is located about forty miles west of New York City, and it has a rich history. In 1779 and 1780, General George Washington and his army endured two severe winters in the encampment of Jockey Hollow, outside of town. The Revolutionary troops suffered through two winters of blizzards, food shortages, and a rebellion. The camp became the nation's first National Historical Park when it was so designated by an Act of Congress in 1933. Near our house was the preserved home and workshop of Steven Vail, who developed the machinery for the first transatlantic steamship there in 1818. Twenty years later, his son, Alfred, and his partner, Samuel Morse, demonstrated the first electro-magnetic telegraph in the house.

It is said that, during the 1920s and 1930s, Morristown had more millionaires than any other city or town in America, on a per capita basis. Most of them lived in mansions along the swanky Madison Avenue, and many of them still occupied these beautiful, enormous homes after we moved to town. Geographically, Madison Avenue and our Franklin Street ran parallel to one another separated only by a couple of blocks. Yet the lifestyles of the residents of the two streets were worlds apart. Papa was working as one of the lowest-paid employees of McGregor Sportswear, and our monthly rent was equal to three-weeks' pay. Mother ironed shirts at home and earned $17 per week. In addition, she took a job as a cleaning lady at Oakleigh Hall, a private school for girls.

As a self-centered teenager, I did not appreciate how difficult life was for my parents. They had left everything behind in Czechoslovakia and came to a place where they had never been and about which they knew very little. Like most immigrants, they were not welcome by everyone because of their strange accents and since they were perceived as competitors for jobs. For my father, especially, this was difficult. He started at the bottom in an industry where (in the northeastern part of America) the lower echelons were dominated by first- and second-generation Italian-Americans. It was difficult for him, a Jew from Central Europe, to gain acceptance and respect. Yet, he managed to do it. Amazingly, my parents never once complained about their plight, while I wondered how we could cope with having gone from being among the richest families in Czechoslovakia to such poverty.

*** *** ***

Although I made a vow to myself the moment I stepped on American soil that I would erase all things European from my memory and that I would become a "100% American," my acculturation was not easy. In addition to learning a new language and getting used to a new name, I spent the first months of my life in America learning about the strange habits of the natives.

Invitations to the homes of my new friends brought about the first shock: food. While subsisting on a near-starvation diet in refugee camps, I had dreamed about traditional Czech meals which I thought would be waiting for me in the U.S.: *řízky* (veal cutlets) with potato salad, *knedliky* (unique Czech bread dumplings) with eggs and ham, *svíčková* (a fabulous Czech national dish consisting of beef slices topped with cream, *knedliky*, and cranberries), *"vepřo-péčo-knedlo-zélo"* (pork, *knedliky*, and red cabbage), and my favorite dessert, *rakvičky* (coffin-shaped tubes) filled with thick cream. But, what was placed in front of me at the American tables? Turkey, with meat so stringy, dry and tasteless that it had to be smothered in gravy. And sweet potatoes. Can anyone really eat a potato that is sweet? And steak. It looked o.k. on the outside, but, when cut, blood actually oozed out of it! I was horrified. Don't Americans cook meat? And what ever happened to Spam? When I fell in love with this CARE-package delicacy in the refugee camp, I expected to see it everywhere in the U.S. I never saw it served at my friends' tables.

And how strangely they ate! Quite properly, they held the knife in the right hand and the fork in the left while they cut their meat. But, then they performed a maneuver which I found incomprehensible. After cutting a piece of meat, they placed the knife on the right edge of the plate, moved the fork into their right hand, stabbed the cut piece, and put it in their mouths. In order to cut the next piece of meat, they switched the fork back into the left hand, picked up the knife with the right, and repeated the drill. This went on until they finished their meal. No wonder I polished off my food in half the time as my American hosts. Why didn't they just keep the knife in the right hand and the fork in the left?

Before dinner, I was offered celery sticks, a strange vegetable I had never seen before. But, the ultimate in inedible foods often came as dessert. Pumpkin pie! What was this horrible stuff on top of a thin slice of dough? Having been brought up to finish everything on my plate and to thank the hostess for a delicious meal no matter how it tasted, I hid my feelings as I chewed my way through the appetizers and main courses. But, when it came to pumpkin pie, I simply could not bear the taste. I declined, claiming that I had filled my stomach on the fabulous meal I had just eaten.

Over time, I was able to develop a taste for most American foods. Some, I began to like (or tolerate) almost immediately; acquiring a taste for steak and sweet potatoes took several years. When I first saw Americans eating steak which oozed blood when cut into, I thought they must be descended from a line of cannibals. I learned to ask for it well done. But, pumpkin pie and that other horrid staple of the American kitchen, peanut butter, remain strangers to my taste buds to this day. I may have become a totally assimilated American, but my stomach has remained decidedly Czech.

Food constituted only the "front line" of culture shock for me. There were many customs and practical matters which surprised me each day. I had not realized that, when Americans greeted me with "How are you?" they did not expect me to explain to them how I felt that day and to tell them about the health of my parents. It took me a while to learn to say "Fine," even when I felt lousy.

A culture shock from which it would take me years to recover was that of crazy American weights and measures. I had grown up with the metric system, a sensible methodology used by the entire world, with the exception of English speakers. In my world, the logic of multiples of ten prevailed. A meter consisted of a hundred centimeters, a kilometer was a thousand meters, and there were one hundred grams in a kilogram. Suddenly, I was thrust into a primitive world, where an inch was based on the length of the tip of an English king's thumb and there were twelve of them in a foot. The latter had been established by measuring the length of the king's footprint. Was his foot really equal to exactly twelve times the tip of his thumb? I found it difficult to remember all the crazy and inconsistent relationships among the various units.

In Czechoslovakia, women's last names had feminine endings, generally attaching the suffix "ová" to the man's last name. For example, while my father and I were named "Heller," my mother was "Hellerová." Thus, it came as a shock to me that American women had "masculine" names. My very feminine mother had become "Ilona Heller." Additionally, it surprised me that many American women gave up their identity entirely when they married and allowed themselves to be called by their husbands' names, with a "Mrs." prefix. Hearing a woman referred to as "Mrs. Robert Jones" struck me as demeaning to the lady who had lost even her first name.

I discovered many other peculiarities in America. When I went to the movies, I noticed that people took off their jackets, spread them on their seats, and sat on them, rather than leaving them at a coat-check. I thought this was uncivilized. Then there was the use of round door knobs, instead of door handles; I could not comprehend why anyone would want to make it difficult to open and close a door. The fact that Americans did not think that real football – or "soccer," as they called it – was the most beautiful, graceful sport of all came as a terrible disappointment. And, later in our first year in the country, I discovered that Americans, unlike Czechs, did not consider December 24, Christmas Eve, the holiest of all days, and that they did not celebrate the holiday until the next day. Moreover, Christmas presents in America were delivered by a funny-looking, fat, old man named Santa Claus, rather than by Baby Jesus.

Finally, there were certain habits of Americans which I found not only strange, but shocking. The most prominent was the amount of waste I noticed in the homes of my friends, no matter how rich or poor their parents may have been. Uneaten food was thrown away in large quantities; paper tissues, rather than reusable cloth handkerchiefs, were used to wipe noses; toys and household items, when broken, were thrown away and replaced by new ones, rather than repaired. I found that Americans slammed doors rather than closing them quietly, and they did not bother to turn out the lights when they left a room.

In our home, we continued to practice frugal, European, ways: lights were turned off, very little waste was generated, and my father insisted in those early days of near-poverty that we limit the use of toilet paper to "three times at three squares each."

Another source of wonder was the Americans' view of themselves as the leading citizens of the world. U.S. world maps had North and South America in the center, with Asia split in half and located on the left and right sides. I had been taught that maps are drawn with the west on the left and the east on the right. Now, countries such as China and Japan were in the west. How odd! Additionally, I found Americans' view of the Second World War, which was still very fresh in my mind, surprising and amusing. I learned that the prevailing opinion was that the United States and Great Britain alone had defeated the forces of fascism. There seemed to be total ignorance of, or perhaps refusal to give credit to, the contributions of the Soviet Union. The facts that twenty-seven million Russians had died in the war, that three times as many German soldiers had fought on the eastern front than on the western front, that seventy percent of all Nazi casualties had come at the hands of the Soviets, and that the true turning point of the war had been the battle of Stalingrad, were either unknown or forgotten by Americans at the beginning of the Cold War. I was no fan of the USSR, but this seemed unjust and ignorant.

※ ※ ※

As a boy growing up in Europe, I had been a good athlete. I excelled in soccer, hockey, skiing, tennis, and table tennis. No doubt, I inherited my father's genes. He was not only an outstanding competitive volleyball player, but he and a friend were co-holders of the European distance record in one-man kayaks. We were a very sports-oriented family, but I had never seen, nor even heard of, the most popular sports in the U.S.:

baseball, American football, and basketball. After all, I came from post-war Czechoslovakia, where these sports were not played and where there had been no television.

Our Franklin Village apartment was directly across the street from a concrete court where, each afternoon and evening, a group of boys played a very competitive game in which they bounced a light brown ball, bigger than a soccer ball, and then tried to throw it into one of two round metal hoops attached to wooden boards located on opposite sides of a rectangular court.

"It's called basketball," my father explained in Czech. "You should go down and join in."

Since I did not know the game, and was embarrassed by my accented English, I refused to go. Day after day, I chose to watch the action from my bedroom window. Finally, after a couple of weeks, I got up the courage to go down. For a few days, I stood on the sidelines and watched, learning a bit about the game from observation. Then some of the older boys – they were mostly fifteen to eighteen years old – began speaking to me and even invited me to play a few minutes at a time.

After several weeks of being the worst player on the court, I began to understand the game and, by the end of summer, I had developed a pretty good set shot, an accurate jump shot, and became a good passer. I was no longer the last player chosen by the captains when they their selected teams.

* * *

As summer came to an end, I worried more and more about starting school. At that point, my formal schooling had consisted of two weeks in third grade in Kojetice, fourth and fifth grades at Palmovka school in Prague, and a half-year of sixth grade in Prague's Libeň gymnasium. Two-and-a-half years of school, while my classmates-to-be had eight years, starting with kindergarten! On top of this, my English was still merely passable. Only three months before the start of school, I had known only two words. Now, I could carry on a conversation, but I made lots of mistakes.

So, I entered eighth grade at Alexander Hamilton elementary school, on the other side of Morristown, full of fear and trepidation. Although a couple of my Franklin Street playground friends were in my class, I was intimidated by all the strange kids who knew each other and who spoke English to one another so fast that I could not understand them. But, one person made my transition far easier than I had expected. She was Miss Agnes Leonard, a tall, portly, gray-haired lady of about sixty, who took me under her wing from day one until my graduation from elementary school. On that first day, as soon as Miss Leonard welcomed the class back from its summer vacation, she addressed the students:

"Children, I want you to meet Charles Heller. He comes to us from a nation called Czechoslovakia, which is in the middle of Europe." She pointed to my native country on a world map. "Last year, his nation was taken over by some really bad people, called communists, and Charles and his parents had to escape. They came to America this summer. Charles is learning English, and I would like all of us to help him learn."

Thus, Miss Leonard set the tone for a wonderful first year in an American school. The kids really did help me, not only by speaking more slowly so that I could understand, but by teaching me American sports and games during recess. In the classroom, I got a pleasant surprise. I found that I was far ahead of the other students in math, science, and geography. Although I had early language difficulties, I became one of the best spellers in the class. But, the subject I enjoyed most was history. We studied the American Revolution, something totally new to me. Miss Leonard used a children's historical novel as her teaching tool, and I was fascinated by it.

Each day in history class, one student would read a passage out of *Johnny Tremain* by Esther Forbes. Johnny was a silversmith apprentice in Boston prior to the war, and he became the messenger who told Paul Revere to watch for a signal from the Old North Church. Some of the passages in the book were stirring and patriotic. I had already experienced cruel treatment of my family and the crushing of liberty of my countrymen by, first the Germans and then the communists. So, it was natural for me to identify with Samuel Adams, John Adams, John Hancock, the fictional Johnny Tremain, and the other Americans who were about to fight for their freedom from oppression. I was moved when James Otis told a gathering of patriots:

"The peasants of France, the serfs of Russia. Hardly more than animals now. But because we fight, they shall see freedom like a new sun rising in the west. Those natural rights God has given to every man, no matter how humble... We fight, we die, for a simple thing. Only that a man can stand up."

From *Johnny Tremain* and the guiding hand of Miss Agnes Leonard, not only did I learn about the struggle which led to the founding of the United States of America, but I developed a deep and abiding love for my new country. To me, Johnny was not a fictional character; he became my hero and my role model.

* * *

My assimilation process had gone relatively smoothly. However, I had one major problem which caused me immeasurable embarrassment. When we moved into our apartment in Morristown, my parents worked long hours. Much of the time, I was left to fend for myself. Intellectually, I understood my parents' preoccupation with scratching out a living; nevertheless, I felt abandoned much the same way I had felt during the war on the farm. As an immediate reaction, I began to wet my bed during sleep. I tried to prevent nighttime accidents by having very little to drink with dinner and nothing at all later, but to no avail. I thought that God was taking revenge on me for the pee showers we had given the poor kid in Switzerland.

My parents had established a close friendship with a pair of recent immigrants from Poland, Edward and Barbara Panzer. Dr. Panzer was a psychiatrist at nearby Greystone State Hospital, and Papa decided to turn to him with my problem. Dr. Panzer came to our apartment one evening and spent a private hour with me, inquiring about the war, the DP camps, and my experiences in the U.S.

"There's no question that Charlie's bedwetting is a result of the trauma he's been subjected to most of his life," he told my parents. "I have no doubt that he'll grow out of it. Just be patient with him."

Mother bought a rubber mat, which she inserted between my sheet and mattress pad. Each morning, I left my bed unmade and my wet pajama bottoms hanging on a chair. Later in the day, when sheet and pajamas were dry, I made my bed. This became my daily routine. It worked fine at home, and my problem remained a secret from the outside world.

But, as I established friendships with boys at school and in the neighborhood, I discovered that American children were fond of something called a "sleepover" – spending the night at a friend's home. Each time I was invited, I managed to come up with an excuse, generally blaming my parents for saddling me with chores. This worked for nearly a year. But, then came the summer of 1950. Dick, a friend and classmate who lived downstairs at the other end of our building, came to our apartment.

"Charlie, my parents have rented a house at the Jersey Shore for a week," he said in front of my parents. "We'd like you to come with us, if it's o.k. with your mom and dad."

I was thunderstruck. On the one hand, I wanted desperately to go to the beach and to swim in the ocean, something which was still a wonderful novelty to me. At the same time, I was petrified. How can I get away with my bedwetting, and what will happen to our friendship when Dick finds out that I, a fourteen-year-old, still pee in my bed? Quickly, I decided that I could not risk being discovered. I looked at my parents, waiting to be rescued by an excuse.

"Oh, Charlie, I think this is a wonderful opportunity for you," Mother said after a long pause. "You'll have a great time. Dick, thank you so much for letting Charlie go with you. And please thank your parents."

I was stunned. For the next few days, I thought about little else than the upcoming nightly misadventures. Finally, it was time to face the challenge. After a two-hour drive, we settled into a little cottage on a beach. It was beautiful. I thought about the fact that, just a bit over a year ago, I had been living in the squalor of a refugee camp, and now I could walk out the door, cross the hot sand, and wade in the Atlantic Ocean which stretched all the way back to the continent from which I had come. And Mother was right. Days of bodysurfing and playing baseball on the beach were capped off by evenings of rides at the amusement park. I had a wonderful time.

But always, the threat of the upcoming night hung over my head like a dark cloud. Despite the fact that heat and hard play made me terribly thirsty, I refused to drink anything after three o'clock in the afternoon. Dick and I shared a bedroom, and each night I kept him awake by talking as long as I could, delaying lights-out until after midnight. After he finally fell asleep, I read with the aid of a flashlight, hoping to stay awake all night. I crept quietly to the bathroom, for one more emptying of my bladder. Finally, totally exhausted, I had to surrender to asleep.

My strategy worked during all but two nights. On those occasions, I woke up in the morning with that all-too-familiar wetness around me. Quickly, I balled up my dry pajama tops, placed them next to the wet spot on the sheet in order to create an air pocket, pulled the top sheet and blanket over it, and finished making my bed. I slid my wet pajama bottoms under the bed and spread them out so that they would dry.

Dick and his parents did not seem to notice my strange activities or cover-up. But I lived in fear of one of them discovering my ruse. When we returned home from our week at the beach, I searched the faces of my friends each time we met. Did they know? Did Dick tell them and they were laughing at me behind my back? I was relieved when there was no sign of my secret having been revealed. Either Dick did not know or he was such a good friend that he remained silent.

Eventually, Dr. Panzer's prediction proved correct. By Christmas of 1950, our second Holiday season in America, the wetting episodes began to subside. In the spring, they stopped entirely. Now, I really did feel like a normal American teenager.

* * *

In the summer of 1950, my parents purchased a home in Morris Township, New Jersey, about two miles north of Morristown. The small, two-story, brick-front house was located on Mill Road, a quiet, leafy street with Route 202 at one end and a traffic blinker at the other. Surrounded by trees and shrubs on a small lot with a manicured lawn, our home had two bedrooms, a kitchen, a bathroom, a living room, and a screened porch on the first floor, and a bedroom, a bathroom, and large attic storage places on the second floor. One half of the basement was finished with wood paneling.

After only one year in America, my parents, both of whom were earning slightly more than minimum wage, were able to save enough money to make a fifty-percent down payment and to take out a five-year mortgage on the balance. Papa had an aversion to owing money to anyone, and he was not going to borrow more than he had to. The cost of the house was $14,500. My father would live in it for the next thirty-eight years and Mother for fifty-one years.

By the time I entered Morristown High School in September 1950, I had lost my Czech accent, and I felt that, whatever roots I may have had in Czechoslovakia had withered and died. I enjoyed school, made many friends, played on the basketball, tennis, and track teams, and participated in school activities. I did not speak about the past, and, for the most part, teachers and students assumed that I was just another kid from Morris County. That was just the way I wanted it.

Every now and then, but only rarely, someone would find out that I had come from Czechoslovakia. A teacher or a fellow student would ask me what life had been like during the war. I would give my standard party-line response: After the Nazis came, my father escaped and joined the British army. Because they knew that he was fighting against them, the Germans put my mother in a slave labor camp, and I was hidden on a farm. The conversation would end there. No doubt, my tone must have discouraged further probing. This had been Mother's explanation to me during the war and it would become my standard answer – my mantra – for years to come. After I repeated it many times, I came to believe that the story of my past was that simple. Of course, it was not.

While I played the role of the All-American boy by day, nights often found me back in Europe. Perhaps because I was surprised by my American friends' lack of knowledge about the war, I was determined to learn as much about it as I could. The ladies at the Morristown library smiled when I walked out with five or six books every two weeks, most of them memoirs and novels of the war. Reading them under the dim light of my bedside lamp, I became a character in each book I was reading, sometimes an American soldier, occasionally a partisan, and too often a concentration camp inmate. Frequently, I awoke in a cold sweat, facing death at the hands of a German. Daylight brought a return to the life of a normal American high-school boy, one who could not share his nightmare experiences with anyone.

My reading did not consist of war books, exclusively. As a sports fanatic, I read everything I could find about baseball, basketball, and football. In the process, I discovered something that shocked me: that, until a year before, Negroes had not been permitted to play major-league baseball alongside whites and that their participation in other American sports was rare. I had dreamed of an American utopia where everyone loved everyone else, a country without the prejudices and hatreds I had witnessed in Europe. Now I was beginning to learn that it was not so. In my library cocoon, I ventured outside the realm of sports to learn more. I read about the decision of my hero, Franklin D. Roosevelt, to remove more than 100,000 Japanese-Americans from their homes to prison camps during the war. Not only did I find this bitterly disappointing, but I wondered why German- and Italian-Americans had not been treated the same way. Wasn't the U.S. fighting against those countries, as well? I was even more devastated when I began reading about vicious American anti-Semitism in the 1930s and, later, America's failure to do anything about stopping the murder of six million Jews in death camps. The books told me that the U.S. government had full knowledge of their existence. Many years later, when I would begin to wonder about the reasons for having suppressed knowledge of my true ethnicity, I would think back on these discoveries. Had I been ignorant of my background, had I been in a state of deliberate denial, or had I simply feared the truth?

* * *

Although I had a number of friends who were girls, I did not have a single date my first two years of high school. Then, late in the summer of 1952, I was invited to come swimming at Mt. Kemble Lake, a private community of homes surrounding a small lake, and home to several kids who attended Morristown High. There, I met a beautiful, tall, dark-haired girl with a deep tan, wearing a blue one-piece bathing suit with white trim. Her name was Susan Elizabeth Holsten. She was going into her sophomore year at MHS, and she lived with her parents, Edward and Viola, within a five-minute walk of the beach. We spoke only briefly, but I could not stop thinking about her after I left. A year later, we began dating and soon were "going steady." When I introduced Sue to my parents, she and my mother found immediate rapport. Things did not go as well with Papa.

"I'm scared of your father," Sue told me one evening when I drove her home from our house. Papa was different from the fathers of my friends. His manner was formal, almost aristocratic, when compared to that of casual, informal Americans. To new acquaintances, and certainly to Sue, he appeared cold and unfriendly.

I played varsity basketball, but I had a rocky relationship with the coach. As a result, my high-school career as a player was quite ordinary. In the early 1950s, it was not unusual for high-school and college basketball players to play in semi-professional leagues and to receive a small salary from team sponsors. Of course, this was against the rules and players used assumed names in order to protect their amateur status. During my last two years in high school, I took the name of Bob Harris, a Boston Celtics forward and a hero of mine because he had starred at Oklahoma A&M College, a school with a long tradition of championship basketball. Playing against accomplished stars, including several former college players who had been implicated in the point-shaving scandals of the period, I began to blossom. I led my team in scoring for two consecutive years, and I was noticed by several college recruiters. I was offered scholarships to three universities, including nearby Rutgers.

I was a voracious reader of sports books and had become mesmerized by stories of a coach who ran a legendary program out in the southwestern prairie: Henry Iba of Oklahoma A&M College in Stillwater. Mr. Iba had never given a scholarship to a kid from the east coast, and he was not about to begin with me. But, he promised to give me an opportunity to walk on to his team. At the same time, Jan and Hana Tuma, our Czech refugee-camp roommates, had migrated to Stillwater, where Jan had become a professor of civil engineering.

It was difficult to leave my parents, and even more difficult to put 1,500 miles between Sue and myself, but I enrolled at A&M in September 1954 as a civil engineering major. I managed to make the basketball team and earn a partial scholarship, although my career consisted of being a practice player and bench-sitter. I made some poor decisions which could have ended my college career prematurely. But, with help from Professor Tuma, my parents, and the good people of the now-renamed Oklahoma State University, I managed to come to my senses. I received the "Outstanding Graduate" award when I got my B.S. degree in civil engineering in January 1959, and I stayed on to get my Master's degree in structural engineering under the tutelage of Jan Tuma.

After I overcame the early hiccups in my education and became a decent college student, my father finally began to consider me an adult. This elevation in status also included my friends and, most importantly,

Sue. Now, she and all my pals got to know the real Rudy Heller, a man with a great sense of humor and a heart of gold. Sue was no longer afraid of him, and they developed a father-daughter relationship to match the closeness between her and Mother.

Sue and I were married on June 3, 1959, one day after her graduation from Trenton State College (today, the College of New Jersey), and we moved to Stillwater, Oklahoma, where I finished my graduate studies. After I earned my M.S. from OSU, we started our adventure in Southern California, where I went to work as an aerospace engineer and my young wife became an elementary-school teacher.

In 1962, we moved to Maryland, in order to be closer to our parents. Our wanderings ended when we discovered the beautiful, historic, sailing town of Annapolis. Our only child, David Arthur, was born there on April 9, 1964. After spending six years on the faculty of the U.S. Naval Academy, and earning a doctorate in engineering at The Catholic University of America during that time, I embarked on an entrepreneurial career, co-founding and running two software companies. I was living the proverbial American dream, and memories of the horrors of my childhood were buried in the deep recesses of my soul.

We live in a moment of history where change is so speeded up
that we begin to see the present only when it is already disappearing.
R. D. Laing

CHAPTER 14

Fateful Eights

For Czech people, major events happen "on the eights" – years ending with the digit, "8." Czechoslovakia became an independent nation in 1918; the country was sold out to the Germans by her so-called allies in 1938; the communists took over the government (and we escaped) in 1948. Now it was 1968.

In early January, a Slovak named Alexander Dubček came to power as First Secretary of the Czechoslovak Communist Party. With him arrived a period which became known as "Prague Spring." After twenty years of oppression, censorship of speech and press was ended. The economy was partially decentralized. Travel to the west was allowed. Young people became westernized almost overnight, with men and boys letting their hair grow long, young people wearing blue jeans and tie-dye shirts and dancing to rock music, and everyone listening to something other than communist propaganda on the radio.

Unexpectedly, the little pilot light of Czech patriotism inside me glowed a bit more brightly, although I was shocked by the fact that the man who became President of Czechoslovakia during this period of freedom was none other then Ludvík Svoboda, the former general whose refusal to support President Beneš in 1948 had assured the success of the communist putsch. Nevertheless, I followed the events intently, even while I was overwhelmed with trying to fulfill my teaching duties at the

U. S. Naval Academy and burning the midnight oil with the last pieces of my doctoral dissertation at The Catholic University of America. Even my parents overcame their cynicism about "socialism with a human face," as Dubček referred to his reforms, and they entertained hopes of going back for a visit.

My joy over the events in my native country was tempered by horrors taking place in another part of the world. The Vietnam War continued to rage. At the end of January 1968, 84,000 Viet Cong guerillas and their North Vietnamese Army allies launched the Tet Offensive by attacking hundreds of towns throughout South Vietnam. This not only turned out to be the turning point of the war, but also the end of the presidency of Lyndon B. Johnson. At the end of March, LBJ announced that he would not run for another term. Four days later, the leader of the nation's civil rights movement, Dr. Martin Luther King, was murdered in Memphis.

Twenty years earlier, in a refugee camp in Germany, I had dreamed of a far-off utopia, a land called the United States of America, where justice ruled and all people loved one another. Not long after arriving on these shores, however, I had discovered that Americans were just as capable of bigotry and hatred as Europeans. I was devastated to read about anti-Semitism, particularly during the pre-war period, when prominent people such as Henry Ford preached that Jews were "the world's foremost problem."

Most of all, I had been disappointed in my adopted country's mistreatment of its black citizens. I had read about lynchings and other cruelties as a boy in Europe, but somehow I had assumed that these had taken place hundreds of years ago. Upon arriving in America, I discovered how recent such events were and that, even in the early 1950s, Negroes did not have equal access to education and jobs; in many places, they were confined to using separate, inferior, public schools and facilities from those reserved for whites. Where as a boy, I had seen signs "Jude," on schools, restrooms, and water fountains, here these signs were replaced by those reading "Colored." The first time I stepped onto the floor of Gallagher Hall, the basketball arena of Oklahoma State University, I was amazed to find that all the other players looked like me – white. In 1954, there had not been a single black athlete at my alma mater.

But I was encouraged by the changes in laws and attitudes which took place under Presidents Kennedy and Johnson. Then, along came Martin Luther King, whose nonviolent appeals for equality for black Americans gained millions of followers, with me among them. Now it was 1968 and he was dead. Disenfranchised Americans not only lost their leader, but they determined that equal rights could not be gained peacefully. They rioted. Nearly one hundred cities and towns throughout the country were on fire. America was in trouble.

We were in the middle of a presidential campaign, and I hung my hopes for sanity to return to our nation and the world on one man, Robert F. Kennedy. Bobby, the younger brother of the late president, was my last remaining hero in public life. If elected, he promised to end the insane Vietnam War and gave hope of a brighter future to black Americans. One day after celebrating our ninth wedding anniversary, Sue and I watched television late into the night of June 4, as the returns from the critical California Democratic primary were being counted. We cheered and drank a toast to Bobby when he was declared a winner, and thus would most certainly be our party's candidate in the general election. I had to get up early the next morning to prepare to march in the procession at graduation of Naval Academy's class of 1968, so we went to bed.

On Wednesday morning, the radio woke us with the same kind of music we had heard after the deaths of JFK and Dr. King. I was startled. *"It can't be. Not again!"* But soon we found out that, indeed, it had happened again. Bobby had been passing through a hotel kitchen in Los Angeles after addressing his supporters, when a Palestinian refugee named Sirhan Sirhan shot him three times. Now, my last hero was lying in a hospital with a team of doctors trying to save him.

Although I was certain that graduation would be cancelled, I drove to my Naval Academy office in Isherwood Hall, hoping to find solace in talking to my friend Bud Carson, a fellow aerospace engineering professor and admirer of RFK. But, the department's offices were deserted. I picked up the phone and called the Academy operator to inquire about the date of the rescheduled graduation ceremonies. To my surprise, I was told that the graduation had not been changed. The offices were empty because my fellow faculty members were forming up for the procession. I sat at my desk, staring at the box containing my rented cap and gown, practically foaming at the mouth with anger at the Navy, the Naval Academy, my fellow faculty – everyone – for their lack of respect for my hero.

Finally, I grabbed a piece of paper and scribbled on it:

"There are those who look at things the way they are, and ask why. I dream of things that never were and ask why not." Robert F. Kennedy.

"Go to hell!" Charles O. Heller

I placed the paper in the box with the cap and gown, closed the box, and threw it on the desk of the head of the Engineering Department. I went home, where Sue and I kept vigil all day and evening. Bobby was still hanging on. The next day, Bobby was dead. I felt as though my world had come to an end. How much more could one take? What kind of a lawless country was this? My idealized vision of America, one I had carried with me on our journey from enslaved Czechoslovakia across the pond, was long gone. I had always prided myself on self-control and coolness under pressure, but, now I felt totally helpless and lost. The following Sunday, I was awarded my doctorate in engineering from The Catholic University of America in Washington. My proud parents, Sue, and our four-year-old son David held a muted celebration. Even after six years of my hard work and Sue's sacrifices, it was difficult to savor the moment of victory under the circumstances.

A few weeks later in Moscow, Big Brother was not happy about the turn of events in Czechoslovakia, that rebellious small country to the west. I was lying in bed a few minutes after midnight on the 21st of August 1968, scanning the dial of my Zenith Transoceanic short-wave radio, searching for news from Prague. The announcement came like a shock wave over the air.

"At eleven o'clock last night, troops of the five Warsaw Pact states invaded Czechoslovakia, brutally violating all fundamental international and human rights."

500,000 soldiers of the Warsaw Pact – Soviet Union, Bulgaria, East Germany, Hungary, and Poland – had invaded Czechoslovakia. Tanks were rolling into Prague. Ordinary citizens tried to persuade the soldiers to leave and attempted to confuse them by changing road and street signs.

"They are going to silence our voices, but they cannot silence our hearts," a woman said on Radio Prague, her voice cracking. I closed my eyes and saw the panorama which is engraved in the mind and the soul of every Czech: Hradčany, the Castle and cathedral, which tower over my native city. Then, on the radio, I heard that sad, beautiful, and haunting melody of the only national anthem in the world which begins with a question. I cried into my pillow, as I sang quietly.

Kde domov _*můj*_*?*
Kde domov můj?
Voda hučí po lučinách,
Bory šumí po skalinách,
V sadě skví se jara květ,
Zemský ráj to na pohled,
A to je ta krásná země,
Země česká, domov můj,
Země česká, domov můj.

Where is my home?
Where is my home?
Water's rustling o'er the meadows,
Pinewoods murmuring o'er the mountains.

PRAGUE: MY LONG JOURNEY HOME

Orchards radiant with spring blossoms,
Earth's paradise on sight,
And that is that beautiful land,
Czech land, my home,
Czech land, my home.

The Czechoslovaks waited for help from the west, but it never arrived. Dubček's government was summoned to Moscow and "re-educated." The Iron Curtain came down again – and hard. Dubček was replaced and put out to pasture. Secret police (StB) provoked riots in order to give the government reason to exercise repression over the citizens. The old controls over newspapers, books, films, radio, music, art, and everything in everyday life were back, with a vengeance. The little pilot light which had flickered inside me grew dim once again, nearly extinguished by a foul easterly wind.

✳ ✳ ✳

My parents were the classic immigrant overachievers. My father, who had started at the lowest rung of the ladder at what had become McGregor-Doniger, a public company and the largest sportswear manufacturer in the world, was now a member of top management. He ran the swimwear division of the corporation out of offices in New York and New Jersey. My mother's story was even more amazing. After a rich-girl finishing-school education, interrupted by great suffering during the war, she had started life in America as a cleaning lady, followed by a stint as a seamstress in a bra factory. A few years later, she went to work at the large pharmacology firm, Warner-Lambert, as a lab assistant. Now, my incredible mother held the title of Associate Scientist. Her closest friend was her boss, Dr. Jane Emele, a Yale-educated lady who had never married and who lived with her parents not far from Mother and Papa in Morris Plains.

The only dark cloud on the horizon was my parents' health. Mother had high blood pressure, a minor heart condition, and arthritis. Papa's problems were more severe. His bout with malaria while fighting in the desert of North Africa during the war left a mark in the form of heart disease and other recurring problems. Every two or three years, he ended up in Morristown Memorial Hospital, ironically located on the site of the former playground across from our first home in America, where I had learned to play basketball and baseball that first year in the United States.

Whenever Papa was hospitalized, Sue and I, and sometimes I alone, drove to New Jersey to stay with Mother and to visit him. On one such trip in 1978, when I drove up alone, I sat with Mother in the waiting room while Papa was undergoing surgery. It was only during such times that Mother, under the strain of concern, would reminisce about the old days. At all other times, our experiences in Czechoslovakia were off limits as topics of conversation. These were exceptions. On this occasion, Mother squeezed my hand as we sat side-by-side in the waiting room chairs.

"Let's go outside," she said. "I have to tell you something."

We took the elevator to the lobby and walked out into the sunshine. When we reached a secluded spot near the parking garage, Mother stopped.

"I have to tell you something about myself that I've never told you before," she started. I bit my lip as I awaited some startling revelation.

"My parents weren't married when I was born," she blurted out. "My Jewish father made a Sudeten Catholic woman pregnant. He sent her to Vienna to have the baby – me. I was born and a few days later my father, your grandfather *Děda*, adopted me. All these years, I've been ashamed of the fact that I was a bastard child, but I felt that I had to tell you now."

Tears were streaking down Mother's cheeks and it was obvious that telling me had been extremely difficult. She must have anguished for a long time over the decision to reveal her secret to me. I was at a loss for a response. On the rare occasions that I thought about it, I had wondered why my maternal grandmother had not lived with us and my grandfather before the war and why she was named Kozuschniková, rather than Neumannová. I had guessed that Mother's parents had never married, but it did not matter to me, so I never pursued it. Now, I was concerned only about not responding in such a way that I might appear to dismiss as trivial something that obviously had been Mother's albatross her entire life.

"Mother," I said finally. "It makes absolutely no difference to me. I love you just as much as before. You know, in today's world, there's absolutely no stigma attached to a child being born to parents who aren't married to each other. You don't have to be ashamed of it. But, I thank you for telling me."

I kissed Mother on the lips, wiped away her tears with my handkerchief, and we walked slowly back to the hospital. In the future, the subject would come up only infrequently, and Mother would treat it in a distant, almost nonchalant, manner. Having told me during that stressful moment at the hospital must have served as successful therapy.

Out of suffering have emerged the strongest souls.
Edwin Hubbel Chapin

CHAPTER 15

Gray Side of Iron Curtain

In 1970, after an absence of 22 years, I returned to Czechoslovakia. The National Academy of Sciences had contacted me and asked if I would be interested in going to Prague as a visiting lecturer. While teaching at the U.S. Naval Academy, I had been at the forefront of research in a new, promising field, called computer-aided design (CAD). Now, I was co-founder and CEO of CADCOM, Inc., one of the pioneering firms in the development of CAD software. Czechoslovaks were eager to learn about this technology, and the Academy wanted me to spend three weeks lecturing on the subject at SVÚT, the country's institute for applied mechanics in Prague.

I was faced with a difficult decision. Only two years before, the Soviet army had extinguished a long-forgotten flame inside me, one which had been reignited for a short time by the promise of Prague Spring. Now, feelings for my native country again lay buried in their customary forgotten corner of my soul. At the same time, I had a young company to run, with my partners, our shareholders, and our employees counting on my leading it through its difficult startup period. How could I possibly pick up and leave for three weeks? Telling no one, I wavered between going and staying put. Finally, I decided that it would be best to decline the invitation. At home that evening, I mentioned it to Sue only in passing.

"What a great opportunity for you to go back after such a long time!"

she exclaimed. Even more surprisingly, she added: "Do you think David and I could go with you?"

"Why would you want to do that?"

"I'd like to see the places where you grew up. And for David, it would be a wonderful experience."

"Aren't you concerned about your safety?" I asked.

"Not really."

"Let me give it some thought," I said.

As I went back and forth again for the next few days, the proposition changed in my mind from that of three weeks of technical lectures to one of adventure. My mind played a trick on me and surfaced only the pleasant memories of my childhood. These came rushing at me now: quaint Kojetice, beautiful Prague, spectacular Krkonoše mountains. In my mind's eye, I saw myself introducing my wife and son to places I had once loved and to people, particularly the Hahn family: Aunt Aša, Uncle Viktor, and their daughter Sylva, whom I had never met.

The decision was made. We were going, assuming that the Czechs would allow an escapee from their regime to come and to bring his American family. After filling out a multitude of forms and waiting for weeks to receive a visa, I was accepted by the Czechoslovak Academy of Sciences. Now came the hardest part. I had to tell my parents about our plans. My father showed some concern; Mother was beside herself. Because the communist government had placed their names officially on the list of traitors, declared them enemies of the state, and revoked their Czechoslovak citizenships, Mother was convinced that I would be arrested as soon as I would arrive and that no one would ever hear from me again. That was before I told her that Sue and David would be accompanying me. When I did, she nearly fainted. But, after speaking to some friends in the New York Czech community, and finding out that a few émigrés from the "class of 1948" had, in fact, visited and returned safely, Mother relented. She was happy that we would see her dearest friend, Aša Hahnová, whom she loved more than anyone outside our family.

So, in October 1970, at the height of post-invasion restrictive conditions, we flew over the Iron Curtain and landed in Prague. To say that it was like visiting another world is no exaggeration. Peter Sís, a Czech artist and author, describes the difference between the two worlds through a picture in his wonderful book, *The Wall, Growing Up Behind the Iron Curtain*. On the western side of the Curtain, he illustrates: inspiration, dreams, respect, love, morality, dignity, liberty, truth, freedom, and happiness. On the other side, he has drawn: stupidity, suspicion, injustice, corruption, terror, fear, envy, and lies. After gathering our luggage at Prague's Ruzyně airport, we entered the world on this other side.

Prague was sad and melancholy, with unsmiling people seemingly rushing nowhere in particular with their heads down. The city was a monochrome movie, black and white with various shades of gray, except for the enormous red flags and banners hanging everywhere, in celebration of some Soviet holiday. As the cab driver who had picked us up at the airport drove through the capital, he pointed at one particularly huge red banner with a portrait of a Russian leader, rolled down his window, and spat.

"*Takový kurvy!*" ("Such whores!") he said under his breath, just loudly enough to let me know his feelings. It was our first sign that the Czech spirit was still alive. Soon we would discover that this was not an anomaly. The *Švejks* had their own way of protesting.

Our government-supplied apartment was on the fifth floor of what was known as a *panelák*, a cheaply constructed pre-fabricated multistory building, made of pre-stressed concrete panels. Such buildings, typical of communist- era "architecture," were the butts of many jokes among Czechs. Some thirty years later, President Václav Havel would refer to them as "undignified rabbit dens, slated for liquidation." But, the apartment, though equipped with cheaply-made, Soviet-style, ultramodern furniture, was clean and comfortable. Also, as I was warned by Aunt Aša upon our reunion, it was bugged. Consequently, whenever we had guests, all of us made certain to say nothing derogatory or controversial. When Sue and I wanted to hold a confidential conversation, either we held it in the bathroom with water running and toilet flushing or we went outside the building.

I commuted each day by streetcar across town to Emauzy, a former Benedictine monastery built in the fourteenth century by Charles IV, and now the home of the institute of applied mechanics. It was also the only historic building in Prague which had been bombed, albeit erroneously, by Allied aircraft during World War II. The setting was bizarre. Instead of researchers, I expected to see monks in black robes when I walked down the dimly lit corridors to the closet-size office assigned to me. There, I was shown to a tiny wooden desk and an old, rickety chair. Other than a small bookcase with a few books, there was nothing but one 25-watt bulb attached to a chord hanging from the white stone ceiling. And, it was cold. As I sat there with my teeth chattering, I thought that it might be appropriate, in this medieval setting, to prepare my lectures by dipping a quill pen into an inkwell. But the ink would have been frozen.

It turned out that I was asked to do very little lecturing about my field of computer-aided design. Instead, my new colleagues were starving for information about engineering, science, and academia in America. What kinds of books were we reading? How fast were our computers? What equipment did we have in our laboratories? Later, when we became better acquainted and lost our mutual inhibitions, my Czech colleagues were more interested in life in the U.S. What kind of house did I live in? Did we really own a swimming pool? What kind of car did I drive? What was available in our shops? How much money did I earn? I had no idea if my fellow researchers had had to join the Communist Party in order to attend university and to obtain their current jobs. To my great surprise, I did not care. Their interest in America was genuine, and, instead of the hatred for "American imperialists" spewed by their government, they expressed nothing but admiration for our justice, freedom, innovation, and accomplishments. They showed me their outdated textbooks and their made-in-Poland computers, equivalent in power and speed to those I had

learned on at Douglas Aircraft Company some ten years before. My heart
went out to these highly-educated, intelligent, hard-working professionals
who did not have the tools necessary to perform state-of-the-art work. I
promised to send them books and papers once I returned to the U.S. I
would keep my promise, but I would never find out if my packages had
reached their destination: the monastery where the famous preacher, Jan
Hus, had once studied.

The best parts of our stay were visits to, and trips with, the Hahns.
Their large, beautifully furnished apartment that I remembered was now
divided in half, with a communist blue-collar family occupying the other
half and sharing the bathroom and toilet. Many years later, I would find
out from Sylva that it was an error by my father that caused the Hahns
to lose one-half of their home. After our escape in 1948, Papa had sent a
postcard to Viktor from Germany. It contained a single sentence: *"Jsme na
druhé straně."* Intended to inform them that we were safe, it stated: "We are
on the other side." Someone at the post office informed the secret police,
who came to arrest Viktor. He spent a month in jail and, while he was
imprisoned, the apartment was divided.

But, Uncle Viktor, the concentration camp survivor, had no fear of the
authorities. His philosophy consisted of: "if the Germans couldn't kill me,
these bastards can't touch me." I wanted to see our apartment building in
Libeň, but I had forgotten how to get there. Viktor offered to accompany
us on a streetcar, and one morning, we found ourselves standing in front
of the building. I pointed out to Sue and David the windows of our former
apartment. The communist red star beneath the window was now bigger
than I remembered it, and the sign over the door read: "Headquarters of
the Communist Party of Czechoslovakia, Praha/Libeň."

"Let's go in," said Viktor.

"Oh, no," I replied. "I don't think we'd be welcome."

"Come on," Victor said. "Maybe they'll give us a tour."

Before I could protest further, he walked in, and we followed. On
the right, behind a small window, sat a uniformed guard. I could see that

he was armed. Immediately, I told Sue to take David outside and start walking away from the building. Viktor stepped up to the window and addressed the guard:

"The owners of the building are here from America, and they'd like to take a look around."

"Oh, shit! I can't believe he just said that!" I thought. *"Now I know that Mother was right. I'm going to end up in a communist prison and no one will ever hear from me again."*

"Uncle Viktor, please," I said in Czech loudly enough so that the guard could hear me. "This building doesn't belong to us any longer, and I don't want to see it. Let's leave."

I turned to the guard and said: "Thank you, sir," and with that, I headed out the door, fully expecting the comrade to come after me with gun drawn. Viktor followed reluctantly, and we continued to walk down the street until we caught up with Sue and David. No one pursued us, and I was relieved when we hopped on a streetcar for the return trip.

My distant cousin, Sylva, was no *Švejk*-like Czech, either. Although she worked for a state-owned savings and loan institution in downtown Prague, she showed her defiance for the anti-Semitic communists by wearing a Star of David necklace everywhere she went. She was raised in her mother's Catholic faith, but she felt compelled to be like her father, Viktor, and to show the communists disrespect.

The Czechoslovak Academy of Sciences people asked me to visit Brno, the capital of Moravia, and to speak to the local university faculty members about my specialty. They gave me a first-class, round-trip, train ticket between Prague and Brno. I boarded the train at what had once been called Woodrow Wilson Station. The conductor showed me to a plush compartment in the first-class car and closed the sliding door when he departed. As the train began to pull out, three communist thugs, dressed in the hated uniform of the St.B., the secret police – long, dark, leather coats and black hats – entered the compartment and occupied the remaining seats. They greeted me politely, and removed their coats before making themselves comfortable. As I stared at them, I began to seethe.

"*These bastards look just like the goddamn Gestapo,*" I told myself. "*In fact, they are the commie version of the Gestapo. I'll be damned if I'm going to spend the next few hours in their company.*"

A few minutes out of Prague, I stood up, put on my coat, pulled my overnight bag from the shelf, and, without a word, walked out the door. I entered a car marked with a large "2." The second-class car was crowded, with people packed onto uncomfortable wooden benches. After a short search, I found an empty seat. I took off my coat and placed my bag under the bench. Soon, the same conductor who had shown me to my compartment came through to check tickets. He did a double-take when he saw me.

"Sir, you have a first-class ticket."

"I know," I said. "But I wanted to sit with my kind of people."

He smiled, winked, punched my ticket, and walked away.

The closest I came to real trouble was when I was invited to a test of a new bridge built over the Nusle Valley in Prague. It was a unique structural trial, in that military tanks were going to be placed in various combinations and positions on the spans, in order to measure deformations of the deck under a variety of loadings. Because the August 1968 invasion by Soviet tanks was still fresh in the Czechs' memories, for several days prior to the test, radio, TV, and newspapers announced the fact that, when these tanks would roll through Prague, they would be Czech, and not Soviet. Even before we arrived in the country, I had been warned that taking photographs of anything military, policemen, trains, and airplanes was strictly forbidden. Yet, I brought my 35-mm Konica to the bridge test.

Because the test was unique, and unheard of in the U.S., I walked along, snapping pictures of the tanks as they were being placed in position. Suddenly, two men in the now-familiar, black leather coats approached me. Without a word, they snatched my camera and led me to the end of the bridge. They pushed me through the door of a construction trailer and told me to sit on a wooden chair. When they began to chide me about breaking the law by photographing tanks, I lost control.

"Do you really think that pictures of these old pieces of shit would be worth anything to Americans?" I asked in Czech. "A couple of our tanks would take out one of your armor divisions in a matter of minutes."

First, there was silence. Then the two secret service guys huddled and whispered to one another for several minutes. I knew that I had made a terrible mistake, chided myself for having lost my temper, and prepared for the worst. Finally, after making me sweat for some time, one of the men opened my camera. He rolled out the film and threw it in a wastebasket. Deliberately, he closed the camera, placed it back in its leather case, and threw it to me.

"Get out, American, and don't come back!" he sneered. I tried to appear nonchalant, but my feet barely touched the cobblestones as I practically ran to the tram station, worried that they might change their minds.

* * *

The Soviet Union's lackeys in Czechoslovakia used the term *normalizace* (normalization) to describe the conformity they had forced on the populace. By the time of our visit, all vestiges of Prague Spring of 1968 had disappeared. Government, universities, and cultural institutions had been purged of so-called enemies of the state. The latter had been imprisoned or downgraded in employment. Secret police goons and their informers watched everyone. "Heretical" books had been taken out of libraries and stores. Centralized management, with its mind-numbing five year plan, was back. A housing shortage had brought about a frenzy of building those cheap, monstrous, high-rise buildings ringing cities and towns. With rent subsidized by the central government, people retreated to their rabbit-wrens at the end of each boring day of uninspired and meaningless work.

"We pretend to work, and they pretend to pay us," was a phrase we heard time and again as old and new friends lamented their situation.

In order to reduce dissatisfaction and prevent unrest, the hard-line communist regime allowed a single pocket of a free-market economy to exist. Czechoslovaks were able to buy materials to build their own tiny, generally one-room, weekend huts. Procuring materials, building and improving, became the downtrodden citizens' only creative activities amid a life of boredom, humiliation, and sadness. With the single exception of Uncle Viktor and Aunt Aša, every single Praguer we met during our visit had such a "piece of the communist paradise." Each Friday evening, a stream of hundreds of plastic East German Trabant cars and old Czech Škodas would stream out of the city. On Sunday evenings, they would return. The tradition remains to this day. On weekends, Prague is devoid of natives; now only tourists roam its streets.

For us, three weeks behind the Iron Curtain were as much as we could bear. When we boarded a British Airways flight to London, I was torn between joyful relief because we were returning to the free world and a terrible sadness for those we were leaving behind in this somber, gray, Godforsaken place: Uncle Viktor, Aunt Aša, Sylva, my colleagues at the institute, new friends we had made during our stay. As the airplane's wheels left Czechoslovakia's *terra firma* and I prayed for them all, I felt a long-lost affection and sorrow for my desecrated native land.

⁂ ⁂ ⁂

On our flight back to freedom, I thought about my boyhood best friend, Vláďa Svoboda, whom I had not been able to find during our visit. Often, in my daydreams, I had imagined our two families escaping Czechoslovakia together, so that Vláďa could have lived the proverbial American dream along with me. Now, having witnessed what had happened to my native country, I wondered how he and his family had been affected by the brutality of the early days of Stalinist communism, the brief period of freedom, and the current return to totalitarianism. It had been twenty years since I had seen my friend, and it would be another twenty-two before we would be reunited. Only then would I be able to find out how he had fared under communism and to begin to grasp where my own life may have led had it not been for the courage and foresight of my parents. Several years following the 1989 Velvet Revolution, Vláďa would reveal some of the travails of his personal journey to me in an interview.

Heller: Back in 1948, I found out from my father that we were escaping the country only when we were near the western border. I couldn't forgive my parents for not letting me say "goodbye" to you and for not letting me give you my bike, my stamp collection, and other things I left behind. How did you find out we were gone?

Svoboda: On March 10, 1948, Jan Masaryk died. The communists claimed that he had jumped out the window of his office, but most Czechs were convinced that he had been pushed. We worshiped the Masaryks, and my mother and I went to Jan's funeral in Prague. They played sad music by Smetana as his coffin, draped in the Czech flag, was pulled on top of a gun carriage, up Wenceslas Square. We took a streetcar back to Libeň, and, when we got to Blanická Street, I told Mother that I'd run up to see you. But, what did I see when I got to your door? Tape across the door and a document with official rubber stamps. Confused, I ran home and told Mother. She explained that the Hellers had probably "gone across the border." That was on March 13, 1948.

Were you as upset as I was?
Oh, yes. Without even a word of parting, a handshake, a smile or a tear, we were suddenly far apart. After that, I thought about you often, but neither one of us knew what and how the other was doing – for many, long years. And neither of us knew if we'd ever see each other again.

What was it like in the weeks after we left?
Life went on. The communists nationalized industry, mines, steel mills, banks. Out in the country, the government took ownership of everything

down to the last horse and cow. No one could own anything. Your family's building in Libeň became the prominent home of the Secretariat of the Communist Party of Prague 8. Throughout the country, terror ruled. People were being tried, imprisoned, and sentenced to death. In school, the anticommunist teachers disappeared and the fanatics who took their places forced us to recite communist poems about the glory of factory workers. Anybody who wanted to study further had to join the communist organization, Pioneer. That included me. They got rid of the selective gymnasium schools and replaced them with something called "Jednotné školy." Here, they mixed the good students from the gymnasium with the dummy children of the new communist "elite working class." My life became easy. What I had learned in one year at the gymnasium was enough to carry me through two years at this new school. I sat in the last row of every class next to one of these dummies. Later on, this guy left school and became a welder in a shipyard. His salary was higher than mine when I became an engineer.

What about your parents?
There was a big change at home, having nothing to do with the stormy political climate. I had been an only child for sixteen years. Now, suddenly, I had a brother, born to my thirty-eight-year-old mother and forty-two-year-old father. They named him Václav, after my dad. When I graduated from high school, he was only two years old. We developed a father-son relationship.

When and where did you meet Marie, your wife?
During the summer between high school and university, I got a job as a surveyor. I was sent north to the Krkonoše mountains, where we worked on a project to construct mountaintop towers. All of us surveyors were living in a small hotel with a restaurant in a ski resort called Paseky nad Jizerou. There, I met the hotel manager's daughter, Maruška. You didn't know that I call Marie by her nickname, Maruška, did you?

No, I didn't. But, of course, I've visited you in beautiful Paseky many times. Was it Marie's home town?

No. She came from a town called Pelhřimov, where her father was an executive chef. After the war, they moved to Paseky, where Marie's widowed grandmother married a businessman. Through him, she was able to buy the little hotel with a restaurant. Marie's parents went to work there. Paseky being a resort meant there was lots of work. Marie helped during summers when she came home from business school, where she was studying accounting. The communists had nationalized the hotel, and her parents were now just managers. Marie, as the daughter of former "bourgeois business owners," was admitted to business school only under the condition that she would "convert" to an attitude of sympathy for oppressed workers. She was allowed to leave the campus only on weekends and during the summer. We went to a movie two days after we met. It was love at first sight.

When and where did you go to work?

I went to work at the big aircraft company, Aero, about fifteen kilometers from Prague. I had a talent for languages and, in school, I had learned to speak Russian very well. In addition to working on the construction of MIG fighter planes at Aero, I taught Russian to other employees.

Did you have to join the Party to get and keep your job?

No, but not joining put my career on a very slow and very limited track. Everybody had to go before a commission regularly, where the chief communist asked questions. One improper answer could mean loss of job —or worse. The first time my turn came, I walked in and gave them their communist greeting. I sat and gave all the proper answers. The final question was: did I consider Egyptian president Gamal Abdel Nasser a democrat or a dictator? I had no idea what they wanted to hear. I started to say: "He's a ddddd…." My questioner helped me: "That's right, don't be afraid to say 'dictator'." I said: "Dictator," and I was out of there, still with a job. All this was very stressful, but I liked my job, and, for the first time, I had some money.

Does that mean you could now afford to get married?

Yes, but it didn't quite happen yet. We had compulsory military service, and I went in for two years. In the meantime, Maruška had graduated and was working in Jablonec, not far from her home in the mountains. Finally, in the fall of 1958, I went back to civilian life. We were married in two places: on December 20th at the little castle in Libeň and a day later in church in Paseky. Having a church wedding was extremely risky, and if the communists had found out, our careers would have been ruined. But, we're both Catholics, and we considered a marriage sacred. Having it officiated by some state flunky, rather than a priest, just wouldn't do. Luckily, no one informed on us. Marie moved to Prague, where we shared the apartment with my parents and my six-year-old brother. I went back to my old job and Marie worked in a savings bank. Over the next two years, I was able to obtain a degree, so my job was upgraded.

Living with your parents and brother must not have been much fun for anybody.

It wasn't. The only way to have a place of your own then was to buy it. There was no such thing as a rental apartment or house. And there was a long waiting list for apartments to buy. We started on the bottom of the list and finally got a place in 1962. It had a bedroom, a living room, a kitchen, a bathroom, and a toilet. We took out a thirty-year loan from the state. The day we moved in, we were given two flags, Czechoslovak and Soviet, with instructions as to when we should fly them from the window. There were informers in the building who made sure everyone complied.

Were you ever able to travel out of the country under the communists?

My first trip was on business, to Dresden, in East Germany. My communist boss allowed me to go there by bus and to bring Marie with me. It was a one-day round trip, for which we were allowed twenty German marks. But, I was thrilled to cross the border for the first time in my life. In 1965, Marie and I applied for a vacation in Yugoslavia. After a lot of bureaucratic stuff, we got permission. We drove our Škoda, with my brother in the back seat, of course. He was like our son. We had no money for hotels, so we camped out in a tent by the sea. It was marvelous! We returned to the same spot the following summer and met a couple from West Berlin. They invited us to visit them, something we considered impossible.

Were you ever able to take them up on their invitation?
Things were becoming better at home in 1967, and, miraculously, we were given permission to go. In May, we went. Of course, my brother went with us. It was a magical trip. We visited department stores, the likes of which we had never seen. We went to a concert by the Berlin Philharmonic. So, this was the west!! When we came back through Checkpoint Charlie, the American soldier at the border noted from Marie's passport that it was her birthday, May 15th. He smiled and wished her a happy birthday. She was thirty that day and had her first-ever conversation with an American!

Tell me about Prague Spring and the invasion that followed.
Things were looking so much better at home when we left for another Yugoslavia vacation in August 1968. After spending ten days there with our friends from West Berlin, we began the drive home. On the Yugoslav-Austria border, we were told by the guards that Czechoslovakia had been invaded by armies of the Warsaw Pact countries. It was August 21st. Not returning home was not an option. As always, we had my brother with us, and our parents were at home. So, we drove back to Prague.

How did the so-called "normalization" affect you?
In a way, we were lucky. They were "purifying" the Communist Party by throwing out members who had stepped out of line during Prague Spring and its "socialism with a human face." Since neither one of us was

a party member, they had no place to throw us *from*. I was called before a commission of "pure" communists and questioned. They asked me if I thought we had freedom. What was I to answer? Of course, I said "yes." So they let me live for a while yet.

Now, it would be another twenty-one years before the Velvet Revolution. It must not have been a very pleasant time.

Hey, you've got to make the best of what you have. In 1969, we managed to buy a 300-year-old house, actually a log cabin, in Paseky. It was cheap because it wasn't in very good condition. We buried ourselves in the project of fixing it up. There was no way to hire anyone to work on a privately-owned house, so we did everything with our own hands – the whole family, weekends, summer vacations, for twenty months. We were spending 500 Czech crowns a month on the project, and we didn't have the money. I got a license for teaching driving and worked this second job three days a week. Making that little cabin into our retirement home became the focus of our lives and was our escape from reality for years.

When was your daughter born?

Jitka was born in 1974. Both of us were older parents, but we were happy parents. My mother had died in 1971 and Marie's father a year later. Having a baby daughter helped us fill the void. Marie took a two-year maternity leave, during which the state paid her 500 crowns a month. I was making 2,000. In short, we were poor. I had to find a better-paying job.

Were you able to find one?

I was lucky to have a good friend who was a director at the headquarters of Czechoslovak Aircraft Industries. Since I wasn't a member of the Party, there would have been no way to get a job there without my friend's influence. I increased my salary by fifty percent. The office was about 200 meters from my old one, but the difference was huge. I left good friends who worked together as a team. Now, I was surrounded by politics, envy, and intrigue. I hated to come to work in the morning. But, because of the money, I stayed for twenty-two years! I traveled a lot, visited most European countries, but always without Marie and Jitka. That's how they made sure I always came back. I kept coming back. Finally, November 1989 arrived.

*Seeking to forget makes exile all the longer;
the secret of redemption lies in remembrance.*
Richard von Weizsaecker

CHAPTER 16

On the Wings of Denial

From the day we arrived in America, my parents made it clear to me that we were not going to discuss memories of Europe in our home. They did everything possible to convince me that the only things that mattered were being alive, being together, and resuming the lives we once had, now in a different country. If we were to have a future, we would have no history. They were determined that I must become totally assimilated in America and that I must do it without carrying any baggage from our difficult past. Perhaps they were trying to say that my European past could not be the defining experience of my life. Maybe they wanted my ignorance of my Jewish roots – a blindness that had been a shield against Nazi murderers – to be a buffer against bigotry in the Land of the Free, a nation which turned out to be not as tolerant as they had expected.

Mother and Papa would have been disappointed had they known that, throughout my adult life, I realized, albeit subliminally, that relatives on both sides of our family had been erased from this earth by German murderers. Though well-intentioned, my parents' actions and words prevented me from learning a great deal about my great-grandfather, great-uncles, great-aunts, grandparents, uncles, aunts, and cousins. It was as if I had never had any. They wanted to isolate me from the tragedies that they, themselves, had experienced and about which they did not want me to know. To oblige them, I forced myself to create a blank space in my memory, one which had once contained the story of the first nine years of my life. But, was I really successful? Or were the pieces always there, and I simply failed to put them together? I do not know and can only speculate.

✳ ✳ ✳

In December 1987, we celebrated my parents' fifty-third anniversary, followed a day later by Papa's seventy-seventh birthday. A week later, our family gathered for its traditional Christmas Eve dinner.

"I'm really happy that you're back in academia," my father said to me, while Mother and Sue prepared potato salad in the kitchen. "I don't have to worry about you beating your brains out anymore as an entrepreneur. Maybe you'll have time to enjoy life more now."

I had cashed out of my last company after eighteen years of starting and running entrepreneurial ventures, and I was now Director of Industrial Research at the University of Maryland. This pleased my parents because, despite (or, perhaps, because of) all the risks they had taken in their own lives, they were extremely risk-averse when it came to our family's economic well-being.

Unfortunately, Papa's feeling of tranquility did not last long. He had been battling heart disease for many years. A few days after the start of the new year, his New Jersey cardiologist called me on the phone.

"Your dad is on a downhill course," said Dr. Stelio Mangiola. "He needs open-heart surgery to replace a valve and to cut away a thickening heart muscle. There are only two surgeons in the country who are considered experts at this procedure."

He gave me the names of the two, and I immediately recognized that of Dr. Denton Cooley. He was world-famous for his pioneering work in heart transplants, and I had seen his photo on the covers of several national magazines. Ten days later, on my fifty-second birthday, Papa, Mother, and I were on our way to the Texas Heart Institute at St. Luke's Episcopal Hospital in Houston, Texas.

Cooley and his staff examined Papa and informed us that they would first perform a cardiac catheterization in order to analyze the situation and determine how to proceed. Mother and I were in Papa's room when they brought him back from the operating room. He was exhausted and weak; his feet and hands were a deathly white from lack of circulation. I rubbed his toes and Mother warmed his fingers while we waited for the doctors. Finally, two of Cooley's associates came in. They informed us that the catheterization had revealed "a severe outflow tract obstruction in his heart due to myocardial hypertrophy." Consequently, Dr. Cooley decided to perform open-heart surgery in two days. Concerned, I asked the older of the two physicians to step out into the hall, out of Mother's hearing range.

"Doctor, did you look at my father? I'm no expert, but he is too weak to be operated on so soon," I said. "I think he needs several days of rest before he'll be strong enough to undergo major surgery."

"I'll speak with Dr. Cooley and get back to you."

An hour later, he returned with the verdict.

"Dr. Cooley sees no problem. He's going ahead with the surgery on the twenty-seventh."

"But, Dr. Cooley himself told me that, because of my father's age and condition, the probability of success of the operation was only seventy-five percent," I said. "Doesn't my father's weakness and exhaustion make that probability even lower?"

"Dr. Cooley has done dozens such surgeries. He's the expert. Leave it to him," he told me.

I said nothing about my concerns to Mother when we checked into the hotel next door to the hospital. Her nerves were already on edge and she did not need additional worries. Two days later, on January 27, 1988, Mother and I spent an excruciating three hours in the waiting room while Cooley and his team operated. Finally, one of the assistants appeared.

"The surgery was a success," he announced. "We replaced the valve and cut away a portion of the muscle. He'll be recovering for the next several hours. Go to your hotel, relax, and we'll call you when you can see him."

Buoyed by the report, Mother and I returned to our adjoining rooms to wait for the call. When several hours passed by and none came, I phoned the hospital. I was told that my father's condition had "deteriorated somewhat and there had been cardiac arrest." I should keep checking on a regular basis. I reported the disturbing news to Mother, and now, after the early encouragement, both of us were petrified. I called every hour and each time received the same report: "no change." The uncertainty and anxiety brought back memories of my childhood and waiting six years for Papa to come back from the war. That empty space in my memory was filling up quickly.

We had a few bites of room-service dinner as we continued the vigil. At three in the morning, we agreed to try to get a couple of hours' sleep. As the sun came up, I resumed my calls; there had been no change. Finally, at ten o'clock in the morning, the phone in Mother's room rang. Hoping to hear encouraging news, I grabbed the receiver.

"Dr. Heller," said the woman on the other end. "I'm terribly sorry to tell you that your father passed away a few minutes ago."

Mother and I held one another for a very long time and cried. At last, we gathered ourselves and walked to the hospital, where a nurse led us into a cold, white, antiseptic room with several beds. One of the beds held a body covered with a white sheet. The nurse pulled back the sheet to reveal Papa's face. He was pale, but looked at peace. His mouth seemed to form the beginnings of a smile.

"Goodbye, Papa. I love you," I whispered, as I kissed his cold lips. The blood rushed from my head, I became lightheaded and felt that I was about to faint. *"You can't do this,"* I scolded myself. *"You must take care of Mother. You've got to be strong!"*

With the room seeming to be orbiting around me, I sat down and held Mother's hand as she gave her beloved Rudy a final kiss. I watched through my tears as my devout Catholic mother made a tiny cross with her right thumb on my Jewish father's forehead.

"Can we leave, please?" she asked.

The flight back to New Jersey seemed interminably long. Mother's eyes were closed throughout the trip. No doubt, she was awake and reliving her life with Papa and trying to visualize how she was going to be able to go on without him. My thoughts now alternated between sorrow and anger. At the hospital in Houston, I had read a magazine with a portrait of Denton Cooley on the cover and with a scorecard containing a record of his successful heart surgeries. I imagined that my father's operation already had been entered in the "win column" of his record. After all, the valve replacement had been accomplished and thus Rudolph Heller would be just another positive statistic for the renowned doctor, despite the fact that my precious father would be lost to us forever. I had warned Cooley's team about Papa's weakened condition, and they had ignored me. Now, the thought of filing a medical malpractice suit crossed my mind. But, before the airplane's wheels touched down in Newark, I dismissed the thought. Legal action would only prolong Mother's agony, and I knew that making her life as easy as possible would be my primary duty for the next few months. Moreover, I recalled that one of Papa's biggest problems with his adopted country was what he called "a sue-the-bastard attitude" – Americans' propensity for litigation. He would not approve of me jumping on this bandwagon.

I had no idea how to handle the funeral service. Throughout his life, Papa had no connection to any organized religion. He had not attended synagogue, and he had not belonged to any Jewish organization. During nearly forty years in America, my parents had never discussed with friends and acquaintances Papa's Jewish roots. Thus, I thought Mother would reject my idea that we should "go public" by having a rabbi preside over the service. To my surprise, she agreed. I found the phone number of a local synagogue in the Yellow Pages, called, and was introduced to a rabbi who agreed to officiate.

I composed a eulogy which I planned to read at Papa's service at Somerset Hills Memorial Park in Basking Ridge, New Jersey, where my parents had purchased notches and urns to hold their ashes. But then I realized that I could not go through with it without breaking down, and I simply gave my written speech to the rabbi to use in his own eulogy for a man whom he had never met. I was sitting with Mother, Sue, and David in the front row and listened to him read it, when I was struck by two sudden realizations.

The more startling one was that I had never dealt with death before and had not attended the funeral of <u>anyone</u> in my family. Other than my maternal great-grandmother Louisa, who passed away when I was a baby, not a single person in the Heller or Neumann family who had lived during my lifetime, had died a natural death. Every single one – at least fifteen of them! – had been murdered by the Nazis in some far-off place. Rather than being honored at the ends of their lives, their bodies had been thrown into ovens or mass-burial holes in the ground. I closed my eyes and saw the faces of those who had been closest to me: *Děda* – my grandfather Artur; *Strejda* – my great-uncle Ota; and *Dědeček* – my best friend and great-grandfather Gustav. I could sense their presence in the stark, cold chapel, and a feeling of guilt came over me because their departures from this world had been so undignified.

"It's all right, Otíčku," Dědeček seemed to be whispering to me. *"Now, at least you're honoring your father properly and recognizing his achievements, his heroism, and his love of family."*

My second realization was that this would be the first time that the great majority of our extended family and friends in attendance would discover that there was a Jewish side to our family. Papa's funeral marked the beginning of my questioning of my own personal burial of this fact for so many years. For now, I was preoccupied with thoughts and memories of my life with my parents, but the seed of new thinking about my past denial had been planted.

Much to my surprise, the discovery that Papa had been born Jewish did not seem to matter one bit to those who had attended his memorial service. In the coming weeks, I paid very close attention to any changes in their behaviors or attitudes toward me. I was amazed to find that they treated me just the same as they had in the past.

I had great difficulties handling the emotional stress of having lost my father and the nonstop pain it caused me. But, I had to be strong for Mother, just as she had been strong for me throughout my youth. I was lucky to have Sue by my side; she not only helped me keep my wits about me, but she cared for Mother with great tenderness. I paused in my relentless, selfish, pursuit of career and personal pleasure, and became more introspective. I thought more and more about my parents and admired their strength, courage, and their ability to adapt without looking back and to appreciate the unconditional love and support they had always given me. I had wondered often why my mother and father were so different from other immigrants who had suffered at the hands of the Nazis and why they were able to provide me with a normal life while I was growing up. Rightly or wrongly, I came upon an explanation that, perhaps, it was because they had *fought* the Nazis, rather than being among the herds led to slaughter. A harsh, and perhaps unfair, conclusion; it was the only rationale I could find.

The fact that I spent a great deal of my time traveling on business by car throughout the Mid-Atlantic region was both a blessing and a curse. My cocoon provided me with the isolation I needed from the world as I mourned my father's passing. I had long conversations with him while hurtling down some six-lane interstate highway. I asked his advice on personal and business matters, and, just as he had when he was alive, he gave me the guidance I sought.

It was in the darkness of night, when returning home from my frequent late meetings, that the past came rushing back at me. As I drove, I recalled wartime horrors and deaths. I wondered how my parents had managed to deal with these memories. After all, Papa had spent six years in combat as a British soldier after a harrowing narrow escape from the Nazis, and all the time had lived with the dread that all of us might be dead. Mother had been tortured by the Gestapo, was imprisoned in a slave labor camp, and spent the war protecting me from deportation to a death camp. After being apart for six years, and discovering that no other

Hellers or Neumanns had survived the war, they were driven into exile by Czechoslovakia's post-war communist regime. Once again, this time in a strange new country, they had to pick up the pieces and start from nothing. After all they had endured, how did they manage to have so much to give and to be so "normal," living lives not dissimilar to those of their unscathed American neighbors on a leafy suburban street in New Jersey? I was in awe of both of them. They had been like two beautiful wildflowers, blooming wherever their seeds had been blown.

With Papa's passing, I came to realize that now I was "the man" in our family. With this came not only new responsibilities, but also a sense of duty to preserve our family story and to pass it to our son David and, ultimately, to his children. But first I had to rid myself of the remnants of denial which still haunted me.

Fortunately, I was at a stage in my life wherein I had achieved some success, and even a bit of fame. This gave me enough confidence in myself to "come clean" – slowly and in bits and pieces to family and friends, more quickly and totally to my own self. As this process evolved, I began to put together the puzzle pieces of the Heller/Neumann family history for the first time.

Emerging from the long period of denial, it was the memory of Gustav Neumann, my great-grandfather *Dědeček*, that haunted me most. *Dědeček* was my friend, my companion, my mentor, and I loved him as much as a young boy can love another human being. Before the war, when I was only three, he took me on long walks in the woods and told me stories about faraway places he had visited. When the Germans took away our factory and our home, he was my only human companion, while Mother toiled in the fields seven days a week and I was not allowed outside the farm walls. He caressed my little hand with his long, calloused fingers and told me how wonderful life would be when our oppressors would be driven out and how I would become a famous explorer whose name would be known throughout the world. I was devastated when the Nazis took him away from me.

Now, I thought about *Dědeček* and our other family victims every day. There were times when I found myself thinking that, perhaps, *Dědeček* had not really died. Despite the fact that he would be well over a hundred years old, I daydreamed that he was wandering around the world looking for me. When I stopped dreaming, I realized that, not only was this physically impossible, but the Nazis' immaculate recordkeeping documented the fact that he had been murdered in the Treblinka death camp. To me, he was a kind, loving, generous friend. To the Germans, he was just another old Jew to be exterminated like some insect. I screamed silently when I read Adolf Eichmann's testimony in an Israeli court about his visit to Treblinka. He described seeing naked Jews being chased by SS men with dogs, whips and clubs through narrow passages between barbed-wire fences to the gas chambers. The Germans called this *Himmelstrasse* ("Street to Heaven"). I wondered if *Dědeček* had been one of the poor souls this murderer had watched with bemusement. And I shed tears of sorrow and loathing when I imagined how the Ukrainian guards at the door enjoyed seeing this once-distinguished and dignified gentleman enter the chamber before they turned the valve for the gas that took his life.

When we first came to America, frequent dreams of the Second World War had filled my nights with terror. As time passed, these nightmares diminished and, eventually, disappeared altogether. But, for children of wars, residual scars never go away. After all the years, war-related fears and nightmares, sleep disturbances, bed-wetting, reactions to explosions, and the fear of bombs raining down on crystal-clear days were gone. I may have had a mild case of Post-Traumatic Stress Disorder for a few years, but life in the United States had provided the cure. But now, thoughts of my great-grandfather and other lost relatives, as well as my own wartime experiences were back. Occasionally, they came as nightmares. By day, they came at unexpected times and under various circumstances. On the street, I would see a gray-haired man with a beard and wire-rim glasses and think that *Dědeček* had found me. In the middle of a business meeting, I would recall the time I ventured outside the farm wearing the Star of David, only to be stoned by kids who had once been my friends. On television, I would see a film about the Holocaust, and I would think about the aunts, uncles, and cousins I no longer had. The incidents came to me as pieces of the puzzle of a proud family history, one which – since the awakening I had experienced upon my father's death – I would no longer deny.

The past is never dead.
It's not even past.
William Faulkner

CHAPTER 17

Coming Full Circle

I discovered that one cannot travel far enough to get away from oneself. November 1989 and Czechoslovakia's Velvet Revolution proved once again that, while there had been no flame of Czech patriotism in my heart, a small pilot light must have been burning somewhere in my soul the entire time. I found myself mesmerized and thrilled, watching on TV as thousands of Czechs held keys above their heads and jangled them like small bells to symbolize the end of communist rule. They rang in freedom on Prague's Wenceslas Square and shouted "Havel to the Castle!" as the smiling playwright, former dissident, and now president-to-be, Václav Havel, waved back from a balcony.

With the exception of a few short weeks in 1968, freedom had been dead for forty-one years in the land of Jan Hus, Tomáš Garrigue Masaryk, and Edvard Beneš. *"Byla tma,"* Czechoslovaks said. "It was dark." No longer now.

The transition from totalitarian communism to freedom had taken ten years in Poland and ten months in Hungary. In Czechoslovakia, it took ten days. My personal transition took less than ten minutes, while Havel spoke words so eloquent and so full of hope that unexpectedly, I felt my past come rushing at me through the opening in the lifted Iron Curtain. I experienced an unexpected surge of pride in my native country and a sudden need to reconnect and reconcile with it. Only, I did not know how.

Then, out of the blue, Czechoslovakia found me. In early 1990, I received an engraved invitation to attend a roundtable discussion at its embassy in Washington. It happened to coincide with a visit from Mother, who was living in New Jersey, and I accepted on behalf of both of us. Rita Klímová, the ambassador, was battling cancer at the time, and her place as host was taken by Irena Zíková, an embassy official who had been Mrs. Havel's interpreter during her husband's triumphant tour of the United States following his election as the first president of the newly-democratic Czechoslovakia.

While various Czech and Slovak officials spoke glowingly and optimistically about their country's near-term prospects, Irena presented a more realistic and pragmatic view of a nation whose economy, environment, infrastructure, morale and morals had been devastated by forty-one years of communism.

"It will be difficult to change our socialist system to a market economy," she told the gathering. "The air is polluted and many buildings are ready to fall down. Thousands of Czechs and Slovaks have no concept of doing business in an honest manner."

Mother and I were impressed by her un-European candor. During the reception which followed the speechmaking, we sought out Irena to compliment her. This led to a long conversation during which we learned each other's family stories. We found out that her husband Oldřich (known as Dick by his English-speaking friends), had studied at Oxford during the Prague Spring period, that their daughter Alena had dreams of becoming a commercial pilot, and that their son Jan hoped to study for an MBA at an American university. Having developed immediate rapport with Irena, we promised to stay in touch.

She took the first step by calling me a few weeks later to inform me that the Czechoslovak government had passed a law of restitution, which might make it possible for us to regain possession of our clothing factory in Kojetice, our apartment building in Prague, and various smaller homes and properties which had belonged to our family. Irena promised to put me on the mailing list to receive information as the details were worked out. Soon, I received the pertinent materials in the mail. The package included a long list of English-speaking lawyers in Czechoslovakia, recommended to guide the claimants through the tedious process. I called Irena to ask for her advice.

"Don't contact any of those lawyers," she instructed. "The government had to pick those who hadn't been members of the Communist Party. This means that all of them are young and inexperienced. Don't forget that we're still a corrupt society, where connections and bribes are the legacy of socialism. I'll get you a lawyer who knows how to work the system."

She explained that she had a friend named Jiří Bedrna, a former schoolmate, who had been a municipal judge during communist rule. As such, he had the necessary connections. He was working with his daughter, Lucie, a recent law school graduate, in private practice. His son, Michal, would join the family firm after completing his law studies. Recovering our Czech properties had never crossed the minds of my parents or me as even the most remote possibility. Thus, I felt lukewarm about the idea of starting the restitution process. Mother was even less enthusiastic. To succeed in America, my family had severed its emotional, as well as fiscal, ties to the old country. Our assimilation was complete, and we felt no need to open old wounds. After a few days of soul-searching, I thanked Irena and told her that Mother and I had no interest in pursuing the return of our properties.

However, all that changed a few weeks later because my boss and friend, Dr. Rudolph Lamone, Dean of the Smith School of Business at the University of Maryland, had a better insight into my heart than I had. From our conversations, he recognized my need to return to Prague. Pretending that it was important to the University, he arranged for me to attend the first major conference on doing business in the "new" Czechoslovakia. To convince me that the trip had value to the business school, Rudy registered to attend along with me. Unbeknownst to me, he had no intention of going and cancelled at the last moment. Quite simply, he was doing a friend a favor.

Since I would be going to Czechoslovakia anyway, I began to rethink the idea of attempting to get back property which was rightfully ours. I contemplated the financial loss suffered by my parents when they chose to start with nothing in America over living under totalitarian rule. A clothing factory, a seven-story office building in Prague, several houses and building lots might be worth millions of dollars. The communists had stolen the factory prior to our escape, and, like the Nazis before them, they took the rest after we escaped. Yet, Sue, David and I were comfortable financially, and my father had made certain that Mother would be well off after his passing. We had little economic incentive to try to get back what had once been ours.

However, two personal traits which have defined my life, competitiveness and an elephant's memory for misdeeds and injustices committed against me or my family, won out over material needs.

"The bastards robbed us of everything we had," I said to myself after a great deal of procrastination. *"I'm going after them!"*

I informed Mother of my intentions. She wished me luck, but made certain that I understood that she was unwilling to rekindle her own painful memories.

"You're on your own," she told me. "I'm the heir to all this, but I'll assign everything to you. I'll be rooting for you, but please keep me out of it."

Promising to fulfill her wish, I marched off into battle. Nothing less than getting the properties back, or at least receiving some form of restitution, no matter how small, would satisfy my need for revenge for the crimes committed against the Heller/Neumann family by Czech communists and their Soviet friends. I called Irena Zíková and set the wheels in motion. I was going on the attack.

* * *

On October 20, 1990, my first night in Prague, after sitting in my room and fighting jet lag, I decided to go for a walk, despite the fact that it was nearly midnight and I had not slept in more than twenty-four hours. Once outside the Hotel Diplomat, I felt as if a magnet was pulling me in a single direction. It drew me toward *Hradčany*, the Castle on the hill above Prague which has been home to kings and presidents for hundreds of years. The Castle's panorama is dominated by a great cathedral, whose soaring spires have served as inspiration for the Czech nation's writers, poets, composers, and exiles.

As I walked up the narrow streets toward *Hradčany*, I noticed that the small, baroque, hundreds-of-years-old, houses were gray. Strange, because I remembered them having had bright colors, mostly yellow and beige, when I was a kid. Under the dim light of street lamps, I could see that the stucco façades were filthy, shabby, and crumbling. Like everything which had no immediate utility to them and their party, the communists had allowed my city to fall apart.

"<u>My</u> city?" I startled myself. "*Did I really say that?*"

Strangely, for someone accustomed to fearing dark streets in America, I felt completely safe here. At the top of the hill, I walked past two guards and through the courtyard of the presidential palace. Suddenly, I was brought back to that magic day in 1945, when I had stood here with my parents, small Czechoslovak flag in my hand, waving to President Beneš, who had appeared in the second-story window on his first day home from World War II exile. Now, I ducked into a passageway illuminated only by light coming through a glass door. The words on the door identified it as *Kancelář Prezidenta ČSFR* (Office of the President of the Czechoslovak Federal Republic). "*Wow!*" I said to myself. "*Can you imagine getting this close to President George H. W. Bush's office, especially all alone and at night?*" This was becoming a new experience. Or was it *déjà vu?*

Emerging from the passageway, I was overwhelmed by the sight of St. Vitus Cathedral, the spiritual center of the nation for six hundred years. The burial place of former Czech kings and home of the crown jewels, the Gothic tower soared toward the night sky. As I stood there alone and stared at the statues of saints looking down at me, I felt as if I had been struck by lightning. *"How much these old gentlemen of stone have seen! Just in my fifty-four years of life, how much oppression have they observed?"* I counted the years of freedom in my lifetime: 1936, 1937, 1938, 1945, 1946, 1947, and now 1990. *"Only seven years out of my entire life! Incredible! How could God let this happen to one small country?"*

I dropped to my knees and began to weep, uncontrollably and for a very long time, alone in this sacred place. I cried for my country, for my fellow Czechs, for my murdered family, for my exiled parents, for the friends I had left behind, for myself.

When, finally, I got up and made my way back from the Castle, I was shocked by the metamorphosis I had just experienced. I realized that I had not succeeded in erasing my childhood memories after all. I had only hidden them from myself. I also knew that now, this trip would be a pilgrimage. For the first time, I wanted to connect with my past in every way possible.

* * *

My visits to Prague became more frequent as I got deeply involved in the training of Czechoslovak businesspeople about life in a free-market economy. At the same time, with the help of our attorney, Jiří Bedrna, and good friend Jitka Thomasová, I continued to recover our family's properties.

On one of these subsequent trips, I visited Josefov, now one of Prague's major tourist attractions, but originally the ghetto which isolated the city's Jews from the rest of the population. Located in the Old Town, the area is surrounded by a high wall and contains a medieval cemetery, synagogues, and a town hall with a clock on a roof gable, famous for the fact that the hands run counterclockwise, following the Hebrew lettering, which is read from right to left. The Nazis had planned a museum in Josefov, recording the history of what they had intended to be the "extinct Jewish race." Ironically, this unfulfilled plan brought about the preservation of treasures, religious objects, and furnishings, which had been confiscated from synagogues throughout the Protectorate. But, I did not go to Josefov to view a tourist attraction. I had heard that the Pinkas Synagogue and Ceremonial Hall now housed a memorial to Czech victims of the Holocaust.

I walked into a sunlit corridor where, on both sides, and as far as the eye could see, names were painted on walls, in the manner of Washington's Vietnam Memorial. There were 77,297 names of Jewish men, women, and children from the Czech lands who perished in the death camps, listed by towns or villages which had been their homes. I rushed to find Kojetice, Kralupy, Luboč. My shaking index finger traced the names: Gustav Neumann, Otilie Hellerová, Emil Neumann, ... My gaze returned to the village of Kojetice, where I searched for "Heller, Ota Karel" – my former name – as my mind played a bizarre trick on me, perhaps reminding me that, but for the bravery of a few people and the grace of God, I could have disappeared up an Auschwitz chimney and into the sky which would have become my cemetery.

Of course, my name was not inscribed on the memorial wall. Yet, I was dealing with demons. Overcome by grief, guilt, and shame, I rushed back to my hotel room. There, I let go of a burden which I had carried for many years deep in my soul. I wept not only out of sadness over the fate of my great-grandfather, grandparents, uncles, aunts, and cousins who had perished at the hands of the Nazis, but from shame for having desecrated their memories by having denied my roots for such a long time. Unlike me, their own kin, at last someone had noted publicly that these members of my family had existed as living, breathing human beings on this earth.

* * *

Over the next few days, I walked the streets of Prague, often with Mother's best friend from years past, Aša Hahnová, the wonderful lady whom I called *Teta* (Aunt). I delighted in hearing the sound of the Czech language, particularly when spoken by children. When I spotted them pouring out of school doors, I stopped, listened, and laughed along with them. Hearing my native language spoken by innocent children was like a concerto emanating from the strings of Itzhak Perlman's violin. The sight and sound transported me back to another time, a time when my boyhood best friend, Vlád'a Svoboda, and I had roamed the streets of Prague after school. Now, I found that my vocabulary was still that of a twelve-year-old. That, after all, was when my Czech language development had ended. But I listened and I understood.

I could not get enough of Czech beer and food. Sitting in pubs with my distant cousin, Sylva, and her friends, drinking my favorite brews, *Plzeňské* (Pilsner) and *Velkopopovický kozel*, brought back memories of stealing sips from a pitcher while delivering my parents' dinner beverage from the tavern across the street from our Prague apartment. Late nights in dark, historic wine cellars, where friends taught me how to make music by rubbing my wet index finger around the circumference of my glass, brought back scenes of Papa teaching me tricks with coasters when I sat with him while he and Mother drank wine, perhaps in the same cellars. Then, there was *svíčková*, that fabulous national dish consisting of thinly-sliced beef topped with sour cream and served with cranberries and *knedliky* – those incredibly delicious Czech dumplings! To Aunt Aša's utter amazement, I ordered *svíčková* in every restaurant we visited, for lunch or dinner.

Seeing familiar buildings and streets in Prague, too, gave me a sense of belonging. I had been robbed of my heritage, but now this beautiful city in the heart of Europe seemed to be saying, "Welcome home, prodigal son. You're still my son." Franz Kafka learned of her power long ago, when he wrote:

"Prague does not let go – either of you or me. This little mother has claws. There is nothing to do but to give in. We would have to set her on fire from both sides…only thus could we free ourselves."

***

After returning home from that first trip to free Czechoslovakia, I struggled silently with my identity and belonging. Had I really become assimilated in America? Was I American or Czech? Could I be both? Most disturbingly, I wondered how I, an educated and well-read person, could not have understood much sooner that the reason for the destruction of most of my family by the Germans had not been the party-line mantra which had been drummed into me: Papa fighting against the Germans with the Allied forces. How could I not have known that the real reason had been the fact that the majority of the Heller-Neumann family had been Jewish?

I began to doubt my own honesty. Could I have really considered myself such a "pure" Catholic that I never gave any thought to my Jewish heritage and genetic pool? Or was this a cop-out I had designed such that I could practice deception with a clear conscience? Did I suppress this information from myself and everyone around me because I was afraid of being tainted and stigmatized, and having my image tarnished, by those drops of Jewish blood? If they had known about my Jewishness, would Sue's parents have permitted her to marry me? Would I have ever stepped onto Oklahoma State University's basketball court? Would I have been admitted into clubs and societies? Would those who became my friends, be my friends? Unexpectedly, after years of being self-assured and even somewhat smug about my successes in America, I began to have doubts about myself, my motives, my integrity.

Perhaps because my training as an engineer has always prompted me to deal with issues in a logical and systematic manner, I began to intellectualize my way out of this dilemma. I came to grips with the fact that, although I had suppressed the knowledge, probably I had understood my Jewishness all along and this awareness had been a hidden source of insecurity and fear throughout my adult life. But, now having recognized it, how should I deal with the guilt which remained?

A visit to Prague which had started as a business trip and turned into a pilgrimage already had helped me end years of denial. Now, another work-related journey would bring my feelings of guilt to an end.

I was a member of a technology trade mission to Israel – my first visit to that country. The second day there was free of meetings, and I chose to visit two places: Yad Vashem in the morning and Jerusalem Old City in the afternoon. At Yad Vashem, I walked up the Avenue of the Righteous and along the way read the names of many of the Righteous: 5,500 European Christians who had risked, and sometimes lost, their lives to save Jews from the Nazis. A tree had been planted in honor of each of them along the Avenue. I searched for a tree honoring our family's heroic, Righteous, Slovak friends, the Šrámeks, but failed to find it.

I entered the Holocaust Museum. Once inside, I struggled unsuccessfully to hold back tears as I stared at photos of bearded Jews being slapped by German soldiers, naked women being herded into showers of gas, dead bodies being thrown onto piles of other skeletal figures. I was overcome with grief when I rounded a corner and suddenly came upon a group of Israeli soldiers. They were swarthy young men and women in uniform, with Uzis strapped to their backs, and they were listening intently to their guide. A force seemed to pull me toward them. I could not understand the guide's Hebrew lecture, but I did not need to. The sight of the soldiers mesmerized me. They were strong, good-looking, athletic – and tough. I looked from one to the other and felt a strange sense of pride and tranquility. I wiped my eyes and managed a smile.

"*It will never happen again,*" I said to myself. Just like the Israelis of biblical times, these Sabras would stand up to any enemy and fight. They would not be led to slaughter like their relatives and mine during the Second World War. As I walked away and back down the Avenue of the Righteous, I felt a kinship with those soldiers. When I got into the cab which had been waiting for me, I sensed a similar connection to the Israeli driver. I felt relief. I was among people from whom I did not have to hide my ethnic background. In the days that would follow, I would meet Israelis to whom I could tell my entire story – the unabridged version, rather than the party-line rendition. They would understand because their own stories would be similar.

Now, I walked through a gate into the Old City of Jerusalem. I stopped at the Western Wall, where I inserted between the stones a note in memory of my Jewish father. I crossed to the east side of the city and began to walk along the *Via Dolorosa* (the Way of Suffering), following in the footsteps of Jesus. Despite the hordes of tourists with their ever-present digital cameras and Jewish and Arab merchants hawking souvenirs, I imagined that I was walking along with Jesus, helping him carry the cross from the place where he had been sentenced to death, to the spot where his mother Mary came out of the crowd to see him, and finally to the place where the Romans had nailed him to the cross.

There, in the Church of the Holy Sepulcher, I thought about Christ's sacrifice and wondered what he would think about the horrors people have imposed upon each other, in the name of religion, over the centuries. Catholics against Jews in the Crusades, Catholics against Jews and Muslims in the Inquisition, Jews against Muslims in Palestine, Protestants against Catholics in Northern Ireland, Muslims against Hindus in Kashmir, Muslims against Christians in Sudan, Sunnis against the Shia in Iraq. I contemplated the perversity of the notion that God favors one religious group over another. After all, if God is everywhere, he touches all of us; if God is not everywhere, then he is not God.

It was here in the heart of a Jewish country, but at the Christian religion's most sacred spot, a place where Roman soldiers had murdered a Jew who was the Son of God, that I made peace with my feelings of guilt. I thought about my parents and how they, one a Christian and the other a Jew, had lived their lives according to the teachings of this Son of God as well as Judaic ethical teachings, despite the injustice and intolerance to which they had been subjected.

I became aware that Rudolph and Ilona Heller, without having verbalized it, had been instructing me that true achievement as a human being does not come from following some dogmas or rituals, or fitting into some Christian or Jewish mold. They had been teaching me to live the best I can under circumstances that require more of me than I think I can give.

Although we did not speak of him in our home, it was understood that God will judge us, not by the church or synagogue we attend, but by our actions. They had been instilling in me the idea of being spiritual – living my life as a decent human being and treating others fairly and humanely – rather than being "religious."

In a rare moment of clarity, I realized that it made not one iota of difference whether I was a Christian or a Jew. Or both. Or neither. Although I recognized the fact that I would continue to search my soul, perhaps for the rest of my life, I felt a new-found peace and self-confidence. I knew that, going forward, there would be no hiding of my background and ethnicity and that I would take great pride in telling the whole story of the Czech-American, Jewish-Catholic, Heller-Neumann family, even as my journey to self-discovery continues.

When I stand before God at the end of my life, I would hope that I would not have
a single bit of talent left, and could say, "I used everything you gave me."
Erma Bombeck

EPILOGUE

Only three years after the Velvet Revolution came the Velvet Divorce. Czechs and Slovaks, who had been brought together in 1918 in a shotgun marriage of two very different cultures, decided to split. In a peaceful, albeit painful, transaction, Czechoslovakia came to an end, to be replaced by the Czech Republic (which included Bohemia and Moravia) and the Slovak Republic.

Through the restitution process, and by suing the Communist Party of the Czech Republic, I managed to win back our factory in Kojetice and our building in Prague, and to receive minor monetary awards for the remainder of our family's properties in our native land. Although Mother chose to stay out of the negotiations and machinations except when absolutely necessary, she gained some satisfaction from getting back what was rightfully ours.

As she approached her ninetieth birthday, Mother was much more comfortable in her role as matriarch of an expanding family in America. She doted on her only grandson, David, and she gave her enthusiastic approval to his choice of Elizabeth Roberta "Bobbi" Bass as his wife. When David and Bobbi gave her three great-grandchildren – Sam, Sarah, and Caroline – Mother felt fulfilled.

Then, on the morning of the ninth of February 2006, I received a terrifying phone call from the Heritage Harbour therapy center in Annapolis, where Mother had been rehabilitating after a hospital stay.

"Your mother went for a walk in the hall this morning and, when she returned to her room, she had a massive stroke."

When I arrived, Mother was being loaded into an ambulance. I was able to catch only a brief glimpse of her impassive face before the doors shut. I could barely see through my tears while following the ambulance to Anne Arundel Medical Center. I sat with Mother for some time in her room, praying for a miracle. But, the only sign of life was the gentle rising and falling of the white sheet covering her body and the graph of her heartbeat on the monitor above her bed.

Soon, Sue, David, and Bobbi arrived. We sat looking at one another without speaking. Finally, Bobbi stood up and walked to the head of Mother's bed.

"Grandma," she said. "Only you could look beautiful lying in a hospital bed."

At that moment, I loved my daughter-in-law more than ever.

The following day, Mother was moved to Room 535. In the afternoon, a kind Indian lady doctor spoke to me about Mother's condition and chances. First, she gave me her official medical opinion: Mother had had a major stroke, she was paralyzed on the right side from the waist up, and she could not speak, eat or drink. Then she touched my shoulder, moved her softened face close to mine, and lowered her voice.

"If things don't improve, let go," she said.

I continued my vigil the next day. All day, I sat next to Mother, watching her face. I recalled my father's reaction each time we came upon a hurdle which seemed too high to cross: "We beat the Nazis, and we beat the communists. We're going to beat this, too." After all that Mother had overcome in her life, I was certain that she would weather this storm. I knew that, suddenly, her eyes would open and she would speak to me.

"Hi, Charlie." Or, perhaps she would revert to our native Czech and the name I had left behind: "*Ahoj, Oto!*"

But, her face remained impassive, even while her heart continued to beat. I had never before attempted to write poetry, but my sadness moved me to do so on that day.

Flowers burst forth from pictures on beige walls,
A mosaic dragonfly relieves the grayness of the floor.
The bed stands a marvel of our electronic age
With switches and chords controlling comfort.
I sit on a colorful settee, surrounded by plush leather chairs
By a window with a view of the Maryland countryside.

In many ways, 535 resembles an upscale hotel room
Even with room service available at the touch of a button.
But, any comparison between Room 535 and one in a Ritz-Carlton
Ends with its physical ambience.
Room 535 is one of the saddest places I have known
Because here my beautiful mother lies dying.

Despite the kind doctor's advice, I was not prepared to let go. Mother and I had been together for seventy years. She had nurtured me throughout the war and suffered torture and harassment in order to protect me from the Nazis. She gave up wealth and comfort and opted to live in refugee camps, rather than live under communism. She worked the most menial jobs when we came to America, so that I could lead the life of a normal American boy. She overcame the terrible grief of my father's death and chose to live a lonely life in the only house my parents had owned in their adopted country. She was the most elegant, kind, and beautiful lady I had ever known. My love for her knew no bounds.

Yet, Mother was not improving in the hospital. On Valentine's Day, February 14, 2006, after consulting with the doctors and my family, I made the most difficult decision of my life – to let go. "Letting go" had a specific meaning in the medical world. All "heroic" attempts to keep her alive would be stopped, and she would be kept as pain-free as possible until the end. In the next few days, in my darkest moments, I kept accusing myself of sentencing Mother to death by starvation. My despair left me unable to function.

But, Mother had one surprise left for us. After being moved from the hospital to a sad place called FutureCare, she began to improve. She became more alert, took in a bit of food each day, and, although unable to communicate, she made repeated attempts to speak with us. She displayed her old feistiness when she became frustrated by the fact that Sue and I could not understand her. Once, she slapped my arm to demonstrate her anger.

We began to rethink the "care-and-comfort" mode, and we discussed restarting various medications. At the same time, we settled in for what we were told might be many months of rehabilitation. Doctors and nurses advised us that we needed to get on with our lives while Mother recuperated. Eager to accept this as good news, Sue and I decided not to cancel a three-day golf trip to Florida. Calls to FutureCare each day were encouraging. On Monday, Mother began physical therapy. On Tuesday, she even took three steps – a miracle, we were told.

When we landed at BWI airport on Wednesday evening, we felt that our decision to "get a life" for three days had been a good one. But then I spoke with Bobbi on the phone.

"Grandma didn't look good, and she didn't respond to me," our daughter-in-law told me about her visit that afternoon.

When Sue and I came to Mother's room on Thursday morning, she did not seem to recognize us. Despite this apparent setback, the staff tried physical therapy again after we left. I returned in the afternoon. As I prepared to leave Mother's room at 4:15 pm, I had the feeling that the end was near, and I said a sad "goodbye" to her.

During her time in the hospital, I had begged God on many occasions to please end Mother's suffering and frustration, without success. This time, when I got into my car in the FutureCare parking lot, with tears streaming down my face, I screamed at God.

"Please stop this! She doesn't deserve this!" This time, God heard me.

At 7:16 the following morning, March 3, 2006, my bedside phone rang. I knew what was coming. The impersonal female voice at the other end said:

"I regret to inform you that your mother took her last breath at 6:29 this morning."

Mother's service was held on March 6, 2006, at the Barranco Funeral Home in Severna Park, Maryland. Many friends and family members came to say "goodbye." Sadly, her best friend, Dr. Jane Emele, was ill and in a convalescent home in Florida, and we kept the news from her. Our friend Henry Green, pastor of the First Baptist Church in Annapolis, whom I asked to lead the service, convinced me that I needed to give the eulogy, despite my conviction that I could not get through the ordeal. I read:

Thank you all for coming to help us celebrate my mother's life. I am overwhelmed by the number of you who came. This was totally unexpected. We chose this small, humble room for the service for three reasons. One, to make it convenient for Mother's good friends… Two, because Mother has not lived here too long, and thus there aren't that many people in our area who know her. And three, because Mother, though a very fine, accomplished lady, was very humble, and an elaborate ceremony in a fancy place wouldn't suit her.

Although I have a whole day's worth of stories – funny, sad, heroic – to tell you about my wonderful mother, I really resisted standing up here for fear of not being able to get through it. But, Sue told me I can keep it short, and Henry Green assured me that "tears are good." So, please bear with me.

First, I must tell you that Mother would get a huge kick out of something ironic today. As Henry already said, we're a strange mix when it comes to religion:

*Mother was a Catholic
*My father was Jewish
*I was raised a Catholic
*My wife, Sue, is a Methodist
*Our son, David, is an Episcopalian
*Our grandchildren are Episcopalians.

Mother got a lot of laughs out of this interdenominational mix we had become, when we talked privately. So, I can hear her laughing in heaven right now and appreciating the fact that her memorial service is being conducted by a Baptist minister. Doesn't quite complete the circle, but it comes close.

Mother would be really happy that her good friends from Sunrise are here this morning. Most of you attended her ninetieth birthday party down the road from here just a little over three months ago... Since Mother's passing on Friday, we've been deluged with messages of sympathy from friends throughout the United States, from Germany, and, of course, from the Czech Republic. The adjectives which describe Mother in these notes and e-mails are: remarkable, brave, inspirational, amazing, great, nice, beautiful, and elegant. I've been greatly moved by this outpouring of love and admiration for my wonderful mother.

You'll notice that the "Surviving Family" list you have in your hands is a bit unusual. Normally, these lists and obituaries show only the surviving blood relatives. Our list includes:

*Sue, daughter-in-law, because she was extremely close to Mother and, as Mother's friends from Sunrise have told us, she referred to Sue as "my angel."

*Bobbi, granddaughter-in-law, might as well have been Mother's granddaughter because of the love the two of them had for one another.

In fact, I could have easily added the entire Bass extended family to the "Surviving Family" list. When David married Bobbi Bass, he gave us a large new family with whom we've been able to share joys and sorrows, just as we are now.

*Of course, there's David. As her only grandson, he was the apple of Mother's eye. I'd be remiss if I didn't tell you how proud Mother was of the wonderful husband, father, and person he has become.

*Finally, let me say something about the little people who provided "Grandma" with incredible joy. My mother's first name was Ilona, her maiden name was Neumann, and her married name was Heller. If you look at the full names of Mother's three great-grandchildren, you'll see that each honors Grandma by sharing her name: Caroline's middle name is Ilona; Sam's middle name is Neumann; and, of course, Sarah — as are all the others — is named Heller.

All of them will be able to remember and honor my mother throughout their lives. I can't think of a better legacy.

Do not stand at my grave and weep.
I am not there, I do not sleep.
I am a thousand winds that blow.
I am the diamond glints on snow.
I am the sunlight on ripened grain.
I am the gentle autumn rain.
When you awaken in the morning's hush,
I am the swift uplifting rush
Of quiet birds in circled flight.
I am the soft stars that shine at night.
Do not stand at my grave and cry,
I am not there, I did not die.
(author unknown)

BIBLIOGRAPHY

Chapter One: *Kde domov můj?* Where Is My Home?
*Honejsek, Václav. *Z dějin nepatrné české vesnice (From the History of an Insignificant Czech Village)*. Prague: V. Kotrba, 1894.
*Kučera, Jaroslav. *Vybrané záznamy z Kojetické kroniky, díl. 5 (Selected Parts of the History of Kojetice, Volume 5)*. Kojetice: self-published, 2007.

Chapter Two: Heart of Europe
*Bryant, Chad. *Prague in Black: Nazi Rule and Czech Nationalism*. Cambridge, MA: Harvard University Press, 2007.
*Čornej, Petr. *Great Stories in Czech History*. Prague: Práh, 2005.
*Hašek, Jaroslav (English translation by Cecil Parrott). *The Good Soldier Švejk and His Fortunes in the World War*. London: William Heinemann Ltd., 1973.
*Heimann, Mary. *Czechoslovakia: The State That Failed*. New Haven: Yale University Press, 2009.
*Holeček, Milan, Josef Rubín, Miroslav Střída, and Antonín Götz. *The Czech Republic in Brief*. Prague: Czech Geographical Society, 1995.
*Kieval, Hillel J. "The Jews of Bohemia, Moravia and Slovakia to 1918." *Slovo*, Vol. 5, no. 2, winter 2004/5.
*MacDonald, Callum and Jan Kaplan. *Prague in the Shadow of the Swastika: a History of the German Occupation 1939-1945*. Prague: Melantrich, 1995.
*Machann, Clinton and James W. Mendl, Jr., eds. *Czech Voices: Stories from Texas in the Amerikán Národní Kalendář*. College Station, TX: Texas A&M University Press, 1991.
*Masaryk, Tomáš Garrigue. *The Ideals of Humanity and How to Work*. London: George Allen & Unwin Ltd., 1938.

*Palacký, František. *Dějiny národu českého, v Čechách a v Moravě (History of the Czech Nation, in Bohemia and Moravia)*. Prague: L. Mazáč, 1936.

*Roberts, Andrew. *From the Good King Wenceslas to the Good Soldier Švejk: A Dictionary of Czech Popular Culture*. Budapest/New York: European University Press, 2005.

*Rothkirchen, Livia. *The Jews of Bohemia and Moravia: Facing the Holocaust*. Lincoln, NE: University of Nebraska Press and Jerusalem: Yad Vashem, 2005.

*Sakson-Ford, Stephanie. *The Czech Americans*. New York: Chelsea House Publishers, 1989.

*Sayer, Derek. *The Coasts of Bohemia, a Czech History*. Princeton, NJ: Princeton University Press, 1998.

Chapter Three: Czech Families Neumann and Heller

*Kučera, *Vybrané záznamy*.

*Sayer, *The Coasts of Bohemia*.

Chapter Four: Occupation: The Nazi Circle

*Lukacs, John. *The Last European War, September 1939/December 1941*. New Haven & London: Yale University Press, 1976.

*MacDonald et al, *Prague in the Shadow of the Swastika*.

*Mackenzie, Compton. *Dr. Beneš*. London: George G. Harrap & Co., Ltd., 1946.

* *Pamět národa (Rememberance of a Nation)*. Projekt: příběhy 20. století (Project: Tales of the 20th Century). www.pametnaroda.cz. Czech Broadcasting, 2009.

*Rigg, Bryan Mark. *Hitler's Jewish Soldiers: the Untold Story of Nazi Racial Laws and Men of Jewish Descent in the German Military*. Lawrence, KS: University Press of Kansas, 2002.

*Rothkirchen, *The Jews of Bohemia and Moravia: Facing the Holocaust*.

*Thomas, Evan. "The Mythology of Munich." *Newsweek*, June 23, 2008.

Chapter Five: Persecution

*Brown, Eva Metzger. "A Child Survivor of the Holocaust Comes Out of Hiding: Two Stories of Trauma." *Psychoanalytic Perspectives*, 4(2), 2007.

*Demetz, Peter. *Prague in Danger*. New York: Farrar, Straus and Giroux, 2008.

*Glazar, Richard. *Trap with a Green Fence: Survival in Treblinka*. Evanston, IL: Northwestern University Press, 1995.

*Gottfried, Ted. *Children of the Slaughter: Young People of the Holocaust*. Brookfield, CT: Twenty-First Century Books, 2001.

*Grove, Andrew. *Swimming Across: A Memoir*. New York: Warner Books, 2001.

*Kieval, *The Jews of Bohemia, Moravia and Slovakia to 1918*.

*Klein, Cecilie. *Sentenced to Live: A Survivor's Memoir*. New York: Holocaust Library, 1988.

*Pressburger, Chava (editor). *The Diary of Petr Ginz, 1941-1942*. (Translated from Czech by Elena Lappin). New York: Atlantic Monthly Press, 2004.

*Rigg, *Hitler's Jewish Soldiers*.

*Tedlow, Richard S. *Andy Grove: the Life and Times of an American*. New York: Portfolio/Penguin Group, 2006.

*Wistrich, Robert S. *Hitler and the Holocaust*. New York: The Modern Library, 2001.

*Wood, Angela Cluck. *Holocaust, the Events and Their Impact on Real People*. New York: DK Publishing, 2007.

*www.HolocaustResearchProject.org. Website of Holocaust Education Research Team (H.E.A.R.T.), Great Britain, 2009.

Chapter Six: Survival

*Brecher, Elinor. *Schindler's Legacy: True Stories of the List Survivors*. New York: Penguin Books/Plume, 1994.

*Kieval, *The Jews of Bohemia, Moravia and Slovakia to 1918*.

*Nicholas, Lynn H. *Cruel World, the Children of Europe in the Nazi War.* New York: Alfred A. Knopf, 2005.

*Pressburger, *The Diary of Petr Ginz, 1941-1942.*

*Roth, Milena. *Lifesaving Letters: A Child's Flight from the Holocaust.* Seattle and London: University of Washington Press, 2004.

*Werner, Emmy E. *Through the Eyes of Innocents, Children Witness World War II.* Boulder, CO: Westview (Perseus), 2000.

*Zapruder, Alexandra. *Salvaged Pages: Young Writers' Diaries of the Holocaust.* New Haven & London: Yale University Press, 2002.

Chapter Seven: Catholics and Nazis

*Akin, Jimmy. "How Pius XII Protected Jews," www.catholic.com/library, 2008.

*Faltin, Lucia. "Czechoslovak-Vatican Relations between 1918 and 1948; a Promising – but Unfinished – Alliance," *Slovo*, Winter 2004/05.

*Glaser, Kurt. *Czecho-Slovakia, a Critical History.* Cardwell, ID: The Claxton Printers, 1961.

*Hellman, Peter. *Avenue of the Righteous.* New York: Atheneum, 1980.

*Henry, Patrick. *We Only Know Men: The Rescue of Jews in France During the Holocaust.* Washington: The Catholic University of America Press, 2007.

*James, "Conversion of Albright's Jewish Family Followed a Well-Trod Path."

*Kieval, *The Jews of Bohemia, Moravia and Slovakia to 1918.*

*Kučera, *Vybrané záznamy.*

*MacDonald et al, *Prague in the Shadow of the Swastika.*

*Margolius, Ivan. *Reflections of Prague, Journeys through the 20th Century.* Chichester, England: John Wiley & Sons, 2006.

*Nicholas, *Cruel World, the Children of Europe in the Nazi War.*

*Pojar, Miloš, Blanka Soukupová and Marie Zahradníková. *Židovská menšina za druhé republiky (The Jewish Minority During the Second Republic).* Prague: Jewish Museum, 2007.

*Rothkirchen, *The Jews of Bohemia and Moravia: Facing the Holocaust.*
*Schvindlerman, Julian. "The Vatican and the Holocaust," www.wzo.org. il, May 2, 2001.
*Tec, Nechama. *When Light Pierced the Darkness: Christian Rescue of Jews in Nazi-Occupied Poland.* New York: Oxford University Press, 1986.
*Werner, *Through the Eyes of Innocents, Children Witness World War II.*
*Wood, *Holocaust, the Events and Their Impact on Real People.*
*Yahil, Leni. *The Holocaust: The Fate of European Jewry, 1932-1945.* New York: Oxford University Press, 1990.

Chapter Eight: Papa's War
*Dickerson, Bryan J. "The Liberation of Western Czechoslovakia 1945," www.MilitaryHistoryOnline.com, June 3, 2006.
*Hrabic, Pavel and Zdeněk. *Muž, který velel mužům: životní příběh armádního generála Karla Klapálka (The Man Who Led Men: Life Story of Army General Karel Klapálek).* Prague: Mladá Fronta, 1988.
*Roučka, Zdeněk. *Američané a západní Čechy 1945, unikátní fotografie (Americans in West Bohemia 1945, Exclusive Photographs).* Pilsen: ZR&T, 2000.
*Shapiro, T. Rees. "The Bazooka Was Just the Beginning for an Inventive Engineer," *The Washington Post,* May 23, 2010, p. C6.
*Smetana, Vit. "Beyond the Myth about Czechoslovakia's International Role in the Second World War," Proceedings of the 2011 Regional Conference of the Czechoslovak Society of Arts and Sciences, New York, NY, June 3-5, 2011.
*Stock, James W. *Tobruk: the Siege.* New York: Ballantine Books, 1973.
*Ströbinger, Rudolf. *Invaze (Invasion).* Prague: Magnet-Press, 1994.
*White, Lewis M., ed. *On All Fronts: Czechs and Slovaks in World War II.* Boulder, CO: East European Monographs, 1991.

Chapter Nine: Revenge and Liberation
*Beevor, Antony. *The Fall of Berlin 1945.* New York: Viking, 2002.

*Jakl, Tomáš. *Prahou pod pancířem povstalců (Through Prague under the Armor of Insurgents)*. Prague: Mladá fronta, 2010.
*Lustig, Arnošt (English translation by Paul Wilson). *Indecent Dreams*. Evanston, IL: Northwestern University Press, 1988.
*Lustig, Arnošt (English translation by Ewald Osers). *Lovely Green Eyes*. London: Vintage, 2003.
*Sayer, *The Coasts of Bohemia*.

Chapter Ten: Short-lived Freedom
*Frommer, Benjamin. *National Cleansing: Retribution against Nazi Collaborators in Postwar Czechoslovakia*. Cambridge: Cambridge University Press, 2005.
*Kovály, Heda Margolius. *Under a Cruel Star, Life in Prague 1941-1968*. New York: Holmes & Meier, 1997.
*Levy, Alan. *Good Men Still Live! The Odyssey of a Professional Prisoner*. Chicago: J. Philip O'Hara, Inc., 1974.
*Malkin, Lawrence. *Krueger's Men: the Secret Nazi Counterfeit Plot and the Prisoners of Block 19*. New York: Back Bay Books/Little, Brown & Co., 2006.
*Margolius, *Reflections of Prague, Journeys through the 20th Century*.
*Roberts, *From the Good King Wenceslas to the Good Soldier Švejk*.
*Sayer, *The Coasts of Bohemia, a Czech History*.

Chapter Eleven: Escape
* *Pamět národa (Rememberance of a Nation)*.

Chapter Twelve: Refugees
*Werner, *Through the Eyes of Innocents, Children Witness World War II*.

Chapter Thirteen: America, the Beautiful
*Tedlow, *Andy Grove: the Life and Times of an American*.

Chapter Fourteen: Fateful Eights

*Levy, Alan. *Rowboat to Prague*. New York: Orion Press, 1972.

*Levy, *Good Men Still Live! The Odyssey of a Professional Prisoner*.

* *Paměť národa (Rememberance of a Nation)*.

*Sayer, *The Coasts of Bohemia, a Czech History*.

Chapter Fifteen: Gray Side of Iron Curtain

*Kimmage, Ann. *An Un-American Childhood*. Athens, GA: The University of Georgia Press, 1996.

*Sís, Peter. *The Wall, Growing Up Behind the Iron Curtain*. New York: Francis Foster Books, 2007.

Chapter Sixteen: On the Wings of Denial

*Brown, "A Child Survivor of the Holocaust Comes Out of Hiding."

Chapter Seventeen: Coming Full Circle

*Bauer, Maria. *Beyond the Chestnut Trees*. Woodstock, NY: The Overlook Press, 1984.

*Hellman, *Avenue of the Righteous*.

*MacDonald et al, *Prague in the Shadow of the Swastika*.

*Munger, Scott. *Rethinking God: Undoing the Damage*. Chattanooga, TN: Living Ink Books, 2007.

ACKNOWLEDGEMENTS

No book is the product of one person's efforts, and mine is no exception. It could not have been written without the assistance, advice, and support of many people – in the Czech Republic and in America – some of whom are close friends, some of whom are acquaintances, and some of whom I have never met. They include all the writers whose books I have read about World War II, the Holocaust, and my native country; my teachers; my editors; my writing colleagues; all my friends; my family.

I am indebted to my Czech friend, Vladimír Svoboda, who had the initial idea for a book. Too numerous to mention are my American friends who said "you must write this book" and who reminded me that my grandchildren may be too young to hear my story from me directly.

In the early stages of writing, my former agent, Elaine Markson, was instrumental in sharpening the focus of the book. Members of my writing group – Karen Cain, Paul Harrell, Ann Marie Maloney, Hank Parker, and Marilyn Recknor – have been my critics, my partners, and my cheerleaders. Karen not only conceived of the book's title, but she was a generous supporter and critic throughout the project; Hank made an enormous contribution by insisting that I was "not telling everything," an admonition that led me to stop holding back memories which were still painful. Marilyn's insistence that "history is not dull" caused me to mix historical information with my own experiences.

I owe a special debt to my writing teachers. After early encouragement and guidance from Mary Bargteil, I received invaluable advice and mentoring from Susan Moger, a wonderful writer in her own right. The book was enhanced by the careful editing and suggestions by the talented and articulate Arlene Swerdloff. John Gebhardt and David Heller helped to make the computer my friend.

Many people gave generously of their time, assisting me in extensive research about my family and my native country. In the Czech Republic, I was aided by my good friend, Jitka Thomasová; the immaculate research and excellent writing of Jaroslav Kučera, the chronicler of Kojetice, was invaluable to me. In America, Steve and Stephen Eisner, as well as the kind and devoted staff of the U. S. Holocaust Memorial Museum in Washington, were enormously helpful. I wish I could thank personally the person who invented the Internet; had I attempted to write this book before the advent of Google and other search engines, the task would have been much more difficult and time-consuming.

I am deeply grateful to Antonín Kočí for his confidence in me and for his belief that my story would be not only interesting to Czech readers, but that it would be of some value to young Czechs who were lucky enough not to suffer under either Nazi or communist oppression. His firm, Mladá Fronta, published my book – so ably translated into Czech by Irena Zíková – in April 2011.

My family cheered me on throughout this project. Each time I became discouraged, I gained my inspiration from a desire to give our son David, our daughter-in-law Bobbi, and – most urgently – our three grandchildren, Sam, Sarah, and Caroline, a connection to the struggles, tragedies, and triumphs of their Czech-American family. It is my fervent hope that they will carry on the legacy.

Above all, I am grateful to my wife Susan Elizabeth Holsten Heller for her love, support, patience, and for providing me with comfort even as she discovered things she never knew about me and the family into which she married more than fifty years ago. Without Sue – my beloved "Sammy" – there would be no book.

ABOUT THE AUTHOR

Charles Ota Heller was born in Czechoslovakia (today's Czech Republic), three years before the country was occupied by Germany. His memoir was translated into Czech and published by Mladá Fronta, in Prague, in April 2011.

He holds three degrees in engineering, and he has had a varied career as founder and CEO of two software companies, faculty member at three universities, venture capitalist, and member of several corporate boards. He was named the first Professor of Practice in the history of the University of Maryland and is recipient of the "Entrepreneur-of-the-Year" award for the State of Maryland, Oklahoma State University's Lohmann Medal, and the Alumni Achievement Award of The Catholic University of America. He is a proud member of the Legacy of Light of the United States Holocaust Memorial Museum.

His writing career began as columnist, then story editor, and eventually editor of the *Oklahoma State Engineer* magazine, which was named the "Best College Magazine" in the nation. He has been a columnist for *Baltimore News-American, Daily Record, The Public Enterprise, The Capital,* and *Washington Business Journal.* The author of a technical book and many columns and freelance articles on business, entrepreneurship, skiing, and sailing, he is working currently on two additional memoirs.

Charlie is married to Sue, has one son and three grandchildren, and lives outside of Annapolis, Maryland.

The author's web site and blog:
www.charlesoheller.com
http://charlesoheller.blogspot.com